A Fire Burns in Kotsk

A Fire Burns in Kotsk

A TALE OF HASIDISM IN THE KINGDOM OF POLAND

Menashe Unger

Translated by Jonathan Boyarin
Introduction by Glenn Dynner

WAYNE STATE UNIVERSITY PRESS
DETROIT

© 2015 by Wayne State University Press, Detroit, Michigan 48201. All rights reserved. No part of this book may be reproduced without formal permission.   a.

19 18 17 16 15   5 4 3 2 1

ISBN 978–0-8143-3813-1 (paper) / ISBN 978–0-8143-3814-8 (e-book)

Library of Congress Control Number: 2014936559

Originally published in Yiddish as *Pshiskhe un Kotsk* by Menashe Unger (Buenos Aires: Tsentral-farband fun poylishe yidn in Argentine, 1949).

Designed and typeset by Adam B. Bohannon
Composed in Chapparral

Contents

Translator's Preface vii
Introduction by Glenn Dynner xi

A Fire Burns in Kotsk by Menashe Unger

1. Traveling to the Wedding 3
2. At a Tavern Outside Ostilye 10
3. Hasidic Cossacks 17
4. In an Attic in Ostilye 24
5. The Dispute in Lublin on Account of a Shirt 33
6. The Fall of the Rebbe of Lublin 39
7. The Paupers' Feast 47
8. The Groom Holds Court Before the Ceremony 55
9. The Ceremony 61
10. The Apter Rebbe Presides 70
11. The Trial 77
12. The Passing of the Rebbe Reb Bunem 85
13. A Fire Burns in Tomashov 92
14. Starting School All Over Again 99

CONTENTS

15. The Vurker Rebbe Goes to Tomashov 112
16. The Hasidic Commune in Tomashov 118
17. Court Intrigues at Kotsk 124
18. The Kotsker Rebbe Forgets to Go to His Own Wedding Ceremony 130
19. The Kotsker Rebbe and the Polish Uprising of 1830 138
20. The Council at Moshe Khalfan's House 144
21. Reb Itshe Meirl Is Arrested as a Spy 150
22. The Kotsker Rebbe Issues a Call to Support the Polish Rebellion 156
23. The Battle Between Maskilim and Hasidim in Warsaw 162
24. "Minister" Montefiore and the Vurker Rebbe 168
25. The Kotsker Rebbe after His Second Marriage 175
26. The Izhbitser Rebbe in Kotsk 182
27. The Contentious Conversation 189
28. The Kotsker Rebbe in His Private Room 195
29. The Society of "Watchers" at the Court of Kotsk 200
30. The Watchers Are Driven Out 205
31. The Kotsker Rebbe Agrees to Open the Door 211
32. The Terrible Friday Night 217
33. The Rebbe of Gostinin Doesn't Know to Whom to Go 221
34. The Kotsker Rebbe Escapes from His Private Room 226
35. The Passing of the Kotsker Rebbe 231

Translator's Preface

In our day, non-Hasidic Jews often view Hasidim through a schizophrenic lens. Sometimes Hasidim are seen as venerable, folkloric, or Other-worldly (in the double sense of belonging to the Old World, and being primarily spiritual). At other times they are denigrated as fanatical relics who refuse to adapt to their times.

Of course, Hasidim who live in our own time indisputably inhabit the same time we do, even as they insist on distinct forms that recall those of the past. We might be reminded of what should be this obvious fact any time, for example, we see a Hasidic gentleman from Williamsburg or Monsey using his cell phone to remind his wife of something that must urgently be taken care of before Shabbes—and when we remember in turn that, for the Hasidim on Shabbes, as for all humans a scant century or so ago, the only way to communicate with a fellow human being was face-to-face.

Hasidim living long ago and far away, in early nineteenth-century Poland, were also people of their times. That is certainly true of the sometimes radically ascetic and seemingly "unworldly" Hasidim who are the subject of this book, stuck to earth often to their own regret, as they struggled to purify themselves by shedding mundane concerns. The tension between that struggle for pure concentration on the search for Truth and hence the divine, and the reality of mortal beings entangled in webs of family, community, and the press of secular history, is the subject of this book. Its author, Menashe Unger, seems never to have lost sight of the humanity that he shared with the Hasidim of Pshiskhe and Kotsk whom he writes about here. Much of the account has the intimate feel of family history passed down orally from generation to generation.

Translator's Preface

These chapters contain little secret lore and no mystical learning. Their lessons about how difficult it is to overcome the blinders of selfishness and to achieve authentic worship are as open to us as they were in 1825. Their down-to-earth depictions of Jewish leaders squeezed between Polish nationalist rebels and the Tsar's generals, of wives and mothers vying with Hasidic rebbes for their husband's loyalty, of the first flush of communal enthusiasm and its seemingly inevitable collapse, should all resonate today.

Unger's gift is a bridge between our world and theirs. His own heirs—Saul Kaiserman, Judy Kaiserman, and Mark Kaiserman—were, in turn, kind enough to grant us the rights to publish this translation, for which we are in their debt. Like any translator, I have had the pleasure of intimacy with his Yiddish text, along with the knowledge that no translation does perfect justice. I have the feeling Menashe Unger would forgive me those imperfections. May his memory, and those of the Hasidim he wrote about so lovingly, be a blessing for us all.

Courtesy of the *YIVO Encyclopedia of Jews in Eastern Europe*.

Introduction

Glenn Dynner

"In my humble opinion, studying with me would not be vital for your current path," Gershom Scholem wrote gently to Menashe Unger in 1927. Unger, a twenty-seven-year-old Polish Jew from a Hasidic family, had already pursued several paths up to this point. Son of the Rabbi of Zabno, in Galicia (Austrian Poland), he had received rabbinic ordination at age 17, left the Hasidic fold, attended the University of Vienna, moved to Warsaw, joined the Labor Zionist movement, worked as a journalist and even as a stone mason. He arrived in Tel Aviv in 1925 but, unable to find work (Scholem regretted to say that he could not find anything for him in Jerusalem), returned to Poland for a few years and then, in 1935, emigrated to America. The "current path" that Scholem referred to was one Unger would stick to for the rest of his career: distilling and disseminating folksy East European Jewish wisdom from hundreds upon hundreds of printed and oral Hasidic tales.[1]

Scholem's advice to Unger was probably sound—the world-renowned professor of Jewish mysticism and the restless former Hasid were not a good fit. For Scholem, Hasidism could only be properly understood by patiently analyzing its early homiletic literature in accordance with strict philological standards. To judge by his famous debate with Martin Buber in 1961, few things irritated him more than an over-reliance on the colorful legends surrounding the movement's charismatic masters.[2] Unger was to devote his entire career to that very genre, drawing upon Hasidic tales for his column "From an Old Well-Spring" in the Yiddish daily *Tog-morgn zhurnal* and his more than ten books. In doing so, Unger did not hesitate to project his own socialist values onto Hasidism, praising what he saw as a proletarian movement that "championed the common man."[3] Unger eventually

Introduction

made so bold as to criticize the works of Scholem and his students, which, to judge by a later letter to Unger, irritated the professor to no end. "Every simple Jew has the right to think what he wants," Scholem wrote him patronizingly in 1960. "And if your wish is to make nice with Hasidim and to heap scorn on their opponents (*mitnagdim*), so be it." But Scholem was "shocked" that Unger had dared to "write about my studies, and those of my students" without having read through all of their works, some of which were available "even in places that a simpleton could access them."[4]

Scholem's harsh assessment is perhaps understandable from an academic perspective. In addition to questioning Unger's mastery of the secondary literature, he might have taken him to task (as he had Martin Buber) for relying on oral and late printed versions of Hasidic tales instead of Hasidic homiletic literature. Still, we must wonder whether a popular, earthbound mystical movement like Hasidism can be accessed solely through its elite literature. Unlike Scholem, Unger had grown up in a Hasidic setting reverberating with oral culture. It was one thing to read a lengthy Hasidic exegesis filtered through transcription, translation, and redaction; quite another to effectively relive Hasidic masters expounding that same wisdom over vodka surrounded by disciples and work-a-day Jews, as occurs within Hasidic tale collections. The tales were for Unger living repositories of folk wisdom, imagination, and ethos spawned and circulated among everyday people and, as such, constituted a reflection of *their* feelings and aspirations. The precise theological development and historical provenance of a text were, for him, rather beside the point.[5]

Perhaps Unger's most impressive demonstration of these tales' capacity is his full-length novel, *Pshiskhe un Kotsk* (1946), which Jonathan Boyarin has translated here under the title *A Fire Burns in Kotsk*. Unger was not the first modern writer to weave Hasidic tales into a novel about the central drama of nineteenth-century Polish Hasidism. The Kingdom of Poland's passionate, contentious masters had already fired the imaginations of some of the twentieth century's most renowned Jewish writers—the most famous attempts being Joseph Opatoshu's *In Polish Woods* (Yiddish, 1921) and Martin Buber's *Gog and Magog* (Hebrew version, 1943).[6] But the novels of Unger's prominent predecessors, unique and beautiful as they are, seem to be missing something. Only Unger manages to serve up Polish Hasidism's full, pungent mélange of wisdom, celebration, prayer, music, scandal, and drunkenness, all the while distilling a single, potent ethos of spiritual authenticity.

That ethos is articulated near the beginning of *A Fire Burns in Kotsk* by its eventual protagonist, the Kotsker Rebbe (R. Menachem Mendel Morgenstern, d. 1859): "If a person goes around proudly feeling that he's already there, he's certainly lost." Warnings against arrogance, pretense, and the consequent loss of striving permeate the novel. A person must be pious in secret, appearing to all the world as a mere commoner. It is better to be a sinner who knows he is a sinner than to be a *tzaddik*—a paragon of righteousness—who knows he is a *tzaddik*. Even the novel's shocking exposés of Hasidic drinking practices promote this message: when the young Pshiskhe Hasidim beat the venerable Reb Fayvl of Gritse until he coughs up enough money for liquor they are also giving him a lesson in humility. When they choose to drink heartily at a tavern instead of reciting psalms like the Kozhenitser Hasidim at the next table, they are deliberately repudiating pious display. In fact, it is better to drink liquor with proper intent, according to one provocative Pshiskhe teaching, than to pray just for show.[7]

But preserving spiritual authenticity is not easy, and this is tragically illustrated through the demise of the Kotsker Hasidic court towards the end of the novel. The now-famous Kotsker Rebbe, the very embodiment of the ethos, retreats into seclusion and finally breaks down under the strain of his own fame and adulation. All he had ever wanted was a few devoted followers, but the Jewish masses have beseiged him and practically devoured him. "They've turned me into an object of worship" he despairs when he finally ventures outside, noticing as well that his court has become opulent beyond recognition.

A Brief History of Polish Hasidism

The Polish-Lithuanian Commonwealth, home to almost three-fourths of the world's Jewish population, had been conquered and partitioned at the hands of Russia, Prussia, and Austria by the time Unger's novel takes place. There had been a brief hope for Poland's complete restoration during the Napoleonic conquest (1807–14), but the tsar soon took over Napoleon's Polish lands and created a technically autonomous Kingdom of Poland in 1815 that remained firmly under his grip, eventually a virtual colony. The situation was unusual: Next door, in the tsarist empire proper, lay the Pale of Settlement, a vast Jewish ghetto consisting of Russia's first Polish conquests that was subject to direct, autocratic rule. In contrast, the tsar's new conquest, the Kingdom of Poland, was for now a constitutional monarchy with a higher degree of urbanization and even higher concentration of Jews. Eventually, after the suppression of two Polish uprisings (1830 and 1863), the Kingdom of Poland would be almost fully absorbed into the tsarist empire. But during the course of Unger's novel, which describes the earlier, 1830 uprising, the kingdom continued to exist as a distinct entity with a pronounced Polish ambiance. Polish Hasidism reflected much of the kingdom's Polishness.

To be sure, Hasidic communities shared certain key elements across geographical boundaries. All Hasidic leaders saw themselves as inheritors of the spiritual path of Rabbi Israel Ba'al Shem Tov (the Besht, ca. 1700–1760), who introduced a radically earthbound mysticism predicated on a non-dualistic consciousness: The divine permeates the material world, he taught, and can therefore be accessed throughout the material world. This did not mean that the world could be enjoyed as an end to itself, but it did mean that a *tzaddik* (or *rebbe* in Yiddish), one who was gifted with the ability to discern the world's underlying divinity and draw the divine flow down into it, possessed the power to sacralize even the most mundane pursuits—eating, dancing, storytelling, imbibing alcohol, and so on. He could even draw down the divine flow to work miracles.[8]

Nevertheless, regional distinctions are discernible. In the Ukraine, Byelarus, and Galicia—formerly Polish-ruled territories now under the direct reign of absolutist Russia and Austria—tzaddikim came to resemble their absolutist monarchs, a tendency that the scholar Arthur Green has termed "royalism." Some established extravagant courts in grand palaces, bearing themselves in a regal manner in imitation of their regions' absolutist monarchs. Most bequeathed their leadership to their sons early on, establishing formal dynasties.[9]

But in the Kingdom of Poland, Hasidism assumed a strikingly different form. During the first half of the nineteenth century, the

Introduction

Kingdom of Poland lacked a direct, absolutist leadership model, thanks to its constitutional framework. Dynastic succession could not take root among Polish Hasidim until the kingdom's full absorption into the tsarist empire during the latter half of the nineteenth century. In addition, the kingdom's comparatively advanced pace of urbanization and industrialization enabled the emergence of a sizeable Jewish mercantile elite, many of whom decided to become patrons of tzaddikim. Several prominent Polish tzaddikim, including R. Simcha Bunem of Phsiskhe (Pszysucha), R. Menahem Mendel of Kotsk (Kock), R. Isaac Meir Alter of Ger (Góra Kalwaria), and R. Isaac of Vurke (Warka), had been merchants themselves before becoming tzaddikim. Their worldliness and intimate contacts with Warsaw's mercantile elites produced a more urban, cosmopolitan, and politically savvy, but also a more tense and factional, Hasidism. Disciples broke off from their masters and established distinctive schools of Hasidism, only to be subjected to a similar fate by their own star disciples.[10] This drama of recurring spiritual rebellions was part of what captivated Unger and other authors of the interwar period who described Polish Hasidism.

Polish Hasidism came to revolve around three courts—Kozhenits (Kozienice), Lublin, and Pshiskhe (Przysucha). The first major Polish Hasidic center, in Kozhenits, was founded by R. Israel Hopstein, known as the "Maggid of Kozhenits" (1733/7–1815). A disciple of R. Elimelekh of Leżajsk, the Galician leader who set the emergent "tzaddik" vocation on a theoretical footing, the Maggid of Kozhenits achieved fame as a physically frail but spiritually mighty miracle worker. Upon his death, part of his following went over to his son Moses Eliakim Beriya (1757–1828). However, his most prominent disciples soon established their own courts.

A second Polish Hasidic center emerged around another disciple of R. Elimelekh of Leżajsk's, R. Jacob Isaac Horowitz, the "Seer of Lublin" (1745–1815). During his master's lifetime, the Seer rebelled and formed his own Hasidic court in Lublin. He promoted a miracle-centered approach to Hasidism, stressing the tzaddik's obligation to magically provide for his followers' material needs. Although that doctrine appealed more to society's lower echelons, his recruiter, R. David Biderman of Lelov (Lelów, 1746–1813), managed to attract scions of rabbinic elites to the Seer's court. The Seer died in 1815 after falling from his window on the eve of *Simhat Torah,* an event which gave rise to a great deal of unkind speculation among Hasidic opponents but receives a more charitable interpretation by Unger.[11] His doctrine of "material tzaddikism" was sustained by his disciple R. Meir of Apt/Stavnitz (Opatów/Stopnica, d. 1827/31).

Among the Seer's more innovative and distinctive disciples was R. Jacob Isaac Rabinowicz, the "Holy Jew" of Pshiskhe (1766–1813). The "Holy Jew" was entrusted with the education of the Seer's scholarly followers, but finally broke away and formed his own court in Pshiskhe. His approach formed a counterpoint to Lublin Hasidism, for he introduced a rigorous Talmudic curriculum, demanded uncompromising self-scrutiny, and conceived his role as less miracle worker than spiritual guide. (Working miracles, as we learn in Unger's retelling, was nothing compared to the difficulty involved in becoming a "good Jew"—hence the virtual absence of miracles throughout the novel.) Most controversially, the Holy Jew counseled followers to delay their prayers until after they had achieved a state of mental preparedness.

The Holy Jew's sons reverted to miracle working and only succeeded in attracting a portion of their father's following.[12] The main inheritor of the Pshiskhe method was the Holy Jew's preeminent disciple, R. Simha Bunem (1765–1827), author of the discourses in Kol Simha (Breslau, 1859). Remarkably cosmopolitan for a Hasidic leader, he had studied in the Matesdorf and Nikolsburg Yeshivas, mastered several non-Jewish languages, traded in Leipzig and Danzig, and had been one of the first Jews in the region to earn a pharmaceutical license. He became the most popular tzaddik of his day, but also the most controversial. At the Ostilye (Uściług) wedding, one of the first scenes in Unger's novel, the elder Abraham Joshua Heschel of Opatów/Międzyboż (ca. 1748–1825), presided over deliberations to possibly ban the school. R. Simha Bunem was exonerated, however, thanks to attestations by several star disciples and his rival, the Holy Jew's son R. Yerahmiel Tzevi.[13]

Upon R. Simha Bunem's death, part of his following, including the future tzaddik Isaac Kalish of Vurke (1779–1848), went over to his son R. Abraham Moses. But typical for Polish Hasidism, the majority shifted their allegiance to his star disciple, the fiery Menahem Mendel of Kotsk. The Pshiskhe approach was pursued in the great Polish

Introduction

Hasidic courts of the late nineteenth century: Kotsk, Ger, Vurke, Aleksander (Aleksandrów Łódzki), Izbica, and Biała. In these courts' theological works, one detects an orientation away from the elitist, "tzaddik-centered" doctrine of early Hasidism towards an ethos of individual self-improvement (*mussar*) by means of humility and submission to the divine, perhaps a deliberate repudiation of the secularist demands for individual autonomy that were gaining currency in the kingdom.[14]

Towns throughout the central and eastern portions of the Kingdom of Poland had become "Hasidicized" to varying degrees by the time the novel takes place. Local Hasidim had broken off from the main synagogues and opened their own prayerhouses (*shtiblekh*), which functioned like satellites of the Hasidic courts, and some Hasidim managed to take over services in local study houses (*batei midrash*) and synagogues. Hasidim even began to inhabit prominent, age-old local communal positions (cantors, ritual slaughterers, rabbis, and so on).

One of the most surprising developments was the ease with which Polish Hasidim penetrated large, industrializing cities, where they created largely Hasidic enclaves containing numerous *shtiblekh*.[15] The memoirist Ya'akov Milkh describes Franciscan Street in Warsaw as a place where "every Hasidic *shtibl* in Warsaw" coexisted, including Kotsk, Ger, Grodzisk, Biala, Warka, Radzymin, Neushtadt, and "even Trisk."[16] While it is difficult to quantify the Hasidic presence in the capital, recent estimates suggest around forty Hasidic *shtiblekh* in Warsaw by the turn of the twentieth century.[17]

In depicting Polish Hasidism's tumultuous history, it is all too easy to let Hasidim and their charismatic masters eclipse the Kingdom of Poland's other inhabitants. Historical analysis proves more sobering. Certain internal Hasidic and external Polish Christian observers agree that the movement attracted about one-third of the Jewish community in the Kingdom of Poland by the time of Unger's story, though their number would rise steadily over the next several decades.[18] Most importantly, there was never a self-contained Hasidic world, not even to the extent that one sees in neighborhoods of Brooklyn or Jerusalem today.

Unger resists the temptation to imagine a hermetically sealed Hasidic Jewry. The most prominent example is his depiction of the impact of the 1830 uprising. Unger introduces readers to non-Jewish Polish leaders like Antoni Ostrowski (1782–1845) who hoped to make Jews an integral part of a future Poland and counted on their support. Ostrowski personally commanded Jewish volunteers in the National Guard and planned to reward them with full emancipation. Alas, as Unger also shows, other Polish leaders were too quick to spurn Jewish participation in the rebellion and hang Jews as spies. Given that mixed message, it is extraordinary that Jews like Yosef Berkovitsh (Jozef Berkowicz) did prove willing to sacrifice their lives for the Polish cause in both 1830 and 1863. Unger's lengthy description of the impact of the 1830 uprising seems a curious departure from the novel's pithy teachings, exuberant weddings, and wild drinking bouts. But the image of the future Kotsker and Gerer *rebbes* imploring their follows to hand over enormous sums of money to the Polish rebels and then fleeing abroad after their defeat constitutes an important reiteration of the book's theme: the inherent self-delusion of security. Despite their illusion of blithe insularity, Hasidic communities and their venerable leaders could be dispersed in an instant.

The industry of repackaging Hasidic tales for an often non-Hasidic and non-traditionalist readership has been subjected to a fair amount of scrutiny by contemporary scholars. Some suspect the authors and redactors of harboring base financial motives or pandering to their audiences' nostalgia for the lost shtetl world.[19] But Unger's novel breathes an unapologetic realism. Who at that time would have truly wanted to know about so many good, bad, and ugly aspects of Polish Hasidism? Not its fervent adherents, not its adamant opponents, and not nostalgic secular American audiences of the late 1940s racked by pangs of survivors' guilt. Perhaps it is we, with our own temporal and emotional distance from the East European era of Jewish history, who are ready to learn what Unger wants to impart.

Notes

1. See Scholem's unpublished letters to Unger in The YIVO Archives, Menashe Unger Collection, RG 509, folder 57. Many thanks to Jonatan Meir for referring me to these fascinating materials. For biographical information about Unger, see the archival finding aid to the collection, in addition to Nathaniel Deutsch, *The Maiden of Ludmir: A Jewish Holy Woman and Her World* (Berkeley: University of California Press, 2003), 38–40.

Introduction

2. See "Martin Buber's Interpretation of Hasidism," in Gershom Scholem, *The Messianic Idea in Judaism,* 234–35.
3. See Menashe Unger, *Hasidus un lebn,* introduction. For a discussion of Unger's socialist Hasidism, see Deutsch, 38–40.
4. Letter from January 18, 1960, Menashe Unger Collection, RG 509, folder 57. Scholem also disparaged Unger's attempts to write about the messianic pretender Shabbetai Tzevi "to inflame the feelings of the masses."
5. Nor was Unger aware of the restrictive, elitist nature of leadership positions within the movement. On Hasidism's elite, populist (as opposed to popular) leadership, see Moshe Rosman, *Founder of Hasidism* (Berkeley: University of California Press, 1996); and Glenn Dynner, *Men of Silk: The Hasidic Conquest of Polish Jewish Society* (New York: Oxford University Press, 2006), esp. ch. 4.
6. On the construction of Buber's *Gog and Magog,* see Shmuel Werses, "Hahasidut be-aspaklariya beleterist-iyunim b'gog u-magog' shel Martin Buber," in *Zaddikim ve-Anshe Ma'aseh: Mehkarim be-Hasidut Polin* (Jerusalem: Mosad Bialik, 1994).
7. On Hasidic drinking, see Dynner, *Yankel's Tavern: Jews, Liquor, and Life in the Kingdom of Poland* (New York: Oxford University Press, 2013), ch. 1, and idem., "'A Jewish Drunk is Hard to Find': The Myth of Jewish Sobriety in Eastern Europe," *Jewish Quarterly Review* 104, no. 1 (Winter 2014): 9–23. Usually, Hasidim were discreet, preferring to drink in their private prayer houses (*shtiblekh*) in contrast to the very public tavern. But pilgrimages and travels to major weddings may have formed an exception.
8. For an introduction to the Besht's thought, see Rachel Elior, *The Mystical Origins of Hasidism* (Oxford: Littman Library of Jewish Civilization, 2006).
9. See Arthur Green, "Typologies of Leadership and the Hasidic Zaddiq," in idem, ed., *Jewish Spirituality,* vol. 2 (New York: Crossroad, 1994), 144; David Assaf, *The Regal Way;* and Paul Radensky, "The Rise and Decline of a Hasidic Court: The Case of Rabbi Duvid [David] Twersky of Tal'noye," in *Holy Dissent: Jewish and Christian Mystics in Eastern Europe,* edited by Dynner (Detroit: Wayne State University Press, 2011), 131–69.
10. See Dynner, *Men of Silk,* chapter 1.
11. David Assaf, "'Ve-ha-mitnaggdim hitlozezu she-nishtakher ve-nafal': nefilat shel ha-hozeh mi-lublin be-r'i ha-zikharon ha-hasidi ve-ha-satirah ha-maskilit," in *Within Hasidic Circles: Studies in Hasidism in Memory of Mordecai Wilensky,* edited by Immanuel Etkes, David Assaf, Israel Bartal, and Elhanan Reiner (Jerusalem: Mosad Bialik Institute, 1999), 161–208.
12. David Assaf, "Hasidut be-hitpashtuta–diyokano shel r. Nehemia Jehiel bibihova ben 'Ha-Yehudi Ha-Kadosh,'" in *Ke-minhag Ashkenaz ve-Polin: Sefer Yovel le-Chone Shmeruk: Kovets Mehkarim be-Tarbut Yehudit,* edited by Israel Bartal, Ezra Mendelsohn, and Chava Turnianski (Jerusalem: Merkaz Zalman Shazar, 1993), 269–98.
13. Aaron Aescoli, *ha-hasidut be-polin,* edited by David Assaf (Jerusalem: Magnes Press, 1999), 89.

Introduction

14. See, for example, Yerahmiel Yitzhak ben Yehiel of Aleksander, *Yismah yisrael* (Lodz, 1913). On Ger Hasidism, see Arthur Green's translation and commentary, *The Language of Truth* (Philadelphia: The Jewish Publication Society, 1998). On Kotsk, see A. J. Heschel, *A Passion for Truth* (Jewish Lights, 1995).
15. In 1827, for example, Isaac Meir Alter, the future Gerer *rebbe*, requested official permission for his Warsaw *shtiblekh* on 1027 Grzybowska Street, 959 Targowa Street, and 1057 Grzybowska Street. Printed in Ignacy Schiper, *Żydzi Królestwa Polskiego w dobie powstania listopadowego Schiper* (Warsaw: F. Hoesick, 1932), 28.
16. Ya'akov Milkh, *Oytobiografishe skitzen* (New York: Iḳuf farlag, 1946), 81–82.
17. Jacob Shatzky's claim that two-thirds of the city's 300 prayer houses were Hasidic by 1880, a figure invoked uncritically in several contemporary studies, is a castle built on air. Eleonora Bergman's data yield a total of only 167 Warsaw prayer houses in 1869, a number that dwindled to 117 by 1910. Bergman reasons that each of the forty tzaddikim buried in Warsaw's Jewish cemetery would have had at least one prayer house in Warsaw (meaning about one-quarter of all the prayer houses), but concedes that there is little concrete data. See Shatzky, *Geschichte fun yidn in Varshe*, III (New York: YIVO, 1953), 364, citing Ya'akov Milkh, *Oytobiagrafishe skitzen* (New York, 1946), 81–82, which makes no such claim. On the repeated use of this fabricated data by contemporary historians, see Dynner, "Hasidism and Habitat," in *Holy Dissent*, edited by idem. See also Eleonora Bergman, *"Nie masz bóznicy powszechnej": synagogi i domy modlitwy w Warszawie od konca XVII do początku XXI wieku* (Warsaw: DiG, 2007), 136–57 and 191.
18. For a good summary of the scholarly debate on the quantitative spread of Polish Hasidism, see Antony Polonsky, *Jews in Poland and Russia*, II, 296–7.
19. See, for example, Joseph Dan, "A Bow to Frumkinian Hasidism," *Modern Judaism* 11 (1991); Steven Katz, "Martin Buber's Misuse of Hasidic Sources," *Post-Holocaust Dialogues: Critical Studies in Modern Jewish Thought* (New York: NYU Press, 1983), 25–39. For more recent and nuanced examinations of Hasidic tales and their redactors, see Justin Jarrod Lewis, *Imagining Holiness* (Montreal, Quebec: McGill-Queen's University Press, 2009), esp. part 2; idem., "Such Things have Never been Heard of: Jewish Intellectuals and Hasidic Miracles," http://home.cc.umanitoba.ca/~lewis2/documents/miracles-skepticism.pdf (accessed on 1.7.14); and Jonatan Meir, *Shivhei rodkinson: mikhal levi frumkin-rodkinson ve-ha-hasidut* (Tel Aviv: Ha-kibutz ha-meyuhad, 2012).

A Fire Burns in Kotsk
by Menashe Unger

1
Traveling to the Wedding

Six years after the death of the "Holy Jew," when his student Reb Simcha Bunem sat in his place in Pshiskhe and led his Hasidic kingdom, all of the Hasidic courts of Poland, Russia, and Galicia began to prepare for the "great wedding" in Ostilye.

Folks began keeping tallies as to which court had received letters of invitation and which hadn't. Among those that had received invitations, they were also curious to learn which rebbes were coming and which ones weren't.

All of these preparations were hardly for naught. After all, the grandfather on the groom's side was the old tzaddik of Apt, Reb Avrohom Yehoshue Heshl,[1] the eldest and most profoundly honored of all the tzaddikim of his generation, the "Holy Grandfather," who was then living in Mezhbuzh. Whole worlds trembled at the mention of his name. The grandfather on the bride's side was Reb Motele[2] of Neshkhiz, also one of the greatest Hasidic masters of his generation.

In the Hasidic courts they knew that the old Apter would certainly be at his grandson's wedding. And which rebbe didn't want to see the old tzaddik, the only surviving disciple of the Rebbe Reb Elimelech[3] of Lizhensk, author of the volume *Noam Elimelech*, who had been the first to bring the "light of Hasidism" to Galicia and Poland, and who left behind a generation of disciples who were themselves rebbes?

That in itself was enough to induce most of the tzaddikim to travel to the "great wedding." But that wasn't the only reason drawing them to Ostilye. They were talking discreetly in the inner circles of the Hasidic courts about the impending trial of the Rebbe of Pshiskhe, Reb Simcha Bunem, that was planned on the occasion of the wedding.

---

1. R. Abraham Joshua Heschel of Opatów/Międzyboż (ca. 1748–1825), known as the "Apter rav."
2. R. Mordecai of Niesuchojeże (1748–1800).
3. R. Elimelekh of Leżajsk (1717–86), tzaddik in Galicia (Austrian Poland), who set the emergent "tzaddik" vocation on a theoretical footing. The honorific "Rebbe Reb" is not redundant, but indicates a master whose disciples became masters in turn.

In most of the Hasidic courts people were upset that he had introduced a new approach to Hasidism—an approach that endangered the way established by the Baal Shem Tov, and which the master's disciples had further developed.

No one spoke openly about the trial that was being prepared, but in quiet they shared their secrets. At the wedding, it was said, the fate of the Rebbe of Pshiskhe would be decided—perhaps he would be excommunicated for having introduced his new approach, and perhaps all of his disciples and Hasidim would be placed under a ban as well, since they were regarded as a new "sect" who might harm the Jewish religion.

And since Ostilye was close to the border between Austria-Hungary and the Russian Empire, nearly all of the rebbes of Poland, Russia and Galicia were preparing to make the journey.

Weeks before the wedding, the imperial highway leading to Ostilye was burdened with hundreds of wagons and covered carts bringing rebbes and their Hasidim.

Every rebbe wanted to impress the old Apter tzaddik not only with his piety and scholarship, but also with his prominence. Every rebbe brought along to the wedding his finest Hasidim, the leading minds and the permanent members of the court. Some of the latter were costumed as Cossacks, with the duty of keeping "guard," to make sure that no ill befell their rebbe, and that no Hasid of another rebbe dared to insult theirs.

The inns on the way to Ostilye were packed full of Hasidim. They drank real Hungarian slivovitz that the Galician Hasidim had brought; real "double mead" from the ancient cellars of Cracow; and precious brandy, pure alcohol, brought by the Russian and Polish Hasidim.

In all of the inns the only topic of conversation was whether the Rebbe Reb Bunem of Pshiskhe would come to the wedding or not. There were rebbes from Poland who had been disciples of Reb Bunem's predecessor in Pshiskhe, the "Holy Jew," and before him of the Jew's own rebbe, the "Seer" Reb Yankev Yitskhok of Lublin. They couldn't stand to see the Rebbe Reb Bunem insulted in public. To tell the truth, they didn't come to spend time at the court of Reb Bunem themselves, but they knew that Reb Bunem was continuing the traditions of the Holy Jew. They couldn't calmly listen when their Pshiskhe way was

A Fire Burns in Kotsk

attacked. Thus everyone sat in the taverns, drinking and talking about the Pshiskhe Rebbe and his fate—but sometimes it came to blows between the various Hasidim as well.

"Do you have any idea who the Rebbe Reb Bunem is?" shouted a Polish Hasid with a flaming copper-red beard and a long brow to a little, skinny Jew from Galicia. "Do you know that Reb Bunem is the son of an extremely well-respected family? That his father Reb Tsvi Hersh was a preacher in Wodzisław, traveled from town to town giving sermons, and wrote the holy books *Asore le'meah* and *Eretz tsvi*?

"And did he study somewhere?" the Galician Hasid wanted to know. "Is he a Torah scholar himself, or does he just rely on his father's merit?"[4]

"He has his own merit," the Polish Hasid said with a broad sweep of his arm. "In his young years he studies at the yeshiva in Mattersdorf in Hungary, under the genius Reb Yermiye,[5] and then in the great yeshiva at Nikolsburg, under the genius Reb Mordecai Banet.[6]

"The Rebbe Reb Bunem," continued the Polish Hasid, "was known as a young genius. A number of communities wanted to install him as their rabbi, but he didn't want to accept a rabbinical post anywhere. And suddenly he became a pharmacist's assistant in Warsaw. Who can understand the ways of the tzaddikim?" (this last to himself). "Then he got married in Pshiskhe, and his business affairs often took him to Germany and Danzig, where he would dress in short, German-style suits."

"Before Reb Bunem was the Rebbe of Pshiskhe," the Polish Hasid continued in a discrete tone, as if conveying a profound secret, "he was friendly with modern[7] Jews in Danzig. When he was there he would often go to the theater with them, and even play cards with them, but not, God forbid, out of moral laxity. He wanted to prevent other Jews from sinning.

---

4. On the charge that Hasidic masters were unlearned or neglected Torah study, a charge undercut by the centrality of Torah study in schools like Lubavitch and Pshiskhe-Kotsk, see *Hasidim u-Mitnagdim*, 2 vols., edited by Mordekhai Wilensky (Jerusalem: Mosad Bialik, 1990). On the importance of familial and hereditary prestige (*yikhes*), see Glenn Dynner, *Men of Silk: The Hasidic Conquest of Polish Jewry* (New York: Oxford University Press, 2006), ch. 4.

5. R. Yirmiyahu of Mattersdorf (d. 1805) became head of the yeshiva there in 1770.

6. Mordekhai ben Avraham Banet (1753–1829), chief rabbi of Moravia.

7. A reference to Jews who had adopted Western styles of clothing and other aspects of the culture of their non-Jewish urban contemporaries.

"And when the Holy Jew passed away during the intermediate days of Succot in 1814, the 'modern' Reb Bunem was chosen by the disciples as his successor, and he began to carry forward the approach of his rebbe, the Holy Jew."

"And what is his path in Hasidism?" the Galician Hasid asked again. "Why do others attack him so bitterly?"

"The Rebbe Reb Bunem teaches us," the Polish Hasid continued in measured words, "that every commandment has to be done in profound secrecy, in the inner compartments of one's own heart. The performance of the commandments must not only be concealed from others, but from oneself as well.

"The essence of worship, says the Rebbe Reb Bunem, is to reach the level of veracity. For every motion, he teaches his Hasidim, that contains an ulterior motive, a false intention, is just like idol worship. 'After all, what difference does it make whether a person worships an alien idol or he worships himself?'

"And similarly, the Rebbe Reb Bunem says, penitence has to be approached differently than it has been up until now. It must be undertaken with a broken heart, and the penitent should demand nothing except that his sins be forgiven, but not the way some Hasidim behave. They shout 'forgive us, pardon us,' and they go right on to demand health and livelihood as well . . .

"Because the Rebbe Reb Bunem stresses the intention underlying the commandment more than the commandment itself, Pshiskhe Hasidim began to focus more and more on the intent to perform each commandment, and that caused them to begin their prayers after the appointed time was over. So other rebbes' Hasidim dreamed up the accusation that when an 'advanced' Pshiskhe Hasid found that he didn't have the right intent, he would skip praying that day altogether. But nobody's ready to testify to that charge before a rabbinical court. But various teachings that the Rebbe Reb Bunem has shared with us show that he does emphasize the importance of coming to recognition of God through concentration on God's works."

"We'll see about that at the trial at the time of the great wedding. By all means, the Rebbe Reb Bunem should come and defend himself."

"Our rebbe doesn't have anything to defend himself against. Every new approach has always been persecuted. Do you know how the

Rebbe Reb Bunem interprets the verse, 'In the beginning God created the heavens and the earth' (Genesis 1:1)? The first thing a Jew has to do, using his own intellect, is to realize that 'God created the heavens and the earth.' You don't only have to believe that, you have to recognize it with your own intellect. That's the new Pshiskhe way. And the Rebbe Reb Bunem also interprets the verse in the morning prayers: "'Always [*leoylem*] a person should fear Heaven in secret." Read *leoylem* hear to mean in public, one should be an ordinary person, but a God-fearer—that, one should be in secret.'"

"It's hard for me to grasp that," the Galician Hasid responded with a shrug of his shoulders. "My brain can't quite comprehend it."

All of the tzaddikim of that generation were afraid that the Pshiskhe approach that the Rebbe Reb Bunem was starting to disseminate among the Polish Hasidim might, God forbid, lead Hasidim to stray from the true path, and they all agreed to place the Rebbe Reb Bunim under a ban of excommunication. They wanted to see to it that this happened at the great wedding in Ostilye.

The leaders of the battle against the Rebbe of Pshiskhe were the two greatest rebbes of their generation. The first was the Rebbe Reb Yaakov Shimon Daytsh of Vizhnitz,[8] who later lived in Zhelekhov,[9] and who, while the Seer of Lublin still lived, persecuted the Holy Jew for having "rebelled" against the Seer. The second was the Rebbe Reb Yosef of Yartshev,[10] who later lived in Tomashov, was a fervent Hasid of Reb Avrohom Yehoshue of Apt, and constantly spoke to his own rebbe against the Rebbe Reb Bunem.

But the old Rebbe of Apt never accepted their gossip, and always said that he would have to hear the other side of the story from the Rebbe Reb Bunem himself. So the two tzaddikim saw to it that the Rebbe of Apt himself should send a wedding invitation to the Rebbe Reb Bunem, so that he would come and they would be able to dispute Reb Bunem. They meant to show the Rebbe of Apt how far the Pshiskhe approach had strayed from the foundations of the Jewish faith.

---

8. R. Simon Deutch of Żelechów/Radzyń, a disciple of R. Abraham Joshuah Heschel of Apt (Opatów), one of the main accusers of R. Simha Bunem of Pshiskhe.

9. Żelechów, a town in the Kingdom of Poland, once home to the Hasidic master R. Levi Isaac of Berdyczów.

10. Little is known about R. Yosef of Yartshev (born in Tomaszów), a disciple of R. Simha Bunem of Pshyskhe.

That would lead the Rebbe of Apt himself to order the excommunication of Reb Bunem and his "sect."

And indeed, the Rebbe Reb Bunem received an invitation from the old Rebbe of Apt, and he decided that he would go to the wedding.

While in all the other Hasidic courts everyone was happily anticipating that they would soon see the holy Rebbe of Apt in person, a gloomy mood reigned in Pshiskhe.

The Rebbe Reb Bunem called for his best disciples, and he said to them: "Although I know that I'll be put through terrible trials there, nevertheless I'm going to go to Ostilye."

"I know," Reb Bunem said further, "that the tzaddikim have betrayed me to the old Rebbe of Apt, but I'll show them who's traveling the true path and who isn't, which is the authentic Hasidic path and which isn't. They consider themselves to be tzaddikim, and they don't know what the Seer of Lublin said in his youth, when he was still seeking his way in Hasidism, rather than just sitting in his chair and working wonders. In his young years the Rebbe of Lublin said: 'Better an evildoer who knows he's an evildoer than a tzaddik who knows he's a tzaddik.' I'll go to Ostilye and have it out with them."

The disciples of the Rebbe Reb Bunem all stood there in mortal terror. They were afraid to dissuade the Rebbe from going through with the trial. They understood that if the Rebbe went to the wedding, no good would come of it. But at that moment the young man from Tomashov, Reb Mendele, later to become the Kotsker Rebbe, called out to the Hasidim:

"Why should we be afraid of them? They say that there will be over a hundred 'white frocks' at the wedding." (The rebbes wore white frocks in those days.) "On market days in Pshiskhe we can also find a hundred white frocks in the tavern." (The peasants living in the countryside also wore a sort of white frock in those days.)

"True, Mendele my dear," the Pshiskhe Rebbe said. "We should be there. We should go, and we shouldn't act arrogantly because a *yid* shouldn't act like a big shot. If a *yid* (the letter *yud*) becomes too big, it stops being a *yid* (it becomes a *vov*).[11]

---

11. The Hebrew letter *yud* is pronounced "*yid*" in Polish Yiddish, and is thus a homonym of the word *yid*, Jew. *Yud* is written as a short, half-vertical line; if extended too far (if it becomes "too big"), it becomes the latter *vov*, written as a full straight line.

A Fire Burns in Kotsk

"And believe me," the Pshiskhe Rebbe continued after spending a few moments in contemplation, "I feel now that I could bring Messiah. But I imagine how Messiah will arrive. First of all, he'll acquaint himself with the leaders of the generation, and all of the tzaddikim will come to greet him. Then all of the tzaddikim together with Messiah will join the old Rebbe of Apt. The Rebbe of Apt will sit at the head; on either side great tzaddikim will be seated, and I'll be down at the very end... Most likely the old Rebbe will ask Messiah right away who managed to make him come. Messiah will point to me and say: 'That one, Bunem of Pshiskhe, is the one who did it!' That will cause the Rebbe of Apt great anguish... And that's why I'm not going to bring Messiah... I don't want to cause the old man pain, but I have to go see him!"

The disciples understood that this was a bit of a jest on the Pshiskhe Rebbe's part... and the Rebbe immediately ordered his Sabbath clothes to be bought, ordered his secretary to harness the horses, and went out into the marketplace to get into the cart.

He was accompanied by his disciples Reb Hirsh of Tomashov,[12] Reb Henekh of Alexander,[13] Reb Yitskhok Meir of Warsaw,[14] Reb Yitskhok of Vurke,[14] Reb Mendele of Tomashov, and many other leading Hasidim.

They all know that they mustn't permit the Rebbe Reb Bunem to go to the wedding, but they didn't know how to prevent his going. They even talked it over with the genius from Warsaw, Reb Yitskhok Meir, who was one of the Pshiskhe Rebbe's favorites, but the genius from Warsaw didn't dare approach the Rebbe to tell him not to go.

And the Pshiskhe Rebbe would certainly have gone to the wedding if Reb Mendele of Tomashov hadn't taken his life into his hands and stopped him.

---

12. R. Hirsz of Tomaszów was the main attendant of R. Menahem Mendel of Kotsk.

13. Hanokh Henokh Hakohen of Aleksander (1798–1870) became the reluctant successor to R. Isaac Meir of Ger.

14. Isaac Meir Alter of Warsaw (1789–1866), later the first Gerer *rebbe*, author of *Hiddushe ha-rim*.

15. R. Isaac Kalish of Warka (1779–1848), known as the Vurke Rebbe, was often regarded as a mild alternative to the fiery Kotsker rebbe. He was also successful as a lobbyist (*shtadlan*) on behalf of the Polish Jewish community.

2

At a Tavern Outside Ostilye

The Rebbe Reb Bunem was standing in his Sabbath[16] clothes next to the cart, one foot on the running board, when he suddenly heard a young man shouting at the top of his lungs:

"I won't let the Rebbe go! Over my body he'll go!"

The Rebbe Reb Bunem, whose sight was already partially gone by this time, recognized the voice, and he ordered the young man stretched out in front of the wagon to be stood up and brought to him.

It was the young man from Tomashov, Reb Mendele.

"What are you afraid of, Mendele?" the Rebbe Reb Bunem said, rubbing the young man's back. "Let's all go and show them, those old tzaddikim who are going to be gathered there, who we are.

"And do you know why we recite the blessings thanking 'God who gives sight to the blind,' 'God who straightens the crooked,' 'God who loves the pious [*tzaddikim*],'" the Rebbe Reb Bunem asked, turning to his Hasidim. "What do tzaddikim have to do with people who have disabilities? The answer is that this, too, is a terrible disability because there's no one more crippled than someone who considers himself a tzaddik!"

"But if the Rebbe goes," Reb Mendele responded passionately, "I will also go because the law is that 'if the master goes into exile, his disciples go into exile with him.'"[17]

"We'll all go!" shouted a number of the Hasidim.

"No! I'm afraid for your sakes," answered the Rebbe Reb Bunem, "and I'm especially afraid for your sake, Mendele, you and your sharp tongue!"

"If so, then the Rebbe shouldn't go either!" shouted the hundreds of Hasidim who had gathered at the marketplace.

---

16. That is, Reb Simcha Bunem dressed in his festive clothes, since he planned to attend the great event. Of course it was not the Sabbath, when he would be forbidden to ride.

17. Babylonian Talmud Makkot 10a.

The Rebbe of Pshiskhe thought for a moment, rubbed his hand across his brow, and then, grabbing the belt of Reb Mendele's frock with his two hands as was his custom, said:

"Absolutely, if we stay together, we've got nothing to fear from them!"

And the Rebbe went back into his house.

Immediately after the evening prayers, the Rebbe of Pshiskhe ordered his leading Hasidim to be brought in to see him. They closed the shutters of the windows so that no one would be able to see what was going on inside, and they began thinking of a way to block the plans of the Austro-Hungarian rebbe Reb Yaakov Shimshon Daytsh and the other rebbes who wanted to convince the old Rebbe of Apt to place them under a ban.

The secret meeting at the home of the Rebbe Reb Bunem lasted until after midnight. It was decided that five disciples capable of combating the other side should be sent to the wedding. They decided that the five had to include a Talmud scholar, a Hasid, a rich man, a gifted speaker, and a wise man.

The Rebbe Reb Bunem chose all five from among his disciples. Their mission was to dispute those who would slander the Pshiskhe Hasidim at the wedding.

For the role of Hasid, he chose Reb Fayvl of Gritse,[18] who had already been a devoted follower of the Seer in Lublin. The wise man—Reb Zishe of Shedlits,[19] who was known for his wisdom among the Pshiskhe Hasidim. The rich man—Reb Yisokherl Horowitz, a scion of a notable family and son-in-law of the well-known, rich, and powerful Temerl of Warsaw.[20] The eloquent one—Reb Eliezer Ber of Grokhovits,[21] whose rhetorical powers were so compelling that the Pshiskhe Hasidim said he could bring a wall together with another wall. And for the Talmud scholar, the Pshiskhe Rebbe indicated the genius from Warsaw, Reb Yitskhok Meir, later to become the Rebbe of Ger.

---

18. Gritse (Grójec) is a town 25 miles south of Warsaw.

19. Shedlits (Siedlce) is a town in eastern Poland, in the Mazovian district.

20. Temerl Sonnenberg-Bergson (d. 1830), patron of Polish Hasidism and benefactor of Warsaw Jewry. In 1787, she married Berek Sonnenberg, the son of the Warsaw plutocrat Shmul Zbytkower.

21. R. Eliezer Dov Ber of Grochowicz is a relatively unknown figure, apart from this episode.

The genius from Warsaw was terrified when he realized that he had been chosen among the five who would have to defend the Pshiskhe Rebbe. In his panic he burst out crying. The Rebbe Reb Bunem approached him and said, "What are you crying for? Do you know why the Talmud says that 'the gates of tears were not sealed?'[22] If the gates weren't sealed, then what are the gates for, and for whom? The answer is: they're for the tears of the fools who often don't know why they're crying. But you certainly aren't in that category, so what are you crying for? Don't be afraid," he continued, caressing Reb Yitskhok Meir's chin, "go and be victorious!"

By the time the Rebbe Reb Bunem accompanied the Hasidim out of his room, it was already quite late. He said goodbye to each one separately, taking time to encourage them. The five disciples, along with the rest of the Hasidim, went to the Hasidic tavern in the middle of the marketplace. Reb Yosl the innkeeper had already gone to sleep, but he heard them knocking on the shutters. He got up, went out in a smock and gave them a bottle of pure aquavit.

The Hasidim toasted each other by moonlight.

Reb Fayvl of Gritse, the former Lublin Hasid, stood by the side, drinking from the bottle and weeping to think that in his old age he would have to travel to someone else's rebbe to defend the Pshiskhe Rebbe. Reb Mendele of Tomashov noticed this, approached him and said: "What are you unhappy about? Let me go in your place and you'll see how I argue with them!"

The other Hasidim also saw Reb Fayvl of Gritse crying, and Reb Henekh of Aleksander approached him and cried:

"What is a Pshiskhe Hasid? A disciple of the Holy Jew should cry? Let him put up some money for liquor, and if not, we'll give him a beating right in the middle of the marketplace!"

And with that, a couple of the Hasidim grabbed him and laid him out across the big stone in the middle of the marketplace. They whipped him with their belts until Reb Fayvele shouted that he would be happy from now on, and that he would treat them to liquor in the tavern outside Ostilye.

---

22. Babylonian Talmud Berakhot 32.

A large cart pulled up into the middle of the marketplace, and the five Hasidim settled into the cart. The genius from Warsaw pushed aside Yantek, the court's usual coachman, took the reins in his hands as he prepared to drive the horses, and Reb Mendele of Tomashov shouted after them:

"Good for you! And you," turning to the other four Hasidim, "tell those guys in Ostilye, those little rebbes from Galicia, that the coachman from Pshiskhe has more Torah in his little fingernail than all of them put together!"

So the Hasidim traveled a night and a day, and late on the second night they arrived at the inn next to Ostilye.

It was so crowded around the inn that one simply couldn't get through. The five Pshiskhe Hasidim stopped the cart on a side street and agreed that they would go into the inn disguised, without revealing their identities.

Inside the tavern it was like a beehive. Hundreds of Hasidim sat at the tables, some drinking liquor, some beer, and some just a glass of tea. The five Hasidim sat down at the side so as not to be conspicuous, and Reb Zishe of Shedlits immediately reminded Reb Fayvl of Gritse that he was obligated to order liquor.

"You know that I want it just as much as you do, but what can I do? I don't have an old penny to my name."

"What do we care about that?" the four disciples responded. "You promised—so give us some booze!"

"But I don't have any money!"

"So pawn your tallis and tefillin!"

"But we agreed that we shouldn't be conspicuous, and if anyone sees us pawning our tallis and tefillin for liquor, they'll immediately figure out who we are."

"Well, but we still want to drink," spoke up Reb Eliezer Ber, the spokesman.

"You know what—I have an idea," answered Reb Zishe of Shedlits. "Let him pawn his tallis and tefillin, but not to a stranger, to Reb Yisokherl Horowitz, the rich son-in-law."

Everyone liked the idea except Reb Yisokherl, but he had no choice. He had to take a silver coin from his wallet and loan it to Reb Fayvl, and Reb Fayvl handed over to him his tallis and his tefillin bag.

"Of course," added Reb Zishe of Shedlits, "when Reb Fayvl needs to pray, Reb Yisokherl will loan him the tefillin bag. He wouldn't want Reb Fayvl to be prevented from praying on his account..."

Reb Yisokherl saw that he'd been trapped, but it was too late. The silver coin was already in Reb Fayvl's pocket.

"Why should I be responsible for guarding your tallis and tefillin?" Reb Yisokherl said to Reb Fayvl. "Take them back already."

The five Pshiskhe disciples sat down at the table and ordered a whole jug of mead.

The inn was so smoky that it was difficult to see. Through the thick air various voices and shouts could be heard.

Right in front of the inn, at a large table, sat several rebbes from Poland and Galicia. People crowded around the table from all sides to hear what the rebbes were saying. From time to time the aides to the various rebbes would begin throwing the hats off the Hasidim to make them stop pushing.[23] A flood of caps, Polish hats, lambskin hats, and wide velvet yarmulkes began to fly across the room. When things calmed down for a few minutes, the five disciples heard various shouts from the area where everyone was crowding in:

"And I tell you that he'll definitely come!" a Galician Hasid shouted.

"We'll see," answered a Polish Hasid.

"What do we need them for," squeaked a Lithuanian Hasid in a high voice. "If they don't come, we'll tell the holy Rebbe of Apt ourselves who they are!"

The five disciples understood what all the conversations were about, but they pretended it had nothing to do with them, and drained the pot of mead to the dregs.

But they wanted to drink even more, and they tried to figure out a way to get the rich man's son-in-law, Reb Yisokherl, to give them another silver coin. Eventually the genius from Warsaw, Reb Yitskhok Meir, had an idea and called to Reb Yisokherl:

"Yisokherl, you need to order liquor because you're sitting at the Rebbe's table."

"At whose table?" asked Reb Yisokherl. "You can't be much of a Hasid if you're that confused after a couple of glasses of mead."

---

23. A classic form of crowd control: remove the head covering of a religious Jew, and he has no choice but to stop what he's doing and retrieve it.

"Don't be afraid, I know what I'm talking about. If I say that you're sitting at the Rebbe's table, I know what I mean! Listen, gentlemen," he said to the other four from Pshiskhe, "don't you agree that our Rebbe should be so famous that the entire world would go to him?"

"Certainly," answered the rest of the Pshiskhe Hasidim.

"Well, so the table would certainly reach from Pshiskhe to here, and since you've merited to sit right there, Reb Yisokherl, you're one of the Rebbe's intimate circle, so I ask you: Shouldn't he stand us a drink?"

All four of the Hasidim were delighted with the Warsaw genius's accomplishment. Reb Yisokherl immediately produced a new silver coin from his wallet and ordered a bottle of pure aquavit, and they went back to drinking.

In the corner, around a small table, stood a few old Kozhenitse Hasidim reciting Psalms. They watched as five Hasidim sat nearby, talking to no one else, but continually drinking. In addition, they could tell that the five Hasidim were discretely laughing at various rebbes who passed by their table from time to time. Eventually one of them, a very elderly Kozhenitse Hasid, couldn't contain himself and shouted at them:

"Wise guys! None of your conversation is about Judaism. Have you ever seen creatures like this? They sit there all night, drink like regular Gentiles and make fun of honest Jews and tzaddikim."

"And what are you doing?" answered the spokesman, Reb Eliezer Ber.

"What are we doing?" answered another old Kozhenitse Hasid. "You can see what we're doing. We're not spending the night in silliness, like you. First we were talking about Hasidism, and now we're reciting Psalms."

"Now that's really something," responded Reb Yitshok Meir. "King David spent his whole life working on those Psalms, and you're going to get through them in one night?"

The Pshiskhe Hasidim, who were already quite tipsy, burst into loud laughter hearing Reb Yitskhok Meir's cleverness. In their anger the Kozhenitse Hasidim came forward and began shouting: "Heresy! It's unforgivable! Out of here!"

Reb Fayvl of Gritse, who was the eldest of the five Pshiskhe Hasidim, immediately understood where this might lead. He wanted to calm the Kozhenitse Hasidim, and he turned to them:

"Don't be offended! You can see that we've had a bit to drink, but the young man didn't mean it as you understood it; he only meant to suggest that the main thing isn't how much you recite but how you do it."

"That's all well and good," answered the old Kozhenitse Hasid, "but what if you don't say anything at all?"

"You must understand," Reb Fayvl began reasoning with the Kozhenitse Hasidim again, "that recitation by itself isn't the main thing; rather, the intent behind the recitation is the main thing. It doesn't really matter what vessel you place your intentions in; so it can turn out that one informs a glass of liquor with the same intentions as you did your recitation of Psalms!"

"That's what you think?" shouted the Kozhenitse Hasidim. "So now we know who we're dealing with here. You're from that gang, that sect—and what are you doing here?"

When the others in the tavern heard that there were Hasidim from the "sect" there, from all sides people began running to the table where the Pshiskhe Hasidim were sitting.

The Pshiskhe Hasidim saw that things were going badly, and that they were about to risk being torn in pieces. Their whole plan to travel to Ostilye might be ruined. Reb Fayvl of Gritse nodded to the other four Pshiskhe Hasidim that it was time to get away. While calls came from every side: "Where are they? Don't let them out!" the five disciples surreptitiously made their way out of the inn, quickly ran to the cart, hurried to harness the horses, and made their way to the imperial road leading to Ostilye.

3

Hasidic Cossacks

The five Pshiskhe Hasidim drove on toward Ostilye through the night, in constant anxiety. It seemed to them that they were being pursued from the direction of the inn where they had barely escaped being beaten once their identity was discovered. By the time they arrived at Ostilye dawn was breaking. All of the roads were full of wagons loaded with Hasidim traveling from various towns and cities to the great wedding in Ostilye.

Every few minutes another wagon would pull into the Ostilye marketplace with much ado, with music and song. From time to time, a proper carriage would arrive bearing a rebbe. They could be immediately recognized by the Cossacks riding around the carriage; according to their various disguises, it was possible to tell whether their rebbe was Polish, Russian, or from the Austro-Hungarian Empire. Every country had its own wedding "Cossacks." The Russian Cossacks were dressed like Circassians, the Polish ones like soldiers from the old Polish army, and the Galicians like Hungarian Hussars.

The Cossacks filled the streets and lanes of Ostilye, and just before daybreak the town looked as though it had been invaded by foreign armies.

When the five Pshiskhe Hasidim arrived in Ostilye, they immediately set off for an inn. But since all of the inns were already fully occupied, they barely managed to get a bit of space in an attic. This worked out perfectly for the Pshiskhe Hasidim because only paupers slept in the attic, and they knew no one would recognize them there.

Quite early in the morning the Cossacks began to go from one inn to another, wherever a rebbe was staying, playing their parts. This is how they did it: An old Cossack rode in front, wearing yellow pants and a Hussar's fur coat, and a pointed cap with a feather on his head. Behind him rode a second Cossack, with his beard combed to either side. In his hand he carried a long stick, a red scarf tied to its end. That served as a kind of flag. The man carrying it was the "conductor" of the Galician Hasidim's Cossack orchestra.

This Cossack had acquired the title of conductor because he was the only one to have traveled with his rebbe to one of the mineral bath spas, serving as a kosher slaughterer—and while there he had heard an orchestra play.

Behind the conductor rode the rest of the Cossack "orchestra." They held little drums. Some of them carried old pots, other pieces of tin or rolling pins, and some of them blew into plain sticks, pretending they were playing flutes. At the end rode the basses, pretending to play on long brooms.

Every few minutes a tumult broke out among the orchestra, when a horse bolted, trying to throw off its Hasidic Cossack rider. The thousands of Hasidim in the marketplace stood watching and doubled over in laughter watching the Cossack struggle with his last ounce of strength to stay on the horse. Eventually the coachman who had loaned the horse to the wedding Cossacks came along, caressed the horse's chin, and immediately calmed it down. Then the orchestra rode further to play at another inn.

More than eighty rebbes came to the wedding, and even more were expected, because the old Rebbe of Apt wasn't supposed to come until the evening, certain to bring several more rebbes in his train. All of the rebbes who were already in Ostilye, along with their thousands of Hasidim, were getting ready to welcome the Rebbe of Apt.

The Rebbe Reb Shimen Daytsh and the Rebbe Reb Yosef of Yartshev had an inn to themselves, along with their own officer corps of Cossacks, who came in every few minutes to report which rebbes had already arrived in town.

Most of the rebbes were from Galicia and Poland. They could be recognized by the style of fur hats the Polish and Galician Hasidim wore. The Galician Hasidim wore *shtraymlekh* made out of fourteen tails, and the Polish Hasidim wore tall *spodkes*.[24] The Rebbe Reb Shimen Daytsh, who was living in Zhelekhov at the time, was also considered a Galician rebbe because he had earlier lived in Vizhnits. He was one of those wearing a

---

24. The *shtrayml*, typically worn by Hasidim on Sabbaths and festivals, consists of a large circular piece of black velvet surrounded by fur, usually sable. Hasidic dynasties deriving from the Kingdom of Poland usually wear a high *shtrayml*, known as a *spodik*.

Galician-style *shtrayml* with fourteen tails, and he was friendly with the rebbes from Galicia. Perhaps in their hearts the Polish rebbes sought, like Reb Shimen Daytsh, to distance themselves from the Rebbe Reb Bunem and his Hasidim, but they still respected Reb Bunem. Reb Shimen Daytsh knew that they wouldn't intervene actively with the Rebbe of Apt in opposition to the Pshiskhe way. So Reb Shimen hurried from one inn to another, lobbying a different rebbe at each one, telling him that the Pshiskhe way was so dangerous that there was no choice except to have the Rebbe Reb Bunem placed under a ban.

Reb Shimen still thought that Reb Bunem would come to the wedding. But when Kozhenitse Hasidim who lived near Pshiskhe arrived and reported that the Rebbe Reb Bunem had decided not to appear before the old Rebbe of Apt, Reb Shimen Daytsh was pleased that he wouldn't have to face a forceful opponent. On the other hand, he regretted that he wouldn't have the opportunity to show the Rebbe Reb Bunem, right in front of the old Rebbe of Apt, that Reb Bunem's way was causing Jews to stray from the true path.

The five Pshiskhe Hasidim spent the entire morning going from inn to inn, discovering who had already arrived, and what the rebbes were saying to each other about Reb Bunem. They had just arrived at one inn where a couple old Hasidim of Reb Meirl of Apt were sitting, when they heard one old Hasid repeat something his rebbe had said about Bunem.

And this is the story he told:

One time a Hasid came to Reb Meirl and told him that he wanted to go to the Rebbe Reb Bunem. Reb Meirl answered him: "It is written, 'Erase me [*mokheni*] from the book You have written'" (Exodus 32:32). I know what everybody says about the Rebbe of Pshiskhe, that he's a *moykh-mentsh*,[25] an intellectual. But my prayer is, *moykheyni*—give me brains, accomplishments, but only from the book that You wrote! From the Torah, that is, not from the merchants who spend entire months in Danzig, going to various illicit places there."

The five Pshiskhe Hasidim heard what was being said about their rebbe, but none of them dared to respond, following the instructions they'd gotten in Pshiskhe so that they would be able to respond

---

25. Yiddish: literally "brain-person."

appropriately to the opponents of Pshiskhe at the wedding. But Reb Zishe of Shedlits couldn't restrain himself, and retorted: "And do you know what the Rebbe Reb Bunem responded, when he was told what your rebbe had said about him?"

"No," answered the Hasidim.

"If so, then I'll tell you," Reb Zishe continued the conversation. "The Rebbe Reb Bunem said: 'I know what the Rebbe Reb Meir of Apt says about me—that a leader can't reach spiritual attainments by going to the theaters in Danzig. But Meir of Apt doesn't know how one sins or what a transgression is. I, on the other hand, have been in the theaters in Danzig. I know how to heal sinners, and to bring my Hasidim to the fear of Heaven."

"But why should you bother to choose the kind of rebbe who can heal sinners? Has everyone sunk to that level?" persisted an old Hasid of the Rebbe Reb Meirl.

"You have to reach a very high level in order to know which rebbe to choose," answered Reb Zishe of Shedlits. "Do you know what the Rebbe Reb Bunem said about the matter of choosing a tzaddik for oneself? It's worth hearing: 'Once I asked my rebbe, the Holy Jew,' said the Rebbe Reb Bunem, 'the meaning of the Talmudic dictum: "Everything that is attached to what is pure is like what is pure." Does a Hasid really become as great as the rebbe he goes to see?' And the Holy Jew answered him: 'Yes! But in order to be attached to a true tzaddik, you have to have reached a very high level yourself because you have to choose the true tzaddik of the generation, and not everyone is capable of that. Many Hasidim choose a tzaddik who is quite unworthy; they err. On the other hand, when Messiah comes,' continued the Holy Jew, 'all the rebbes will go to meet him, accompanied by their Hasidim. But when Messiah sees the kind of rebbes these are, he'll be terribly disappointed, and he'll send them all away from his presence. All of the Hasidim will fall at the feet of our Tzaddik Messiah and weep: "Is it our fault? Our intentions were good. We thought they were true rebbes!" But Messiah will have no regard for them, and won't listen to their weeping. He'll answer: "You should have really thought it over before choosing a rebbe for yourselves. But you were satisfied with your first look, and for that you deserve to be beaten!"' That's what the Rebbe Reb Bunem told us," concluded Reb Zishe of Shedlits.

"Good," interjected other Hasidim, "we're blind indeed, and that's why we seek first of all a rebbe who is careful about his observance of Judaism and makes sure he won't go outside the boundaries. And to which rebbe do you go?" they asked, turning to the five Pshiskhe Hasidim.

"I've been around long enough that I used to go to the Seer of Lublin," responded Reb Fayvl of Gritse, utterly confusing the questioners because all of the Hasidim instantly respected someone who had been in the presence of the Seer of Lublin.

"But if you afflict your body, if you fast and say Psalms," answered the Hasidim, "you can hope that you will reach a high enough spiritual level that you'll merit to choose the true tzaddik of the generation!"

"Fasting doesn't always do it," answered Reb Fayvl of Gritse. "And do you know how a disciple of the Baal Shem Tov interpreted the verse, 'This is the law of the burnt-offering, of the meal-offering, and of the sin-offering, and of the guilt-offering' (Leviticus VII:37)? That the Torah can sometimes be a burnt-offering or a meal-offering for someone, but other times it can be a sin and a source of guilt . . ."

"What more can you do besides fasting?" asked an old Hasid. "We know that fasting purifies us."

"Are you sure you know that?" answered Reb Zishe. "You know what they say about the Baal Shem Tov and his horses? What? You never heard the story?" He looked at them in surprise. "If you want, I'll tell you."

"By all means!" voices were heard, "we have time, it will still be quite a while before we go to greet the holy Rebbe of Apt."

"Well, if you're asking me, I'll accede to your request.

"It's related that once the Baal Shem Tov had to travel by supernatural means,[26] so he ordered his coachman to harness the horses, and he began to fly over mountains and valleys, straight as an arrow from the bow. But the horses saw that they were traveling past one inn after another without stopping. So with their equine minds they thought that they must be great spiritual masters who were committed to fasting. But as they continued to travel, passing by a few more

---

26. Known as *kvitzat ha-derekh* ("short-cut"), a magical technique originating among pre-Hasidic mystical practioners called *ba'alei shem* ("Name-masters").

inns without stopping to feed them, the horses began to think that they must be really extraordinary figures, since they didn't seem to need to eat at all. Eventually, when they had passed yet more inns, the horses thought that perhaps they were actually angels. And the Baal Shem Tov concluded by saying that as long as they were driving and the horses didn't eat, they were indeed in an angelic state, but as soon as they stopped at an inn and the horses started eating, they stopped being angels and returned to being horses."

The old Hasidic stranger understood whom Reb Zishe had in mind when he related the story about the Baal Shem Tov.

Meanwhile it started growing dark outside. In every window the residents placed silver candelabras with burning candles to illuminate the path the holy Rebbe of Apt would be riding. All of the rebbes began preparing to greet the old Rebbe of Apt.

And in order to please the old Rebbe, the younger rebbes agreed that they would dress up as Cossacks themselves, and ride up to meet the Apter.

More than eighty rebbes set out from Ostilye disguised as Cossacks, riding on horses and carrying sticks in their hand instead of flutes. They played a melody which has remained a standard melody until this very day. Every rebbe was surrounded by hundreds of Hasidim with burning torches in their hands, and they rode along singing for miles, until they arrived at an inn. They stopped there, waiting for the coach carrying the old Rebbe of Apt and the thirteen-year-old groom. The Hasidim lined up along both sides of the road, carrying the burning torches. In front of them stood the Cossack-rebbes, and when they saw the Apter Rebbe's coach, the rebbes and the Hasidim began singing a lively tune with the words, "David, King of Israel, lives!"

The Apter Rebbe ordered the coach to be stopped. He climbed down. Every rebbe individually greeted him, and then the Hasidim began pushing forward to meet him. When it was the turn of the five Pshiskhe Hasidim, who had also come to greet the Rebbe of Apt, the latter suddenly stopped, held back his thin, bony hand, looked at them sharply and asked:

"Who are you?"

The Pshiskhe Hasidim felt for a moment that all was lost. They didn't want to say who their rebbe was, but they also didn't want to lie. They simply answered: "We are Polish Hasidim."

"I don't care for *'poyelishe'* rebbes.[27] Can they really accomplish anything for their Hasidim?" asked the old Rebbe of Apt with a smile. Before the Pshiskhe Hasidim had a chance to answer, they were carried along in the stream of Hasidim who wanted to greet the old Apter. The Pshiskhe Hasidim were hardly troubled at the brief interview, since they hadn't wanted to reveal their identities.

The old Rebbe of Apt immediately began telling his tall tales, as was his custom. He retold that for his son's wedding he'd ordered a fur to be made. Its hairs had been so deep that a Cossack riding a horse and holding a dagger in his hand could hide inside it, and the pelt was also so soft that the entire fur coat could be hidden inside a walnut shell.

The rebbes and Hasidim immediately began meditating, trying to understand what the Apter Rebbe had meant. It was well known that the Rebbe of Apt habitually concealed the true intent of his words. The Rebbe Reb Borukhl of Mezbuzh had said of him, "He weighs every word." It was also said of him: "He has a golden scale in his mouth, and he does not utter a single superfluous word."

Meanwhile the horses were unharnessed, and the Hasidim began singing and pulling the coach themselves. And when they arrived in Ostilye, the five Pshiskhe Hasidim heard the Rebbe Reb Shimen Daytsh saying to a couple of Polish rebbes: "If we can arrange it, then tonight, at the 'groom's meal,'[28] we'll begin telling the Rebbe about the Pshiskhe Hasidim. Let Blind Bunem hide in Pshiskhe; we'll still show him what we can accomplish . . ."

"And we'll see who wins!" a voice was suddenly heard.

The Reb Reb Shimen Daytsh looked around to see who had said these words, but he couldn't find their source.

---

27. A pun on *poyln* (Poland) and *poyeln* (to accomplish).

28. The groom's meal (Yiddish: *khosns tish*), held at a table laden with food and drink, is an occasion to toast the groom and sing. The groom attempts to offer a discourse but is customarily interrupted with singing and clapping to protect him from potential shame should he be unlearned. A wedding jester (*badkhn*) then sings toasts to the groom in rhymed couplets.

4

In an Attic in Ostilye

The old Apter Rebbe was brought to Ostilye with much singing and music.

Hasidim besieged the house where the Apter was staying. They were ready to tear the house apart to see the Rebbe, but soon the Rebbe's chief secretary came out of the Rebbe's private chamber and said: "The Rebbe is very tired from the journey and begs you to leave him in peace now. Tomorrow the Rebbe will receive people."

And that was enough to convince the Hasidim to return to their inns, or to celebrate with their rebbes. For the same reason, the groom's meal was postponed.

In the attic of the inn where the five Pshiskhe Hasidim were concealed, a lantern burned after midnight, and a broken shard of window glass nearby threw great shadows on the sharply angled walls of the roof.

Down the entire length of the attic poor folk lay on the floor, shirtless, wearing nothing but old patches, soundly snoring. It hardly mattered to them that the Pshiskhe way was about to be on trial at the wedding. The old Rebbe himself was to sit at the pauper's feast, personally handing out silver rubles to each and every pauper there.

For the moment they were comfortably snoring, these paupers who had walked for miles in order to arrive on time at the great wedding in Ostilye. The five Pshiskhe Hasidim were off to a side, thinking about how to defend the Pshiskhe way before the Apter Rebbe. They were trying to decide who would speak first in the Pshiskhe Rebbe's behalf.

"If they want to talk about scholarship," spoke up Reb Fayvele Gritser, "then you, Itshe Meirl, should immediately intervene, so they'll know that thank God we know how to study. And you, Zishe Shedlitser, should help him, you're the wise one. And finally you, Eliezer Ber, should come in, and we'll all help out."

"Why should I be first?" asked Itshe Meirl in a trembling voice. "Who am I to speak up among such scholars? Whenever I look at Reb

Shimen Daytsh, with his dirty looks, I get completely terrified! In addition, they're preparing so hard for the dispute, and I can't understand why they hate us, why they call us a 'sect.' What do they see in us that makes them harass us so?"

"Really," added the wealthy young man, Yisokher Horovits. "Why do they make up such slanders about us?"

"Oy, Itshe Meirl," Fayvl Gritser sighed into his gray beard, "you're still two young pups, and you don't know everything that happened before this. You, Itshe Meirl, really should remember, since you lived in Kozhenits. But you, Yisokherl, are still quite young, you showed up when it was all in place, but don't think that it was always like this. It took a long time before the Rebbe of blessed memory, the Holy Jew, was ready to break with the Seer of Lublin. But you've probably heard about that?"

And although all of them certainly knew the story, they still wanted to hear from Reb Fayvele from beginning to end how the Holy Jew had torn himself away from Lublin, for Reb Fayvele was an eyewitness. He himself had traveled to the Seer. All of them began asking Reb Fayvele to tell them once again how the great dispute had begun in Lublin.

"If so," answered Reb Fayvele Grister, "if you want to hear the story how the dispute began, you have to promise me that you'll sit and listen to the end, and in the meantime you have to give me a bit to drink because discussing Hasidism without a drink is like reciting the daily rabbinic readings without Psalms."[29]

Reb Zishe Shedlitser happened to have a bottle of pure liquor which he'd stashed away three days earlier. The five Pshiskhe Hasidim poured themselves large glasses of it and quietly wished each other "lechaim." Reb Fayvele Gritser warmed himself a bit and began relating:

"There was a time when Poland hadn't heard about the great light of Hasidim, until the Rebbe Reb Elimelech and Reb Mekhele Zlotshever spread the Baal Shem Tov's way among the Polish Jews. After them came the student of Rebbe Elimelech, the Seer of Lublin.

"And then the storm began throughout Poland. They lit candles in the synagogues, they placed us under a ban, using the well-known

---

29. The reference is to two components of the traditional morning service. The first, known as *karbanot* (sacrifices) consists of Biblical and Rabbinic discussions of details of the sacrifices in the Temple in Jerusalem. The second, *pesukei d'zimrah* (verses of praise), is a selection from the Book of Psalms.

formula: 'to rise up impetuously, to oppose the terrible sinners who pray using the Sefardic rite[30] and who introduce new customs,' just the same as today's Hasidim say that we are, God forbid, who knows what, so they want to excommunicate us. But the tzaddikim in those days didn't care about the big tumult their opponents made, and they attracted more and more Hasidim. The rebbes understood that the common folk didn't have time for studying like the scholars do, so rather than distancing them, like the opponents do, they should be drawn close. The tzaddikim knew that the common people were overworked, worried about earning a livelihood, and they don't have much left over for spiritual matters. It's enough for them if they go to a rebbe for the Sabbath, listen to his teachings, soak in a bit of the warmth, and have enough strength afterward to withstand all of the trouble they get from the Polish noblemen and the Jewish magnates and notables who still continue to persecute us.

"The first rebbes indeed tried to do only good things for their Hasidim, even to work miracles, as long as they could make their lives a bit easier.

"Among the first rebbes in Poland were some who would virtually risk their lives for another Jew.

"And who was the Holy Jew's first rebbe? Reb Moyshe Leyb of Sasov,[31] who said: 'Nine Moyshe Leybs don't constitute a minyan, but ten tailors do.' What he meant to convey was that ten simple tailors are worth more to the Master of the Universe than nine scholars like Moyshe Leyb.

"You can imagine what the opponents of Hasidism thought of him. Even the Holy Jew, who was at that time the head of the yeshiva where Reb Moyshe Leyb lived, was at first unable to grasp the new path, befriending every simple Jew and teaching him that he must always be cheerful, for 'joy is the dew of life,' as he used to say. When the Holy Jew himself discretely became a Hasid, his master Reb Arye Leyb,[32] the great scholar and author of the *Novellae of the Mahara,*

---

30. This is the name given to the slightly modified liturgy adopted by Hasidim, based on innovations attributed to the sixteenth-century Safed Kabbalist Isaac Luria (d. 1572).

31. R. Moshe Leib of Sasov (Sassow, 1745–1807), mentor to R. Jacob Isaac, the "Holy Jew" of Pshiskhe.

32. R. Aryeh Leib Harif Heilpern, Rabbi of Opatów and Sochaczew, and then in Warsaw, author of *Hidushe maharah* (Lemberg, 1866).

wept a glassful of tears. And who was Reb Dovid Lelever,[33] who made the Holy Jew a Lubliner Hasid? A Jew who used to spend years wandering among the Jewish settlements, just like the Rebbe Elimelech of blessed memory, in order to understand the troubles of the Jews living in isolated villages.

"And even when Reb Dovidl became a rebbe, he still maintained a grocery store in Lelev. They say that whenever anyone came to his store to shop, he would first list all of the other grocery stores in town and advise them to buy from another Jew; but when he saw that the customers didn't want to buy from anyone but him, he thought it over and calculated how much he would need to get through each day, and once he had earned that amount, he immediately closed the store in order to avoid causing losses to the other Jewish storekeepers in town.

"And Reb Dovid Lelever used to shout at his Hasidim: 'How can you call me a rebbe, while I still love my children more than I love other Jews?' You understand? He wanted to reach a point in his love of fellow Jews where he would no longer feel any difference between his own children and unrelated Jews.

"And it wasn't only people that he loved so much, but all of God's creatures. He would go into the marketplace and feed a horse if the peasant forgot to do it himself.

"Reb Dovidl once said to a Jewish coachman who had beaten his horse severely: 'You know, in the World to Come the horse will summon you to court for beating it. How's it going to look when you have to go to the Heavenly Court to defend yourself against a horse?'

"And maybe you think that his Sabbath homilies challenged his Hasidim? His homilies consisted of mere interpretations of verses, but they were such as found their way deep into his listeners' hearts. I remember how he once interpreted the phrase 'v'heyisem li am segula' [And you shall be for Me separate from all the nations (Exodus 19:5)]. God says to the Jews: 'You should remain before me as the vowel sign *segol*—it's a triangle of dots, so no matter which way you turn it, it remains a *segol*. That's how you Jews should be to Me.'

"And once at the festive Sabbath table he said: 'One cannot find fault in a Jew. Whenever we see a bad person who's a Jew, that's just

---

33. R. David Biderman of Lelow (1746–1814), a disciple of R. Jacob Isaac Horowitz, the Seer of Lublin, was a highly effective recruiter of scions of prestigious rabbinic families.

the Gentile part of him, but in the part that's Jew there can't possibly be any bad.'

"You should know that this Reb Dovidl blew the shofar in Lublin. Once it happened on Rosh Hashanah that the Seer was waiting for Reb Dovidl to come in and blow the shofar, but he hadn't yet appeared. Reb Yitskhekl Vurker went out to look for him, and do you know where he found him? He was with the horses! It was a market day in Lublin, so he went among the horses giving them oats from his big fur hat. Only when he was finished did he come into the synagogue to blow the shofar. People thought the Seer would be upset with him over this, but the Seer said at the festive table: 'Dovidl made us happy with the way he blew the shofar!'

"Now you know why the Holy Jew became a Hasid, when tzaddikim like that attracted him to Lublin.

"Once he arrived in Lublin, he was surrounded by all of the young scholars, the intellectuals who went to the Seer but could no longer tolerate the kind of Hasidism that consisted in just working miracles and displaying supernatural inspiration. In fact that kind of Hasidim really wasn't for the common people. But the intellectuals wanted to immerse themselves in the ways of Hasidism and raise themselves to the level of the Rebbe, rather than having the Rebbe descend to their level...

"So the Holy Jew created in Lublin a 'sacred society' devoted to scholarship.

"Many learned Hasidim belonged to the sacred society, including just about the best disciples of the Seer. Among them were Reb Dovid Lelever himself, Reb Shaye of Pshedborzh, Reb Kalmish of Cracow, Reb Note of Chelm, and others.

"Anyone who was invited into the sacred society first had to donate a pot of mead. The sacred society would sit in the study house, study together, and discuss Hasidism amongst themselves.

"The Seer himself ordered many of his disciples to join the sacred society.

"It was the heyday of Lublin Hasidism. Hasidism took on again the brilliance it had once had, as the Hasid Reb Zekharye Mendl had described Reb Elimelech in a letter where he writes: 'I've been among these tzaddikim for a few years already. They never let a penny stay in their pockets overnight. For years on end they are busy with good deeds, arranging weddings for orphans and widows. Hasidim are very fond of each other, true unity reigns among them, they have a single shared treasury. The love among them is so great that one can scarce discern who is whose father and who is whose son.'

"The disciples of the Holy Jew reached the same level, and the same unity reigned among the members of the sacred society.

"At first the Holy Jew often traveled to Lublin and stayed for a few weeks at a time. The Hasidim who belonged to the sacred society began increasingly to belittle wonder-working: 'It's no big deal to be a miracle worker,' the Holy Jew taught his followers. 'The trick is to be a real Jew.'

"They began to focus on having the proper intent when they prayed, and anyone whose thoughts weren't pure wouldn't go through his prayers by rote, but rather prepare himself until his thoughts were appropriate.

"The Hasidim of the sacred society began traveling to be with the Holy Jew in Pshiskhe. And who knows how wonderful a generation of disciples the Holy Jew would have nurtured if Satan hadn't become involved and ruined things.

"People began to report gossip to the Seer of Lublin, saying that the Holy Jew wanted to become a leader while the Seer was still alive. They argued that the path the Holy Jew was teaching was only for exceptional individuals, that the Pshiskhe way was bold and risky, that it places into question the fundamentals of Judaism and that if this path were disseminated among the common folk, it might eventually lead to apostasy.

"And thus it happened that a number of the disciples of the Seer who are today rebbes themselves gathered together and began to attack the Holy Jew.

"Our lives in Lublin were embittered. As soon as anyone found out that a certain Hasid knocked on the door of the Holy Jew, they would start examining him to see whether he prayed. And once Reb Yehuda Leyb of Zaklikov[34] said in public in the Lublin study house, while the

---

34. Judah Leib of Zaklików, author of *Hidushe maharil* (Lemberg, 1862) and disciple of R. Elimelekh of Leżajsk. Zaklików is located 113 miles SSE of Warsaw.

Holy Jew was there: 'There is a simple way to serve the Creator, to do all of the commandments as the Most High ordered, to pray communally with joy, that is the path of the tzaddikim. But there is another way as well, which is: Not to pray communally, sometimes to miss the set time for prayer altogether, in order to be able to pray later with pure intent. That path is called the way of the evildoers, who claim they are doing it for the sake of God.'

"This was intended as a stab at the Holy Jew.

"All of us wanted to rush at Reb Yehuda Leyb and tear him like a fish, but the Holy Jew restrained us and said to the band of Hasidim who stood around him:

"'In every generation a new light arises, shining for the Jews and showing them a new path in Judaism. That's how it was with the prophets, the tannaim, the kabbalists, and the last light was that of the Baal Sehm Tov, may his merit shield us, but his light has dimmed over time as well. That light has to be kindled once again, but not with miracles. And tell him,' he turned to us with a bit of humor, 'that it is written: "Signs and wonders in the land of Ham (Psalms 105:27)"—even folk-healers [*khames*] can perform wonders.'

"Reb Yehuda Leyb ran in to see the Seer and began to shout that the Holy Jew was mocking the Seer right in the study house, that he had come to Lublin in order to steal Hasidim.

"Libels began to fly. Reb Shimen Daytsh, who's now the ringleader at this wedding and who prepared the whole case against our way, was the main tale-bearer back then.

"It came to blows in the Lublin study house; once I myself was thrown out, along with Reb Yitskhok Vurker and Reb Mendele Tomashover. But the Holy Jew ordered us to accept everything graciously and not to respond at all.

"And we kept going to Lublin, until there broke out a bitter dispute over a shirt that the Holy Jew had received from the Seer. They reported back to Lublin that he had intentionally given it away to a drunk. This lead to a big fight, and to the 'great downfall' of Lublin.

"But probably you know all that," concluded Reb Fayvele.

"No! Tell us more!" the Pshiskhe Hasidim begged Reb Fayvele Gritser. Although they had certainly heard the story before, they wanted to hear it again.

But a few of the paupers, aroused by their shouts, began complaining:

"Have you ever seen such a thing? They sit there and chatter all night long! We've been on the road to Ostilye for three days, haven't slept a wink, and here they won't let us sleep. They just talk and talk and talk. You need to be rested tomorrow, too, so you can earn a couple of dollars and be at the pauper's meal," said the paupers to the Pshiskhe Hasidim, assuming that they too were beggars who had come from Ostilye to be at the pauper's meal.

"Right! Right!" answered the Pshiskhe Hasidim, in order to avoid suspicion, and Reb Fayvele added: "Ah, young folk, when we start talking about the old times, I never want to stop. The world was really something back then! But now let's go to sleep, and we'll finish the story tomorrow."

"But really, first thing tomorrow," the rest of the Pshiskhe Hasidim asked Reb Fayvele, stretching themselves out on their hard beds.

▲▼▲▼▲▼

Before dawn, when a bluish light began to shine into the attic through the window in the roof, the paupers awoke from their hard beds, gathered up their packs, and set off across the town.

The five Pshiskhe Hasidim also quickly arose and got through their morning prayers.

Reb Yisokher Horovits wanted the old Pshiskhe Hasid Reb Fayvele Gritser to finish his story about the fight over the Seer's shirt but Fayvele answered: "Another time. Now we have to go to the Rebbe of Kovel, Reb Leybele, the son of the old Rebbe of Neshkhiz and a brother of the groom's father-in-law, Reb Yosele of Ostilye. Our Rebbe told me that I should look him up. He's certainly arrived by now, and we have to find the inn where he's staying."

"What do we need him for?" asked the Pshiskhe Hasidim, feeling somewhat more confident now. "We aren't afraid of anybody. As the old Rebbe of blessed memory put it: 'Anyone who is contemptuous of himself doesn't have to care what the world thinks either.'"

"True," answered Reb Fayvele, happy that the Pshiskhe Hasidim were feeling encouraged again, "but the Rebbe told me to do this, and we have to carry out his will. The Rebbe put it this way: 'Tell him that I send greetings and remind him of the verse "And you shall bring Me a separation" (Exodus 25:2), which Rashi interprets thusly: "To Me—means for My sake."'[35] The Holy Jew added his interpretation: Is it a big deal to be a wonder worker? Anyone who's spiritually accomplished can overturn heaven and earth—but being a Jew, that's really tough."

"Well, if the Rebbe told us to do it," answered the Pshiskhe Hasidim, "he probably knows what he wants."

But the Hasidim couldn't fathom why they had to remind him of Rashi's interpretation.

The marketplace had been packed with Hasidim since before daylight.

From time to time a late-arriving coach would come bearing a rebbe. The Hasidim pushed closer to every coach as it arrived, in order to see which rebbe had come.

---

35. Rashi's interpretation of this Biblical verse was used by other Hasidic masters to justify their lavish lifestyles. Hence, the Holy Jew's argument that "being a Jew" is the real task is meant as a challenge to the threat of decadence.

5

The Dispute in Lublin on Account of a Shirt

The wedding caterers led cartloads of chickens to the slaughterhouse near the study hall. The five Pshiskhe Hasidim made their way through the throng to the inn where the Kovler Rebbe was staying. They found him sitting alone in his room.

The Kovler Rebbe sat in a large, overstuffed chair, wearing a flowered frock. He smoked a long pipe, emitting large clouds of smoked that filled the whole room until it was difficult for anyone entering to see the Rebbe sitting there.

Evidently the Rebbe hadn't been sitting by himself long. He was quite taken aback to see people entering suddenly so early in the morning, and he asked: "Who are you and what do you want?"

"I'm bringing you greetings," answered Reb Fayvl on their behalf, "from the Rebbe Reb Bunem of Pshiskhe. And he told us to mention Rashi's interpretation of the verse, 'And you shall bring for Me a donation:' 'For Me—means for My sake.' And he also ordered us to relate that the Holy Jew said: 'Is it a big deal to be a wonder worker? Anyone who is spiritually accomplished can move heaven and earth. Being a Jew—that's hard!'"

The Kovler Rebbe, Reb Leybele, was deeply impressed when he heard these words. He jumped up from his chair and began spanning the room, rubbing his hands over his large skullcap, which reached to the tops of his ears:

"Wow! Wow! That's what the Rebbe Reb Bunem said? How did he know about my doubts? For a few days now I've been looking for the plain meaning of the verse 'And you shall bring for Me a donation,' and trying to figure out why some of the tzaddikim were wonder workers and some weren't. And now you've answered both of my questions at once. Rashi's actually right. 'For Me' means only 'for My sake;' 'being a Jew—that's hard.' But how did your rebbe know that?" He couldn't stop wondering. "If that's how it is," he continued, "we won't let him fall. We'll help him in any way we can."

"That's exactly what we want," said Reb Fayvl Gritser, "but for now our presence here must remain secret."

"Of course," the Rebbe Reb Leybele answered, "first we have to know how Reb Shimen Daytsh and Reb Yosef Yartshever are going to argue. We've heard so much about the new Rebbe of Pshiskhe that it's hard even for us to know where the truth lies. We've heard reports that the Seraph, Reb Uri of Strelisk,[36] said: 'The Holy Jew wanted to introduce a new direction in Hasidism, to consist of the unity of Torah and prayer. Such a thing has never existed in this world. But the Holy Jew was suddenly taken from us, and his new direction was not fully articulated. It's possible now that by trying to follow his path, one might God forbid easily be led astray, leave the true path and slip.'"

"The Holy Jew didn't die prematurely because he was trying to introduce a new path," answered Reb Fayvele. "Rather, through his death he tried to help the Seer bring redemption."

"How can that be?" wondered Reb Leybele. "He mocked the Seer, and even gave away the Seer's shirt, which had been a gift to the Holy Jew, to a Jewish drunkard?"

"Not true!" shouted Reb Fayvele. "'They' made up that story. It was the Devil's work, intended to drive a wedge between the rebbe—the Seer—and his disciple—the Holy Jew. But if you wish, I'll tell you how it happened."

"By all means, let's hear it," answered Reb Leybele.

Reb Leybele approached the large, unheated oven as though it were wintertime and he was trying to get warm. He buried his hands in the wide belt of his frock and leaned against the oven. The Pshiskhe Hasidim made a half circle around Reb Leybele, and Reb Fayvele began his Hasidic discourse:

"The whole world knows that one Sabbath before the Holy Jew came to Lublin, in the middle of delivering his homily as the Hasidim were gathered at the Seer's table, the Seer said: 'It is written, "Let the Lord, the God of the spirits of all flesh, set a man over the congregation, who may go out before them, and who may come in before them" (Num.

---

36. R. Uri ben Pinhas of Strelisk (1757–1826), in eastern Galicia, a disciple of R. Shlomo of Karlin.

XXVII:16–17). I also prayed to the Master of the Universe that He show me who would be my successor, and I received an answer from Heaven that his name would be the same as mine—Yankev Yitskhok.'

"Later, when the Holy Jew first crossed the threshold of the Seer, the Seer got up from his chair and happily greeted him, saying: 'You've comforted me because a few days ago a Hasid was here by the name of Yankev Yitskhok, and I was terrified because I feared that he might be my successor. But now that you've come, I'm reassured.'

"That was the Seer's initial reception of his disciple, the Holy Jew; he immediately saw the Jew as his successor.

"We also know that later, the Holy Jew had attracted the attention of the greatest scholars in Lublin, and indeed of none other than the Rabbi of Lublin himself, on account of his brilliant scholarship. That was when the great genius, the 'Iron Head,' Reb Azriel Halevi Hurvits,[37] had been involved in an ongoing dispute with the Seer. Yet, when the Holy Jew began coming to Lublin, the Iron Head made peace with the Seer. He figured that if the Seer could have a scholar like the Holy Jew as his disciple, 'Well then, let him be a rebbe.' Can you understand this from an opponent of Hasidism? He regarded the Seer as a legitimate master simply because he had such a great disciple. On the other hand, he remained an opponent of Hasidism, and the Iron Head never thought all that much of the Seer. When he had a chance to score a point against the Hasidim, he did. Once the Holy Jew went to see the Iron Head and proposed a match between the Iron Head's daughter and the Seer himself, who was at that time (may we be spared!) a widower.

"The Iron Head answered as if naively, 'It's against the Torah.'

"'What do you mean by that?' answered the Holy Jew.

"'The Torah says,' he replied, '"I gave my daughter to a man"' (Deut. XXII:16) 'and you Hasidim keep shouting that your Rebbe is an angel.'

"The Holy Jew didn't say anything to him, but turned to the Hasidim and said, 'an opponent remains an opponent.'

"Yes, when you start thinking about the past, you feel like telling more and more stories," sighed Reb Fayvele, "but let's not get distracted. We were talking, I believe, about the greatness of the Holy Jew

---

37. R. Azriel Halevi Horowitz of Lublin (d. 1819), known as the "Ironhead," was the main opponent of R. Jacob Isaac, the Seer of Lublin, and of Hasidism in general.

in Lublin. Yet the Devil interfered, gossip mongers became involved and cooked up the whole dispute.

"In addition to Reb Shimen Daytsh and Reb Yosef of Yartshev, there were another two Jews involved. The Holy Jew said that Satan kept his eye on them for forty years so they might later serve him loyally. They were Ber Kintsker and Yekusiel. The Holy Jew humorously interpreted a verse from Psalms as referring to them: 'A boor [*b'er*] will not know and a fool [*ksil*] will not understand' (Ps. 92:7). They set out to cause trouble for the Holy Jew and for all of us.

"At first the Seer didn't want to hear any of it, and even gave the Holy Jew his old shirt, as was his custom when he was extremely fond of a disciple. Once a wandering beggar came to the Holy Jew and asked him for clothing. The beggar said he never had anything to wear but rags, and sometimes lacked even a shirt. The Holy Jew's heart was touched, and he handed over the shirt that the Seer had given him.

"But the poor man was a drunk. He took the shirt, went into a tavern and sold it to a Gentile for a bottle of liquor. It's a wonder that the gossips later found out about this. It may be that they had a hand in the incident itself, but in any case they made a big deal about it, claiming that the Holy Jew had done this intentionally in order to publicly insult the Seer of Lublin.

"After this incident, the Seer began listening to the slanders against the Holy Jew, and after a number of such reports the Seer ordered the Holy Jew not to come see him again.

"When the Holy Jew was asked why he had given away the Seer's shirt, he replied: 'It is written, "skin for skin, and everything a man has he should give away for his soul" (Job 2:4). For the redemption of souls, one must give away one's last shirt, even if it is his most precious.'

"The Holy Jew disregarded the order, and continued to go see the Seer. He went into the Seer's private room, but the Seer did not want to greet him. But when the Seer saw the Holy Jew standing in a corner and weeping, he walked over to him and made up with him. The Lubliner Hasidim even say that the Seer asked him not to cross his threshold. But it's been reported to us that the Seer and the Holy Jew had a conversation at a very exalted level, the sort of thing that's utterly mysterious for simple people like us. And as a result of that conversation, the Holy Jew died so young, at the age of just forty-six. Later came the great 'fall' in Lublin, but it was all on account of the Devil's work.

"And this was the story," continued Reb Fayvele. "The three greatest tzaddikim of that generation—Reb Yisroel, the Kozhenitser Magid; Reb Mendele of Rimenev;[38] and the Seer of Lublin—were determined to bring the Redemption prematurely.

"But that generation wasn't worthy, and perhaps their approach was overly ambitious. That was the cause of the great 'fall' in Lublin. And if it weren't for the fact that 'the wise man of the Rebbes,' Reb Naftoli Ropshitser,[39] hadn't caught on in time and said, 'Leave me alone,' then it might have caused the destruction of the world.

"But these three leading saints of the generation didn't want to be deterred. They made a pact that they would not join in the celebrations on Simchat Torah until they received a heavenly promise that the Jews would be freed from their bitter exile.

"In addition they knew that they weren't alone. The Tzaddik of Berditshev, Reb Levi Yitskhok[40] (may his merit shield us), had already been in Heaven for three years. He always tried to intercede with Heaven on behalf of the Jews, and before his soul departed he promised that he would not rest in his grave, nor would he cease appealing to all of the saints in Paradise, until with their help he could bring the final Redemption.

"But in order to remind him of his promise and arouse him, the three tzaddikim agreed to send a special messenger to the Berditshever. They cast lots among themselves to determine who would be that messenger, and the lot fell to the Seer of Lublin.

"The Seer began preparing for the journey. However, the Holy Jew found out about this and came to see the Seer. After their long, secret conversation, the Seer of Lublin agreed that the Holy Jew would carry out the mission.

38. R. Menahem Mendel of Rimenev (Rymanów, 1745–1815), in Galicia, disciple of R. Elimelekh of Leżajsk and R. Jacob Isaac, the Seer of Lublin. Known for his stringency in matters of dress and his opposition to Jewish tavernkeeping.

39. R. Naftali Tzvi of Ropshitz (Ropszyce, 1760–1827), in Galicia, disciple of R. Jacob Isaac, the Seer of Lublin, and R. Menahem Mendel of Rimanov. Known for his compassion and sense of humor.

40. R. Levi Isaac of Berdichev (Berdyczów, ca. 1740–1809), disciple of R. Dov Ber, the Great Maggid of Mezheritch and author of the seminal *Kedushat Levi* (Berdichev, 1811). R. Levi Isaac was rabbi of Żelechów and Pinsk before settling in Berdichev.

"After that, the Holy Jew made his pilgrimages to Kozhenits and to the Rebbe Reb Mendele in Rimenev. The Seer's Hasidim actually say that he went to them to ask if they could mediate between him and the Seer. But we know that there were deeper purposes involved in the journey, and indeed in that very same year, the fall of 1813, the Holy Jew passed away.

"And the three tzaddikim prepared to bring the Redemption."

Reb Fayvele sighed and prepared to continue his narrative about the origins of "the great fall in Lublin." But Reb Leybele, who had been standing near the oven the whole time with his eyes closed, swaying back and forth, suddenly took his pipe out of his mouth and said:

"You're giving us pleasure. You're telling stories we've never heard before. But you're strangers here. You probably haven't had a bite to eat, so we've got to offer you something." And the Rebbe called out:

"Ahron Moyshe!"

In came the Rebbe's secretary, Ahron Moyshe, a Jew with a carefully groomed, broad gray beard and long brows that were sharp as spears.

"Bring in some snacks," the Rebbe ordered in a commanding voice.

Ahron Moyshe, the secretary, cast an angry glance at the five Pshiskhe Hasidim, a look that said: "We won't see a red penny from them, and we have to offer them refreshments?" He quickly left the room.

"When we've eaten something, you can continue telling the story of the fall in Lublin," said the Kovler Rebbe, Reb Leybele.

6

The Fall of the Rebbe of Lublin

The secretary Ahron Moyshe brought in a silver platter with honey cake, liquor, and jam. The Rebbe Reb Leybele poured cups of liquor for the five Hasidim.

The Pshiskhe Hasidim toasted "lechaim" to the Rebbe, and Reb Eliezer Ber, the gifted talker, jokingly said: "We've heard from our Rebbe that hard liquor is another one of those good things that have no prescribed limit because the Hebrew initials *yud-shin* can mean *yayin sorof* (brandy) or *yiras shomayim* (fear of Heaven)."

"Well, if so," answered Reb Leybele, "then pour it for yourselves and drink as if you were at home, just as if you were with your Rebbe Reb Bunem."

The five Pshiskhe Hasidim realized that Reb Leybele was entirely on their side. Out of great joy they began drinking one cup of liquor after another.

Later, once they had already done some drinking, the Rebbe Reb Leybele spoke up: "I haven't even prayed yet. But it is known that one time the Rebbe Reb Ber of Mezritsh was passing by the study house at night, and he saw a fiery column shining forth from within. The Rebbe Reb Ber went into the study house to see who was sitting there, and he saw a couple of Hasidim discussing Hasidism. 'Now I understand why I saw a fiery column shining from the study house,' said the Rebbe Reb Ber to the Hasidim."

"Certainly discussing Hasidism is an important topic," answered Reb Zishe Shedlitser after the Pshiskhe fashion. "It purifies the mind. And you have to pray when your heart reaches the appropriate level, when your heart yearns for prayer."

"You must know the old Pshiskhe song?" asked Reb Fayvele Gritser.

"No, haven't heard it," answered Reb Leybele.

"If so, we can sing it now," answered Reb Zishe Shedlitser enthusiastically.

"By all means, we want to hear what kind of song it is," said the Rebbe Reb Leybele.

But even before Reb Leybele finished his sentence, the Pshiskhe Hasidim quickly moved away from the table, as if a hidden force had suddenly tugged at them. They threw their hands above their shoulders and began dancing, singing the old Pshiskhe song:

We didn't pray, we didn't study—
As long as we didn't anger God.
Why should we worry
What may happen tomorrow?
Better let's set right
What we ruined yesterday.
Oh, maybe, maybe we'll be able to fix it
Oh, maybe, maybe we'll be able to fix it.

The Hasidim danced, first quietly and slowly, with concentration, but the tune grew ever faster and more fiery, until the Pshiskhe Hasidim lost all self-consciousness, began to spin as fast as a whirlwind, and their feet barely touched the ground.

At first the Rebbe Reb Leybele looked on in amazement at the level of intensity these Hasidim possessed. But then—and he himself didn't know how it happened—he found himself in the circle, singing, "Oh, perhaps, perhaps, we'll be able to fix it!"

Who knows how long they would have danced like that if the secretary Ahron Moyshe hadn't come in. Seeing the Rebbe dancing with these strange Hasidim, he quickly closed the door again. The banging door interrupted the Pshiskhe Hasidim's dance.

Reb Fayvele Gritser was the first to realize that the Pshiskhe tune could be heard in the street and that they might soon be caught. And Reb Itshe Meirl muttered, wiping the sweat from his face with his big kerchief: "Who could have imagined that here in Ostilye we could have danced the Pshiskhe way so enthusiastically?"

The Hasidim sat back down at the table, and the Rebbe Reb Leybele said: "If so, you have to finish the story about the 'big fall in Lublin,' which you started telling earlier."

"True, true," said Reb Fayvele, passing his hand over his great gray beard, separating it into two points. He began relating:

"Yes, we had reached the point just after the death of the Holy Jew, who was supposed to bring a message to the Berditshever Rebbe in Heaven, that the three tzaddikim had taken upon themselves the task of bringing Messiah that year.

"And at that point, the real work began among the three tzaddikim.

"'Pray to God that I may survive the year 5575,' Reb Mendele of Rimenev said to his Hasidim as they sat in the sukkah. 'And you can be sure that you will merit hearing the shofar of the Messiah and sitting in the sukkah made of the skin of Leviathan.'

"'Who is ready to go to war alongside me?' asked the Seer of Lublin before the Rosh Hashanah shofar blowing that same year.

"Reb Kalmish Nayshteter stood by the Rebbe's right hand and Reb Naftoli Herts, the Berezhaner Rebbe, at his left side. The Ropshitser Rebbe, Reb Naftoli, saw how things stood and quietly stole away. He recited the additional prayers somewhere in a tailors' synagogue, and indeed never came to the Seer again until after the 'fall.'

"'A wise man is better than a prophet,' they said of the Ropshitser after the fall.

"And that year, while the shofar was being blown, the Seer battled Satan. A couple of times he took the shofar out of the hands of the Zaklikover Rebbe, who was then the shofar-blower in Lublin. He held onto Reb Kalmish Nayshteter and Reb Natfoli Herts, and couldn't bring a sound out of the shofar.

"'But what we aren't able to do with the shofar,' said the Seer, 'with God's help we will be able to carry out with the power of the Torah. The power of joy,' added the Seer, 'is much greater and stronger than the power of fear.' Of course, the Seer was referring to the joy of Simchat Torah.

"Yet Satan darkened the holy eyes of the Seer, and he didn't perceive that immediately after Rosh Hashanah, on the eve of Sukkot, the Kozhenitser Magid passed away.

"Before his death the Kozhenitser Magid had actually called in his son, Reb Elyokum Beriya, and ordered him to tell the holy Seer that for God's sake, he should call it off. He should no longer arouse the supernal spheres with his intense worship because the generation wasn't worthy of it. But the Seer was not told of the Kozhenitser Magid's death and about what he had said. They hid everything from him, and unfortunately that gave Satan the power to defeat him.

"Who can convey a picture of the joy of Simchat Torah every year in Lublin, and that year especially? A few hundred Hasidim came to Lublin that year. Their joy was boundless and impossible to relate. Throughout the day on Shemini Atzeret the Hasidim drank vast amounts of mead and other kinds of alcohol. The Rebbe himself had practically ordered everyone to drink.

"After the morning of Shemini Atzeret the Seer told the Hasidim, 'Drink and be happy with the Torah, and I promise you that just as we've had a joyous Simchat Torah, we will also have a joyous Tisha B'Av.'[41]

"The Hasidim obeyed, and they drank. Heavy pots of mead and large containers of wine were brought into the study house all day long. But no one spotted the Seer. From early in the morning he stayed alone in his private room. He placed his secretary at the door and told him to guard it carefully, to make sure that no one came in. The secretary was also to pay close attention to the Rebbe and not let him out of his sight.

"Meanwhile they were dancing and living it up in the study house, one dance after another, and their joy was redoubled because they knew that the Seer was going to accomplish something new through the power of his worship that night.

"They danced like that until late in the night. Reb Kalmish Nayshteter and Reb Naftoli Hertz danced in their white socks on the tables, with the large crowd of Hasidim surrounding them.

"And while the Hasidim were dancing in the study house, steeped in joy as the Seer had commanded, the Seer was pacing back and forth in his private room, performing certain rituals of unification, arranging divine Names,[42] preparing for the time when the Hasidim would take out the Torah scrolls and dance with them, when he would completely defeat Satan and bring the true Redemption.

---

41. Tisha B'Av (the ninth day of the Hebrew month of Av) is a fast day commemorating several national disasters, especially the destruction of the Holy Temple. Anticipating its transformation into a day of joy is thus anticipation of the Messianic age.
42. A reference to various techniques of practical Kabbalah.

"But a terrible disaster happened. The secretary, who was supposed to guard every step of the Seer, suddenly dozed off for a moment. And as soon as he woke up, he saw that the lights had gone out and the holy Seer was no longer in the room. He immediately opened the door and shouted into the study house at the top of his lungs: '*Where is the Rebbe?*'

"The Hasidim immediately interrupted their dance. All at once their joy disappeared. They began searching for the Rebbe in every room of his house, and when they brought a candle into the Rebbe's private room, they saw that all of the windows were closed. Only one small window, upon which a number of bottles stood, lay open.

"The Hasidim spread out throughout the entire courtyard with their heads bowed, like mourners, seeking the Rebbe. It took almost an hour until one of the leading Hasidim, Reb Hershele Stashever, saw by the light of the moon the figure of a human being, lying on the ground far from the study house.

"'Who is there?' cried Reb Hershele in great terror.

"'*Yankev Yitskhok ben Maytl,*' a weak voice was heard.

"In his great fear Reb Hershele Stashever first ran to announce to the Hasidim that he had found the Rebbe. Everyone burst out weeping and wanted to set off for the place that Reb Hershele indicated.

"'Absolutely forbidden,' a voice was suddenly heard coming from somewhere near the door of the study house. 'No one must move at all except for the Rebbe's leading disciples.'

"The entire crowd stayed near the study house.

"Immediately the leading Hasidim, the 'sharp minds,' cast lots to see who would have the merit to carry back in the tzaddik of their generation.

"The disciple Reb Shmuel Makarover, who won by lottery the right to hold the Rebbe's head, later related that while he was carrying the Rebbe he saw the Seer's lips constantly moving; and when he bent very close, he heard the Rebbe reciting the series of Psalms known as Tikkun Leah.[43]

"As we approached the study house, the Seer suddenly opened his eyes, looked around in amazement, and seeing that his disciples were carrying him, he quietly said: 'Oh, why did you withhold the terrible

---

43. A series of Psalms that form one component of the prayers known as Tikkun Chatzot, recited by some Jews close to midnight in commemoration of the destruction of the Temple.

news from me? The Kozhenitser Magid is no longer in this world, and I knew nothing about it!'

"The Seer had learned about the death of the Kozhenitser Magid thus: While he was being miraculously ejected through the small window (upon whose sill stood a number of bottles, none of which fell), the Kozhenitser Magid arrived and grasped him by the waist of his shrouds. The Seer himself is supposed to have related this later to his disciples. But other Hasidim said that his mother, the holy Maytl, stretched out her shroud and saved him.

"And from that time on, the Seer remained dangerously ill.

"On the morning of Simchat Torah, when the opponents of Hasidism in Lublin found out about the Seer's fall, they were very happy. They drank and got drunk all day long and vowed that on the day the Seer died they would make a second Simchat Torah, with a big feast.

"But the Seer summoned his disciple, the doctor of Pietrkow, Khayem Dovid Bernard, and said to him: 'The entire Dark Side gathered together to conduct war against me, and in Heaven they did not agree to bring the Redemption . . . But they, the opponents, are looking forward to my death, they look forward to making a holiday to celebrate my passing. But they're greatly mistaken. Not only will they be unable to rejoice on the day of my death, but they will sorrow together with you. On that day not only won't they drink wine, they won't even have a sip of water.'

"At the time the Hasidim didn't understand the Rebbe's pronouncement.

"But alas, that same year the great light was extinguished, and on Tisha B'Av of 5775 the Seer passed away. So the opponents of Hasidim in Lublin likewise had to mourn, and couldn't even drink a drop of water . . .

"That was the end of the great fall in Lublin," concluded Reb Fayvele with a deep sigh.

"You have opened our eyes," said Reb Leybele. "Now we know why the Holy Jew died prematurely. But it's still hard to understand why Reb Shimen Daytsh is so determined to bring your way to trial here at the great wedding, where so many tzaddikim have gathered. What does it have to do with you?"

"Probably Satan has something to do with it, since he doesn't want our path to spread. Reb Shimen Daytsh already had complaints against the Holy Jew. Once the two of them were traveling to Lublin. On the way Reb Shimen Daytsh said to the Holy Jew: 'We see that the Rebbe is not at home.' However, the Holy Jew convinced him to go further.

"When they had traveled another few miles, Reb Shimen Daytsh repeated, 'We definitely see that the Rebbe has left the city.' But the Holy Jew once again talked him into continuing on their way together.

"When they arrived in Lublin, Reb Shimen Dayth learned that the Seer had indeed wanted to leave the city but at the last minute he changed his mind.

"Reb Shimen Daytsh asked the Holy Jew why his foresight had been mistaken. Answered the Holy Jew, 'I saw in you a certain degree of haughtiness, and wherever there's arrogance, even a tiny bit of it, Holy Spirit cannot prevail.' Since then Reb Shimen Daytsh has been angry at the Holy Jew, and that's why his hostility is so great."

But suddenly, in the middle of this Hasidic conversation, the door of the Kovler Rebbe's room burst open. A band of Hasidic Cossacks pushed their way in. They filled the whole room. They arrayed themselves like a wedding band and played a joyful tune on their own instruments, consisting of sticks, brooms, pokers, rolling pins, platters, and pots. The wedding jester Reb Zanvl announced in rhyme that the father-in-law on the bride's side, the Rebbe Reb Yosef of Ostilye, and the grandfather of the bride, the Rebbe Reb Mordkhe of Neshkhiz, along with the father-in-law on the groom's side, the Rebbe Reb Dan of Radvil, and the groom's grandfather, the Holy Grandfather Reb Avrom Yehoshue Heshl, were inviting the elder brother of the father-in-law, the Rebbe Reb Leybele, to the paupers' meal, which would soon be held in the large shop which had been set up for the wedding feasts.

And the jester finished with the familiar rhyme:

Everybody be ready
For the paupers' feast
Together with all the great ones
He's coming, he's coming, he's coming.

When the jester finished his rhyming invitation to the paupers' meal, the Hasidic Cossacks played another "mazel-tov" tune. It was the wedding tune that the old Apter Rebbe's musician had composed for the occasion, and it was sung everywhere. The Hasidic Cossacks demanded a tip for their playing, and Reb Leybele gave them a whole silver ruble. They ran out in a tumult. They proceeded to another inn, to invite another rebbe to the paupers' feast.

The Rebbe Reb Leybele requested that the five Pshiskhe Hasidim take their leave, for he had yet to pray before setting off for the paupers' feast. Before they set off he promised that he wouldn't tell anyone that they had come to the wedding, and most importantly, that he would help them defend the Pshiskhe way at the trial, if they asked him to.

"We won't allow the in-law, the holy Apter, to be taken in by gossip," said the Kovler Rebbe. "We will remind him of the Hasidic interpretation of the binding of Isaac. The question is why the order to 'take your son' (Gen. 22:2) was given by God Himself, while 'do not stretch your hand unto the lad' (Gen. 22:12) was uttered by an angel, as it is written just before that: 'And the angel called to him' (Gen. 22:11). The answer is: we can rely on an angel to save someone. But on the other hand, when a Jew is about to be slaughtered, you can't listen to anyone, even an angel. That, you have to hear from God alone. Especially," concluded the Rebbe Reb Leybele, "when it comes to slaughtering an entire congregation of Jews, God-fearing, with integrity, and true tzaddikim.

"We will help you! Don't be afraid!" the Rebbe Reb Leybele called after the Pshiskhe Hasidim, as they were already by the door, about to set off for the paupers' feast. As they left they heard the Rebbe Reb Leybele humming the tune:

We didn't pray, we didn't study—
As long as we didn't anger God.

"He's come over completely to our side," Reb Fayvele Gritser said happily to the other Hasidim.

7

The Paupers' Feast

Since early in the morning the streets of Ostilye had been packed with paupers and beggars making their way in droves to the giant hall that had been set up for the wedding guests, which was the site of the paupers' feast as well.

The doors of the hall had been opened quite late, and the crowd of paupers pushed their way in with a great tumult. They shoved in through doors and windows, everybody trying to grab the best possible place at the tables, arranged in the form of three sides of a square. There was plenty of cursing, pushing, and shoving. Eventually all of the paupers were seated. Various rebbes who had arrived for the wedding began the table service. The rebbes walked around on the tables in their blue and white socks, the front of their silk caftans stuffed into their belts. Over their shoulders were hung large baskets of rolls, which they distributed to the paupers.

Other rebbes carried silver platters bearing multicolored bottles of various liquors, such as plain brandy, caraway brandy, green wormwood brandy, aquavit, wine, and wishniac, to which they treated the paupers. And some of the rebbes distributed honey cake, fruit layer cakes, strudel, and various jams.

The paupers sat comfortably at the tables, feeling quite well honored, as if the entire wedding in Ostilye had come to pass solely on their account, and the more than eighty rebbes who had come from various countries were present only to serve as their waiters.

From the nearby stalls that had been set up came the smells of saffron, cloves, sharp caraway, of roasted meat, and gefilte fish.

The secretaries of the various rebbes were there, together with the wedding caterers, preparing all of these dishes for the paupers.

Dozens of secretaries and waiters hurried, sweating, their arms full of platters that they distributed among the paupers. There was a great tumult in the hall as the paupers rushed forward from every side. The secretaries resented their inability to scold the paupers for their affrontery because their rebbes had earlier told them to be friendly to the paupers.

Among the various beggars and homeless folk were the five disguised Pshiskhe Hasidim, in tattered long jackets. They sat at one end of the long table and spoke little amongst themselves, so that no one would notice that they were together...

Hasidim went to and fro among the paupers with big dishes and heavy copper two-handled jugs, hand towels over their shoulders, bringing the paupers water so that they might ritually wash their hands.

Every second another rebbe approached a pauper, warmly asking him whether he had enough to eat and what other dish his heart might desire.

And none other than the Rebbe Reb Shimen Daytsh approached the corner where the five Pshiskhe Hasidim were sitting. He asked them what sort of liquor they would like.

"We drink everything," responded their spokesman, Reb Eliezer.

"Perhaps you would like wormwood brandy?" Reb Shimen Daytsh asked again.

"Doesn't matter to us, that's fine," answered Reb Fayvele Gritser, so that Reb Shimen Daytsh would go away as soon as possible without looking closely at him.

It seemed to Reb Zishe Shedlitser that a certain Hasid, who was standing in back of him the whole time, was looking at him too closely, so he naively turned to the Hasid: "Perhaps you could tell me what wormwood brandy is, and how it's made?"

"You don't know what wormwood brandy is or how it's made? You take plain grain alcohol, you add a certain herb that's called wormwood, you leave it standing for twenty days, and it becomes spicey and turns green, and that's called wormwood brandy."

"But still I don't understand," said Reb Zishe Shedlitser with a smile, "how it becomes wormwood brandy. What do you mean, 'you let it stand for twenty days?' Who has the self-discipline to let brandy stand for so long without drinking it?"

The Hasidim standing behind Reb Zishe's back burst out laughing, and one Hasid responded: "Oh, you must be a real drunkard if you can't understand how someone can let brandy stand for so long without touching it..."

That delighted Reb Zishe because now he was certain that they didn't recognize who he was and who his comrades were.

Meanwhile the rebbes were bringing all sorts of dishes to the tables: chicken broth with noodles, chicken with egg barley, and chicken with sliced brown dumplings, roasted and boiled chickens, roasted geese and ducks, and other roast meats. The Hasidim of the various rebbes crowded around the tables to grab bits of the food left over by their rebbes. The crowding was endless. A band of Hasidim hovered above Reb Fayvele Gritser, waiting to pounce on a plate from which the Rebbe Reb Shimen Daytsh had tasted. Reb Itshe Meirl, the genius from Warsaw, sensed that the elderly Reb Fayvele Gritser was being crushed by those Hasidim. In addition, he resented the fact that the Hasidim were so avidly drawn to none other than Reb Shimen Daytsh. He called to a couple of Hasidim who were leaning on the old Reb Fayvele's back:

"Why are you leaning so heavily on a Jew you don't know? You know that every Jew is compared to a Torah scroll, and you're not allowed to lean on a Torah scroll?"

"Is that so?" responded a fiery Hasid. "You want to show that you're a learned fellow, and in fact—may we be spared—you don't know what you're talking about. If every Jew is comparable to a Torah scroll, then one Torah scroll is just like another and you can lean one Torah on another one."

"Yes, that's true," responded Reb Itshe Meirl, "but every Jew must believe in his heart that only his fellow Jew is as holy as a Torah scroll, while he himself is utterly worthless."

"He got you there!" other Hasidim cried, giving the fiery Hasid a friendly clap on his head, nearly making his shtreiml fall off. "Look, he's still a young man," they pointed to Reb Itshe Meirl, "and a traveling beggar, and he gives such clever responses."

Meanwhile the press in the hall had continued to intensify. Hasidim began pushing in from all sides, jumping through the open windows, nearly bursting the walls. Every now and then the cracking of a broken bench could be heard. And voices were heard in the distance: "Behave yourselves! The groom and the in-laws are coming!"

And although it seemed that the hall was already so overcrowded that you couldn't have found enough room on the ground to drop a needle, hundreds of Hasidim crowded into the hall and nobody shouted "I'm getting crushed" because all eyes and everyone's thoughts were turned toward the door through which the fathers-in-law, the holy tzaddikim, were to enter with the groom.

Hasidic Cossacks ran in breathlessly, beginning to clear a way in the hall. Hundreds of shtreimlekh flew on all sides. The Hasidim brandished their wooden swords on all sides above the heads of the Hasidim, and voices were heard: "To the side, slobs. Show respect! Make way! The in-laws are coming!"

The musicians arrived playing the groom's melody, and "Tall Raphael" appeared with his drum from the Land of Israel. He wore broad, red Arab pantaloons, and a Turkish shawl thrown over his shoulders like an Arab cloak, with a fez on his head. He danced facing the groom and the in-laws, who walked behind him.

Tall Raphael had inherited the drum from his grandfather Reb Sender Tsfaser, who had joined the great Hasidic emigration to the Land of Israel in the year 1777. At that time hundreds of Hasidim had banded together, and together with the Rebbe Reb Mendele of Vitebsk,[44] they had left the diaspora and ascended to the Land of Israel.

And when the Hasidim arrived in Safed, as Tall Raphael used to relate, the Rebbe Reb Mendele's joy was so great that he danced in the streets of Safed and drummed on that very same drum. Later Reb Sender Tsfaser returned to Poland as an emissary of the Rebbe, taking along the drum that the Rebbe Reb Mendele had personally played. Eventually the drum was passed on to his son and then to his grandson, Tall Raphael.

From that time on, it was Tall Raphael's custom to attend every major wedding among the rebbes' families, dress up as a Turk, and play his Land of Israel drum. He always kept apart at these weddings, both from the musicians and from the Hasidic Cossacks. He considered himself to be more distinctive than they. At every wedding among the rebbes' families, he was always the one who announced that the groom or some great rebbe who was an in-law was arriving.

---

44. R. Menahem Mendel of Vitebsk (Witebsk, 1730?–1788), prominent disciple of R. Dov Ber, the Great Maggid of Mezheritch, known for leading an emigration to the Land of Israel in 1777.

Behind him meekly walked the fourteen-year-old groom, Shmelke. He had a long, pale, childish face. Two long and twisted Galician-style sidelocks hung like little bottles to his shoulders. By their stiffness it was clear that they had just been curled with plum syrup. The groom wore his silken clothes and a Galician shtreiml with points, which fell over his ears. At his right hand strode his grandfather, the old Apter Rebbe. He kept his eyes closed, and his lips moved constantly, as if he were murmuring some prayer. At his left side was the bride's grandfather, the tzaddik Reb Motele Neshkhizer. Behind them, the fathers-in-law: the Ostilyer Rebbe, Reb Yosef, father of the bride, and the Radviler Rebbe, Reb Dan, the father of the groom. And behind them there were rows of rebbes, relatives on both sides. They were all surrounded by a chain of hands formed by the Hasidic Cossacks so that no outsider could make his way in.

When the in-laws and the groom had sat down, Leyzer Leyb, the old Apter Rebbe's secretary, shouted: "Sha-a-a-t!" And suddenly everything was so quiet that you could have heard the wings of a flea buzzing.

The old Neshkhizh Rebbe took a plate of food and handed it to a pauper who was sitting next to him, so that he could personally fulfill the commandment of hospitality, and then he turned to the Apter Rebbe:

"In-law," said the Neshkizher Rebbe, "we must praise the Creator for making arrogance a sin because if, Heaven forfend, it were a commandment, how could we fulfill it? How can one possess an ounce of arrogance when he remembers that we are but dust and ash?"

"True, true," answered the Apter Rebbe with his eyes closed. It seemed that he had been interrupted in the midst of a deep thought, and suddenly he turned to the rebbes who were walking around the tables in their socks, feeding the paupers:

"Everyone enjoy himself! When I married off my son, Yitskhok Meir, there were so many Hasidim at the wedding that there were three cartloads of straw for toothpicks, and the eggs? They took the shells and made a causeway over the river . . ."

And the Apter Rebbe became lost in thought again.

The rebbes knew that every word uttered in the Apter Rebbe's exaggerations contained profound secrets of the Torah. They immediately began to interpret the Apter's words, explaining the insights contained in these exaggerations, yet immediately the musicians and the Hasidic Cossacks began playing a cheerful tune, just as the Apter Rebbe had commanded.

They took away the tables and benches. The Neshkhizer Rebbe took the groom by the hand, and began dancing with him in a circle, together with the hundreds of paupers. The circle grew larger and larger. No one was allowed to dance now except for the groom, the in-laws, and the paupers. Every pauper wanted to dance close to the groom and the Neshkhizer Rebbe. The old Apter Rebbe no longer had the strength to dance, so he simply stood up from his chair and clapped with joy.

By now it had grown quite late. The Neshkhizer Rebbe continued dancing with beggars until his son, Rebbe Reb Yosef of Ostilye, pulled him out of the circle, together with the groom. Only then was the beggars' dance interrupted. Liquor was distributed once again. At the table appeared an old beggar with a wide gray beard and a high cap on his head. He took out from inside his frock an old fiddle, which he had been playing for decades in the various Hasidic courts. He stuck half of his beard into the fiddle, so that it looked as though the beard and fiddle were interwoven. He began singing a song with gentile words, playing his own accompaniment.

It grew very quiet and the melody with the gentile words stretched out like a prayer:

Abraham, Abraham,
You, our great-grandfather,
Pray to God,
Pray to God,
It's time to go home.
It's time to go home.

The old beggar walked back and forth on the table, playing his fiddle, singing the praises of our forefathers, telling in the sweet tones of his fiddle about the bitter exile, and bringing the message that it is high time for the Jews to be redeemed. Eventually people noticed the holy Apter Rebbe wiping his eyes with his kerchief, and the Neshkhizer

Rebbe sighing from time to time so deeply that one's heart could break for sorrow, so the Hasidic Cossacks climbed onto the table and began singing a wedding march, until the faces of the two tzaddikim began to shine again and the mood in the hall became more joyful. The secretary Leyzer-Leyb then called out that the bags of money had been brought, and that no one should push because everyone would receive alms.

The secretaries of the Neshkhizer Rebbe and the Apter Rebbe came in. They placed the sacks of silver coins next to both seats. The two rebbes began distributing the alms. The paupers proceeded past them one by one. Some of the paupers tried to get in line a second time in order to receive double alms, but the Apter Rebbe, whose eyes were shut the whole time, said to anyone who tried that: "Don't embarrass me. Don't test me. You've gotten yours already!"

It took a long time to distribute the coins, and when all of the coins in the sacks had been distributed and all of the paupers had gotten their alms, the Apter Rebbe arose from his seat and, in his weak voice, he addressed the paupers: "And now, pray for something for yourselves! Say what your petition is!"

Various responses were heard: "Livelihood," "We should get better alms," "The poorhouses in the towns should be renovated." Most of all was heard, "We want the Rebbe to see to it that the Jews are not driven from the villages. We won't be able to get from one town to another if there are no Jews in the villages, with whom we can rest from our endless journeys."

But louder than all of these could be heard a powerful, weeping voice: "We petition that there be no disputes among Jews, and that there be no division in God's camp!"

The Apter Rebbe's quiet blessings could not be heard. Immediately the Rebbe Reb Shimen Daytsh and a handful of Hasidim made their way toward the corner from which that voice had come, as if they wanted to tear that person limb from limb. But Reb Fayvele Gritser, the one who had called out, disappeared among the hundreds of paupers, and Reb Shimen Daytsh and his Hasidim could no longer find him.

Reb Shimen Daytsh left the hall in a foul mood together with the other rebbes, sensing that disguised Pshiskhe Hasidim were at the wedding, intending to disrupt the trial.

Late at night the thousands of Hasidim hurried home to their inns, so that the next day, Friday, they would be able to get up as early as possible. They didn't want to miss the ceremony, and they wanted to celebrate with their rebbes, with the groom and the Apter Rebbe, and they wanted to be there early to grab a good spot near the wedding canopy. And the five Pshiskhe Hasidim climbed up to their attic, together with the rest of the paupers. They were glad that they had put their petition to the Apter Rebbe out loud: "There shouldn't be any division among the Jews!"

8

The Groom Holds Court Before the Ceremony

The town of Ostilye was topsy-turvy from early in the morning on Friday, the day before the wedding ceremony. Rural Jews from the surrounding settlements came to town with their wives and children, as if for the start of the High Holiday season. Most of the village folk brought along wagons full of harvest goods as wedding presents, and some of them brought ducks, geese, and young calves for the nightly ritual meal and special blessings throughout the week following the wedding.

The village Jews looked curiously at the Hasidic Cossacks, who ran from one inn to another all day long. The Cossacks arranged the tables in the big hall, where the groom was to sit with the unmarried young men before the wedding. They repaired the benches that had been broken during the paupers' feast. They actually expected that the groom's feast was to come that same day, but since the old Apter Rebbe was feeling weak after the previous day's paupers' feast, the in-laws agreed to cancel the groom's feast.

Loud voices could be heard in all of the inns where the various rebbes were staying, but the loudest noise came from the house of the Rebbe of Ostilye himself. The Ostilye Rebbetsin, the bride's mother, hurried from room to room in outrage that the wedding dress wasn't yet finished and the seamstresses hadn't completed the entire costume. For more than a week already the three seamstresses and female tailors had been sitting in the Rebbetsin's room, doing nothing but sewing the wedding clothes.

And when the seamstress did finally bring in the white silk wedding dress, a large number of female in-laws and Hasidic women were together with the bride in her room. They immediately sent for the two elderly grandmothers, the Nekhshizer Rebbetsin and the Apter Rebbetsin, who arrived in the same coach, accompanied by a pair of Cossacks. The wedding musicians came, and the elderly Nekhshizer

Rebbetsin took out a couple of old, worn-out silver coins that she had inherited from the old Mezhbuzher Rebbe,[45] placed them into the stuffing of the groom and bride's bedding, and murmured various prayers as she did so. Only then did the elderly Hasidic women make the last stitches in the cover.

For her part, the elderly Apter Rebbetsin took the silken wedding dress, secretly murmured a spell, and sewed into the front of the dress an amulet which had come down to her from the Baal Shem Tov. They had a poor girl of marriageable age from town put the dress on, as was the custom, and only then did they dress the thirteen-year-old bride in her wedding dress. Then all of the female in-laws and Hasidic women led the bride to the women's study house, where she sat until the ceremony.

While the bride sat in the women's study house and the town girls performed various dances, the fourteen-year-old groom sat in his quarters at the inn, holding court.

The largest crowd was assembled at the groom's door. The Hasidim of Radzivil, Apt, and Neshkhiz all wanted to convey their petitions to the groom before the wedding. The emaciated young groom didn't even know how to respond properly to such petitions, but nevertheless Hasidim reported that he "knows how to read a petition."

Women from the countryside crowded around the door as well, wanting just like the men to hand the groom a petition before the wedding. The groom stood there, pale from fasting all day long, asking the women the same questions he'd heard his grandfather, the Apter Rov, ask in similar situations.

The five Pshiskhe Hasidim made their way into the groom's room to confirm with their own eyes that the fourteen-year-old really had the nerve to take petitions. The Pshiskhe Hasidim saw the young groom taking the petitions in his hand just like a rebbe. At his side stood Leyzer-Leyb, the old Apter's secretary, who was in charge of the proceedings and who indicated which of the women the groom should see first. Then Leyzer-Leyb quickly pushed each one away, shouting, "Let somebody else in! There's no time!"

---

45. Probably referring to R. Barukh of Miedzyboż (ca. 1756–1811), a Hasidic leader in Podolia (the Ukraine). Barukh was the younger son of Odl, the Ba'al Shem Tov's daughter, and one of the first tzaddikim to assume a royal bearing.

But one woman was stubborn and didn't want to back away. She stood in front of the young groom and wept in a high-pitched voice, relating that just one week after her wedding her husband had left her. For ten years now she had been a grass widow and childless.

But the groom didn't hear a word the woman was shouting at him and asked: "Pregnant, nursing?"

"Don't you hear me, holy bridegroom?" the woman sobbed. "I'm a grass widow without a child!"

"Yes, okay," repeated the groom. "But 'pregnant, nursing?'"

It was the same question he'd often heard from his grandfather when a woman was in an audience with the latter.

The woman didn't understand what the groom meant, and she remained standing with her mouth open, as though her capacity to speak had suddenly vanished.

But at that point the secretary Reb Leyzer Leyb got involved. He murmured something into the groom's ear. The groom blushed somewhat, lowered his eyes in embarrassment, and right away offered his blessing:

"Go in good health, and you will be helped!"

The woman wanted to weep some more and tell the fourteen-year-old groom how cruel her husband was, but the secretary Leyzer-Leyb didn't let her stand any longer. "Go already, go! There's no more time, the groom gave you his blessing; you see that other women want to hand him notes."

The five Pshiskhe Hasidim watched the whole drama of such a young child listening to petitions and giving his blessing, and Reb Itshe Meirl, the genius from Warsaw, quietly said to Reb Isacharl Horovits: "Evidently, with them it's not at all difficult to be a rebbe. We really thought that you have to work on yourself until you become a tzaddik. They make it really easy . . ."

And with that the five Hasidim left the groom's room and went out into the courtyard.

But here as well, in the courtyard of the Ostilyer Rebbe, there was a great throng of Hasidim and country Jews.

From all sides the country Jews found their sleeves tugged by people enticing them toward the various rebbes.

The voices sounded like a market day:

"You need a blessing so you'll have a son? Come to our rebbe, the Ziditshover,[46] who's famous as a wonder worker."

"Do you have a sick child? Come to our rebbe, the Premishlaner.[47] He's just about able to resurrect the dead."

In this fashion the country Jews were encouraged to attend the various rebbes who had come to the wedding.

The five Pshiskhe Hasidim wanted to make their way out of the commotion in the big courtyard as soon as possible, but suddenly a heavyset Jew with a red beard accosted Reb Itshe Meirl and pulled at his sleeve:

"Young man," he addressed Reb Itshe Meirl, "what's the trouble that you need help with? Come to my rebbe, the Gliner! What do you lack, livelihood? Children? At my rebbe's place, miracles are scattered around like dust."

"What I lack is something your rebbe certainly can't help me with," answered Reb Itshe Meirl with a sardonic smile, and the five Hasidim left the Ostilye court.

They walked through the marketplace, which was full of Hasidim, and Reb Fayvele Gritser turned to Reb Zishe Shedletser: "Is it any surprise that they persecute us? They've brought Hasidim down to such a low level. They do business in wonders, magic healing, and amulets, just like a Gentile folk healer."

"It will make our task at the trial that much harder," Reb Zishe Shedlitser said with a deep sigh.

"But conveying a petition to the old Apter Rebbe before the wedding ceremony is still something we have to do," said Reb Fayvl Gritser. "One thing has nothing to do with the other! To attend the Apter Rebbe is a great thing now."

The whole house was besieged by gangs of Hasidim who pushed in through the doors and windows, trying by every means to make their way into the Apter Rebbe's room. In every room scribes of sacred scrolls as well as simple petition-writers sat at long tables, writing out petitions with goose quill pens. At this busy time the petition-writers didn't want to write out the detailed petitions the Hasidim were used to handing in.

---

46. R. Tzvi Hirsh Eichenstein, known as Hirsh Zydaczower (1763–1831), was a disciple of the Seer of Lublin and R. Menahem Mendel of Rimenev.

47. Meir Hagadol of Premishlan (1703–73), disciple of the Baal Shem Tov.

"Keep it short," the petition-writers stormed at the Hasidim who stood before them pouring out their bitter hearts, "You can tell it all to the Rebbe when you see him. Just tell me the name of this cruel nobleman and his mother's name. What's that—'Jan Bronislaw ben Kasha Maria?' I've got it down; go and may you be helped."

Each Hasid left the petition-writer a few coins and made his way to the door of the Rebbe's room.

But in front of the door stood a whole staff of secretaries, dictating who could be let in and who couldn't. Those who handed a more valuable coin to the secretary were let inside first.

The five Pshiskhe Hasidim pushed toward the Rebbe's door as well. Leyzer Leyb, the chief secretary, rubbed his fingers together to indicate to them that they had to pay. When Reb Yisokherl Horovits, the wealthy young man, handed the secretary a promissory note for a large sum, the secretaries pushed the rest of the crowd aside and the five Pshiskhe Hasidim were admitted to see the Rebbe.

The old Apter Rebbe sat in his Sabbath clothes on an upholstered chair, smoking a large pipe. Two candles burned on the table, next to a glass of water. Before reading each petition the Apter Rebbe dipped his fingers into the glass, rubbed his forehead, and quietly murmured something. Hasidim stood by him in attendance.

When Reb Itshe Meirl laid his petition on the table, the old Apter Rebbe took it in his hand and turned it from side to side.

"What kind of petition is this?" the Apter asked in wonder. "It's entirely empty."

Only by the light of the candle did the old Apter Rebbe see the words that were written there: "Yitskhok Meir ben Khaye Sore, for fear of Heaven and spiritual healing."

The Apter Rebbe read the petition a few times and then said in astonishment: "Wow! A petition worthy of the Baal Shem."

He turned to the Hasidim and began shouting:

"You see the petition the young man brought me? He's not asking for livelihood. He's not giving me a headache about business and assorted vain things. All he asks for is fear of Heaven! It's a long time since I had a petition with those kinds of concerns."

And the Apter Rebbe took Reb Itshe Meirl by the hand and said to him, "Young man, you've revived me."

Then he uttered his response quietly, so that no one would hear what he said.

The other four Pshiskhe Hasidim wrote nearly the same thing in their petitions.

The whole time the Apter Rebbe repeatedly clasped Reb Itshe Meirl's belt with his hand. When the five Pshiskhe Hasidim finished their audiences with him, the Apter fell into deep thought, rubbed his large, creased forehead with the silver tobacco holder that he held, meanwhile dipping his finger from time to time into the glass. And he suddenly began telling all of the Hasidim present how many times he had been in this world, how he remembered being a high priest when a Jew came into the Temple to bring a sacrifice but the cow ran away and the Jew chased it, spreading his broad sleeves, until he caught the cow.

The old Apter then turned to Reb Fayvele Gritser and quietly said to him:

"When the light of the saintly Baal Shem Tov arose in the world, Satan may his name be eradicated was profoundly perplexed, and he asked: 'What am I going to do now?' ... And an idea came to him: He went to the saints of that generation and said to them, '"Let me assign to you some of the people that are with me" (Genesis 33:15). Since you don't have many Hasidim, I'll provide you with some Hasidim from my side' ... The saints of that generation, however, didn't take this good advice from Satan. It's different today. The doors have been opened and there's a mixture. There are some Hasidim who come from 'his' side ... That's why your petitions revived me," he said to them quietly.

9

The Ceremony

The five Pshiskhe Hastidim were pleased with the old Apter Rebbe's statement, and they were doubly pleased that none of the other Hasidim had heard the Rebbe's last statements.

Next to the table stood the elderly secretary, Leyzer Leyb's assistant, casting angry looks at Reb Itshe Meirl and the other four Hasidim who were detaining the Rebbe so long and preventing others from approaching. The old secretary came up closer to the Rebbe's table and murmured into his long beard: "The crowd is waiting!"

"I won't receive anyone else!" the old Apter Rebbe suddenly declared, as if tearing himself away from another world. "I've just had five petitions worthy of the Baal Shem! Okay, hand over my frock and we'll go find the groom and take him to the veiling ceremony."

The press of the huge crowd of Hasidim surrounding the Rebbe's room and the rooms nearby was unimaginably dense. The secretaries opened the door and Hasidim pressed their petitions into the old Apter Rebbe's hand. The Rebbe immediately handed the petitions over to the secretaries who were standing nearby. He merely shook the hands of the Hasidim, wished them well and said, "I'll read the petitions later." And the great crowd of Hasidim had to retreat and make way for him.

The five Pshiskhe Hasidim mingled with the rest of the Hasidim so that they wouldn't be recognized. Throughout the town word spread that the old Apter was on his way to the "groom's meal."

In the large hall sat the groom and the rest of the young unmarried men.

The fourteen-year-old groom sat at the head. Next to him on either side sat ten- to twelve-year-old children of other rebbes, in high sable caps. Some of these were grooms themselves already, while others were expected, on the occasion of the wedding gathering, to be examined in Torah scholarship by the rebbes who were their prospective in-laws, or by their Hasidim who were specially trained to conduct such examinations.

The unmarried young men had their own Cossacks, who served the various rebbes' children and served the groom as bodyguards. They were to watch him from the time he was ceremoniously called to the Torah in the synagogue as a bridegroom and didn't let him out of their sight for a second. The power of the Other Side is very great at such times, and Satan's minions are always looking for a way to seize the groom.

The young Cossacks were dressed in the same clothes as the married Cossacks. But they could easily be recognized because none of them had any facial hair.

The young Cossacks took money for liquor from every rebbe who came to offer a mazel tov to the groom. They ordered a ceremonial happy song to be played for him. The chief of the young Cossacks, who was learning how to be a master of ceremonies, offered rhymes that he had invented for the occasion, and then ordered the choir to sing "And he will be like a groom departing the wedding canopy" (Psalms 19:6).

Between one tune and the next, various youngsters of extraordinary scholarship delivered a brief Torah analysis. The youngsters disputed various issue in their studies, tossing in references to passages in the Talmud, difficult statements of Maimonides, showing off the range of their learning, and sharpening their minds.

When they were done talking about their studies, a troop of young Cossacks climbed onto the table and began singing a Hasidic song, accompanied by all of the other lads. The Cossacks asked:

"The splendor and the faithfulness, to whom does it belong?"

And the other youngsters answered: "To the One who lives eternal."

The young Cossacks asked further: "Who is He and what is He?"

And the other youngsters responded: "A great God are you."

And they continued until they'd recited the entire hymn "The Splendor and the Faithfulness."[48]

The Hasidim who filled the great hall kept their distance, as if they wanted to let the youngsters have a last good time with the groom, for the moment the wedding ceremony was completed the groom would no longer be part of their company.

---

48. A traditional hymn associated with the festival of Simchat Torah.

But the groom paid little attention to the younger children. He sat there with his face pale from the daylong fast, and from his recitation of the afternoon prayers for the day before Yom Kippur. He was tired from his earlier reception of the hundreds of Hasidim and Jewish women. And his heart was banging in anxiety over the task of climbing the mountain that loomed before him—he had to deliver the "groom's lecture" to the youngsters.

For more than a month already his personal teacher, Reb Yoysef Maytls, had been rehearsing with him the two speeches he would have to deliver—one under the wedding canopy, and one on the "great night." All of his comrades, his assistants and bodyguards, already knew the two speeches by heart, since he had recited them so many times. Yet now he was still afraid when he looked out and realized he would have to recite the speech in front of so many hundreds of strange young men and Hasidim.

The slight young groom sat the whole time, his eyes covered with a scarf, quietly rehearsing the speech. He was sweating profusely in his new silk clothes. He opened up the shirt, which was tied with two ribbons, repeatedly lifted up the heavy Galician-style fur hat, and runnels of sweat flowed down his pale cheeks.

The whole time his teacher, Reb Yoysef Matyls, stood nearby, ready to help him out should any problems arise, ready to rescue him from any danger . . .

And when the boys had finished their various tunes, the teacher winked at the groom, to let him know it was time to start.

Little beads of sweat immediately appeared on the groom's brown, wetting the lowest hairs on his fur hat. The youngsters and hundreds of Hasidim approached the head of the table, where the groom was sitting. In a thin, shaky voice, just barely loud enough for the words to be heard, the groom began:

"The Talmud says, 'Said Aba, one who betroths with a loan, the woman is not betrothed to him . . .'" (Kiddushin 10a). And he immediately posed a question about the commentary of Tosafot, and resolved a difficult statement of Maimonides.

The hungry groom began his speech on this topic fluently, engaging with the Talmud's discussion of the requirements for a transaction between a potential bride and bridegroom to permit licit relations between the two later on, elaborated a line of reasoning according to "this one's approach," responded to it with a citation from the commentary Pnei Yehoshua,[49] drew in the views of many earlier and later commentators, and responded to them further with a quote from the Noda BeYehuda.[50]

His cheeks began to flush, his eyes took on a sharp aspect. He began talking louder and faster, and one could sense that he himself understood not a whit the meaning of all the laws he was debating. Eventually he stumbled when he was discussing the Talmud's question: "They asked him whether the beginning of intercourse accomplishes the acquisition of the bride, or the end of intercourse accomplishes it" (Kiddushin 10a). He kept looking at his teacher with pleading eyes, as if asking the latter to help him out because the danger was so great. He was on the point of bursting into tears when suddenly everyone heard the rumble of Reb Refoyel's drum and his voice announcing: "Let the in-laws proceed to the reception!"

The groom didn't manage to finish his speech.

Suddenly a crowd of Hasidim tore their way into the hall. The married Cossacks pushed their way in from all sides, and shouts were heard: "Let the in-law, the old Apter Rebbe, through! Make room!"

Soon the young boys were pushed away. Now there was no particular deference shown toward the young Cossacks, and their places were seized from them.

The Cossacks called out in Hebrew: "A groom is like a king!" And right then the following were brought in on a silver platter: a new, heavy Turkish tallit with its broad silver adornments; a large white ceremonial robe with a golden, Spanish-style yarmulke, and a belt woven of silver thread, which the groom's father-in-law had inherited from his own father, the Rebbe Reb Mikhele Zlotshever.

The groom's father, the Radziviler Rebbe, arrived. He approached the groom together with a Hasid of his, an orchard manager who had a broad, combed beard covering his homely face and long, grey brows. He wore a worn-out fur hat and a torn mohair caftan, from whose

---

49. Commentary and novellae on the Talmud by Rabbi Jacob Joshua Falk (1680–1756). Consists of four parts, the last published in Furth, 1780.

50. Famous collection of responsa by R. Ezekiel Landau of Prague (1713–93).

sleeves long fringes dangled. He spoke with a hard "r," and his clothes were scented with the perfume of fruits.

The Rebbe stood the orchard manager, Reb Shakhne Dovid, next to the groom, and he addressed him in front of the entire assembly:

"In-law Reb Shakhne Dovid, thirteen years ago I sold to you my son Shmuel. At that time he was very sick, may we be spared. At that time I accepted 18 gulden from you in exchange for my child. You were to take the child into your home and raise him together with your eight children. But you agreed to leave the child with me and I raised him. I consulted with you when the discussions began about a possible match for him, and it was actually your celebration when he began to put on tefillin.

"Now, when both of us have been granted the merit to raise the child and to live to see him married, I would like to buy my son back from you. Tell me, how much do you want for him?"

The simple Jew Shakhne Dovid felt terribly awkward among all these rabbis, but he stood up straight like a real father-in-law. He recited in a hoarse voice and a lower-class "r" the entire answer that had been taught him:

"The truth is that this child is very dear to me, even though, thank God, I have, no evil eye!, eight children. But since the Rebbe has had terrible sorrows in the matter of children and has not been blessed in this matter, I will agree to sell the groom Shmuel back to you. I know that there isn't enough money in the world to match what this groom is worth, but since the Rebbe raised him for me, provided him with the best teachers, provided him with all the best and didn't take a penny from me for all this, I will take all of that into account and will ask now as his price only eighteen gold ducats."

The Radziviler Rebbe took his old silver etrog case, which was full of golden coins, and counted out eighteen gold ducats into Shakhne Dovid's hand. The Rebbe turned to the whole crowd and said, his voice drawn out and full of tears:

"You are all witnesses that I have repurchased my son from Shakhne Dovid, and from now on the child is mine."

"We saw it! We saw it!" came shouts from every side.

"Mazel tov, mazel tov," the jester cried out, and the Hasidic Cossacks played the congratulation melody.

Then the groom was led to the Apter Rebbe, who sat in a chair on the side the whole time. The groom lowered his head, the Apter Rebbe raised his trembling hands, lowered them onto the groom's head, and blessed him.

The two attendants, the Ostilye Rebbe's brother and the Radziviler Rebbe's brother, approached the groom, who stood utterly drenched in sweat. They ordered him to give away all of the money and all of the gold or silver items that he might possess.

The groom fished out of his pockets a few coins to give them away. The attendants then took the groom's golden chain and watch with a zipper, which he had received as a gift. They dressed the groom in the long white robe, which was twice as big as he was. They folded it in two, bound it with Reb Mikhele Zlotshever's belt and put the golden Spanish cap on his head.

The father-in-law, the Kovler Rebbe, placed under the cap a bit of ash that lay on a gold plate, and in a quiet voice with a grieving heart said the verse: "If I forget you, Jerusalem, let my right hand forget . . ." (Psalm 137:5–6), which all of the Hasidim repeated after him.

All at once everything grew quiet. Suddenly there could be heard the murmuring of a melody, which the Kovler Rebbe sang with these words:

"Once again will be heard in the cities of Judah and in the streets of Jerusalem the voice of gladness and the voice of joy, the voice of the groom and the voice of the bride" (Jeremiah 33:10).

The melody drew out lonely and sorrowful, the notes were filled with pain but not with despair; rather they expressed a quiet, longing hope.

The Apter Rebbe sat the whole time with his eyes half-glazed, wiping away his trears with his kerchief.

The Neshkhizer Hasidim placed their hands on each other's shoulders, clustered tightly together, and swayed as they sang together with the Rebbe.

All at once the leader of the Apter Cossacks, "Black Yosl" from Rove, who stood outside the hall, shouted: "What is it, today—Tisha B'Av? What are you lamenting like that for?"

A Cossack from among the Ostilye Hasidim, a tough guy, heard this and angrily shouted back: "Respect, you nervy character, or I'll let you have it!" And indeed he immediately made good on his words.

A battle soon broke out between the Ostilye and Apter Cossacks. All of the Galician Hasidim were on the Apter's side and all of the Polish Hasidim on the Ostilyer's side. They tore the Cossack braids, stepped on the Hussar caps, pulled off the Russian epaulets, and who knows what might have been the outcome had not Ahron Dovid, the chief commander of all the Hasidic Cossacks, ridden up on a horse. He drew his hand across the two halves of his broad beard, waved his wooden sword two and fro, and the dispute calmed down.

The Kovler Rebbe and the Hasidim in the hall kept singing for quite some time, until Reb Leyzer Leyb, the head secretary of the Apter Rebbe, shouted: "The groom doesn't have the strength to keep fasting, why aren't we going to the veiling ceremony!"

Only then did the Kovler Rebbe stop singing. The Apter Rebbe asked: "Has the bride been seated already? Let's go to the veiling!" And he turned to the groom's grandfather: "In-law, let us meet the saints who are already in the True World and who came to the ceremony!"

And in the meantime, while the in-laws were getting ready for the veiling, the bride was formally seated on a chair in the middle of the women's hall. Young wives waiting to get their households established approached the even younger bride and braided her hair. While they did this they quietly wept into her ears, pouring out their bitter hearts to the bride.

The female in-laws, the rebbes' wives, went about amongst the women with platters of hops and wheat, distributing them to the crowd.

The old Apter Rebbetsin held in her hand the white silk veil that she had received as an inheritance from Adel, the Baal Shem Tov's daughter. And the master of ceremonies sang to the bride, until a call was heard: "The groom is coming."

The women moved off to the side, with the rebbes' wives standing as a barrier between the men and the women. They stood dressed in their various headdresses, holding handfuls of hops and wheat.

The organizers, together with the elderly rebbes, entered with the groom. Almost all of them shielded their eyes with their hands, looking down to see where they were going, until they reached the place where the bride sat. The old Apter Rebbetsin handed the groom the veil, and he quickly shielded his eyes, and hastily tossed the veil onto the bride.

The Rebbes called out: "Our sister, be the mother of thousands of ten thousands" (Genesis 24:60). The women showered the bride with hops and wheat, the musicians played a tune, and the designated bridesmaids led the bride to the canopy.

The canopy stood in the middle of the market on four posts that were deeply embedded in the earth. The entire marketplace was occupied by Hasidim. On all of the surrounding rooves sat Jewish men, women, and children. The Cossacks worked diligently to make way for the bride, for the mothers-in-law, and for the groom.

The whole town was filled with one song, which carried across all the rooves, from one end of town to the other.

Women held their children in their arms, so that they might remember having the merit to see the ceremeony at the "great wedding."

And though the sun shone bright on the town, Jews placed candelabras in their windows. Hundreds of Cossacks preceded the groom, with burning havdalah candles in their hands.

The press was so great that the old Apter Rebbe had to be brought in on a chair carried by a group of Hasidim.

Every minute a commotion could be heard from a different corner. Women fainted, thousands of candles burned on all sides, and every time the name of a rebbe was called out as one honored with conducting the ceremony, or with reading aloud the wedding contract, or with another ritual honor, the press increased afresh.

As soon as the Seven Blessings[51] were completed, the Hasidim wove themselves together and began dancing.

Thus dancing, they led the bride and groom into the room where they would spend some time in seclusion. Old women danced in front of the doorway with braided challahs, and while the bride and groom sat in seclusion eating the traditional soup, the Hasidim danced in the marketplace with enthusiasm and passion, beside themselves with ecstasy.

Many Jews danced in their bare yarmulkes, holding their fur hats in their hands.

People danced on the rooves and porches. Tipsy Jews took flasks of wine, tied them to their belts, and joined the circles of dancers. The

---

51. The last and crucial part of the Jewish wedding ceremony.

rest of the dancers leaned down to the flasks, took a sip, and danced on.

A troop of Cossacks carried the Apter Rebbe on his chair and danced with him into the study house.

The sun began setting behind the town's hill.

Long shadows appeared on the walls of the brick houses. The panes of the old synagogue's windows burned with golden fire. The light of Sabbath candles could be seen from some houses.

Women behind schedule ran with pots of cholent to the bakery, where the pots would be placed in the big oven.

Jews from the city hurried to the mikvah with packages of clean clothes, and in the middle of the marketplace the dancing continued.

And apart from the whole crowd of dancers, the five Pshiskhe Hasidim danced with the Kovler Rebbe.

The crowd of dancers in the marketplace grew thinner and thinner. Jews hurried to the study house to greet the Sabbath, and the five Pshiskhe Hasidim kept dancing with the Kovler Rebbe in the marketplace, until the prayer leader could be heard from the study house beginning the afternoon service: "Praise the Lord for He is good, for His mercy is eternal . . ." Only then did the little bands of dancing Hasidim, including the five Pshiskhe Hasidim and the Kovler Rebbe, dance right into the study house and there begin to pray with fervor.

10

The Apter Rebbe Presides

On Friday night the five Pshiskhe Hasidim prayed in the anteroom of the study house. That's where the simple Jews, the artisans, the homeless wanderers, and the beggars prayed.

Reb Itshe Meirl, the Warsaw genius, paced back and forth across the anteroom, his hands tucked into his belt, and anxiously cast his eyes back and forth across the anteroom.

To the side stood Reb Yerukhem Sofer with a few other Hasidim. The Rebbe Reb Yankev Shimen Daytsh asked them to watch carefully to find out whether the five strange Hasidim who were wandering around the wedding, acting like paupers, and submitting petitions that (as the old Apter Rebbe had said) were in the spirit of the Baal Shem Tov, might not actually belong to the "sect" that they were planning to bring to trial.

So Reb Yerukhem Sofer didn't let his eyes stray from the five Pshiskhe Hasidim for a second.

In the anteroom they could hear the sounds of a march coming from the study house. The Galician Hasidic choir was singing the Friday evening hymn Lecha Dodi. To the Pshiskhe Hasidim it sounded like the army had come to town.

Reb Fayvele Gritser discussed Pshiskhe Hasidism with Reb Zishe Shedletser as they sat on a bench in the anteroom. Meanwhile the Hasidim in the study house paused between each verse, singing each phrase of the march a few times.

"Do you know?" Reb Zishe Shedletser asked Reb Fayvele Gritser. "Before we left Pshiskhe Mendele Tomashover told me something that's wormed its way into my bones."

"What did he say to you?"

"He said, 'You should know that every commandment a Jew fulfills must be for its own sake; you can't do it just to be humble.'"

"A worthy saying," Reb Fayvele smacked his lips, "Wow! A worthy saying."

A Fire Burns in Kotsk

"He's going to be something, that Mendele."

"And how!" answered Reb Fayvele. "Sometimes I sit with him at the table in Pshiskhe, and I'm happy that the crowd is growing and the way of Pshiskhe is becoming better known, and suddenly I notice Mendele Tomashover. He whispers a secret to me: 'If a person goes around proudly feeling that he's already there, he's certainly lost.' I tell you, dear Zishe, he got me right here!" Reb Fayvele indicated his heart. "So go tell that crowd," he nodded toward the study house, "what Pshiskhe Hasidism is."

The genius from Warsaw, Reb Itshe Meirl, meanwhile made his way to the library and climbed up the ladder that stood before the big bookcases. He took out a volume, climbed back down, became absorbed in the book, and remained standing there with one foot on the first rung of the ladder and the other on the floor. His big Polish fur hat was pushed toward the back of his head, his hand resting on his intelligent forehead, and he swayed from side to side, squinting his right eye as though he were aiming at something far, far away . . .

Reb Yerukhem Sofer slowly and casually approached the ladder. He came closer to the genius from Warsaw, took out a pair of tin wire eyeglasses, placed them on the end of his nose right next to his nostrils, and connected them to his ears with some thread. Raising his shoulders, he gave a sideways glance at the volume the Warsaw genius was studying. Then he took out his large, flowered handkerchief and blew his tobacco-filled nose so loudly that it soundly like a long blast from a hoarse, dirty shofar. The sound was intended to let the Warsaw genius know that someone was standing next to him.

But Reb Itshe Meirl was too interested in the book and didn't hear anything. So Reb Yerukhem Sofer came even closer to Reb Itshe Meirl and saw that he was looking at the volume *Tevues Shor,* covering the laws of kosher slaughter.

"Humph!" muttered Reb Yerukhem Sofer through his clogged nose. "What an odd idea that young man has, to look at *Tevues Shor* in the middle of the Sabbath eve prayers."

The genius from Warsaw was startled, as though he'd been cast down from another world, and he saw standing before him an old, undernourished Jew, angry enough to swallow him whole.

Reb Yerukhem Sofer lifted his shoulders and repeated the same words: "What an odd idea, for a young man to look at *Tevues Shor* in the middle of the Sabbath eve prayers."

"What's bad about *Tevues Shor*?" the Warsaw genius wondered.

"Sssss . . ." Reb Yerukhem hissed through his toothless gums. "It's not right! What, are you, studying to be a slaughterer so you need to study *Tevues Shor* right now, in the middle of prayers?"

"First of all, no one's praying now," answered Reb Itshe Meirl. "They're just tapping along to march tunes. And second, I am indeed studying to be a slaughterer. For years I've been studying the central principle of the laws of slaughter—that a slaughterer must be a God-fearing Jew. But I still haven't quite gotten it down yet."

Reb Yerukhem Sofer didn't answer. He sighed deeply, "Oh!" No one knew what he meant by that sigh.

But Reb Yerukhem Sofer wasn't satisfied by the strange young man's answer. He approached Reb Shimen Daytsh's lookouts who were supposed to be watching the five strangers. He told them what the young man had said.

"We know the kinds of things they're up to," the Hasidim answered. "Sure, that just shows you that we really have to keep an eye on them."

And all throughout the Friday evening service the Hasidic investigators watched the Pshiskhe Hasidim as they prayed. They saw the five strangers walking back and forth around the anteroom, lost in thought, barely murmuring their prayers.

But when the service was ended and the crowd set off back to their inns to make Kiddush, the investigators saw the five strangers going up to their attic room and putting on fresh shirts. The shirts they had worn for the prayers were soaked with sweat from their intense worship.

The investigators watched the strangers throughout the Sabbath. They wanted to catch them doing something wrong, but they didn't come up with anything to report to Reb Shimen Daytsh. They could only tell him about the strangers' odd behavior—they kept close to the masses, to the artisans and beggars; in the middle of services they might be engrossed in a volume of responsa or chat with each other, so that they might not appear to be praying at all. And yet after the prayers they have to change their shirts, since their devotion is so great.

But the Rebbe Reb Shimen Daytsh kept insisting that this was precisely the way that "sect" of Jews behaved. At first they would behave like God-fearing Jews and only years later, when they had caused great damage among the faithful, would they appear in their true colors.

The various Hasidim and their rebbes quickly ate the Friday night meal. They all wanted to get to the hall where the Apter Rebbe was conducting the ceremonial table.

Masses of Hasidim crowded into the hall to hear every word the Apter Rebbe said.

The Apter Rebbe sat wearing a flowered robe. He kept his silver tobacco box in his hand the whole time. He tasted a bit of every Sabbath dish, then quickly pushed the dish away. The rebbes distributed the Apter Rebbe's leftovers to their Hasidim. After the meat course the Apter's chief secretary told an old Apter Hasid to sing the Friday night hymn "How Precious Is Your Rest." At the verse "the Sabbath rest is part of the World to Come," they heard the Apter Rebbe repeating the words over and over. He kept rubbing his right temple with the silver tobacco box. His face was shining like a torch. He leaned his head back on the chair and was overcome with enthusiasm.

The older Apter singer had long finished the hymn and the Apter Rebbe still sat with his head leaning back. In the whole hall it was so quiet that you could have heard poppy seeds being sown.

And the old Apter Rebbe was heard humming the "Torah melody."

At first only isolated words could be heard, coming through in a sweet melody. The melody flowed into the words and they became one.

And finally they heard the old Apter singing with passion:

Aba-ba-ba ba ba
Ba-ba-ba ba
The several orders of angels
All ask, "Where is God?"
Ahh-ahh,
How to answer them?
There is no place that is without Him

There is no thought that grasps Him at all.
Oh-ay-oh-ay-ay,
No thought grasps Him at all.

The old Apter Rebbe repeated the last words a few times, more and more quietly, until he was entirely lost in thought, as if he were hovering in the higher worlds. Then everyone heard, "The letters of the Hebrew word for love have the same numerical value as those of the word for 'one.'"

The Apter Rebbe was discoursing in Torah.

Everyone pushed closer, standing on top of one another.

They pricked up their ears to catch every word and every sigh that came out of the old Apter Rebbe's mouth, and they tried to see every motion. And the Rebbe repeated: "Love has the same numerical value as one. There is higher love and lower love. Thirty days before a soul is born, it is decreed in Heaven which one shall unite with which one.

"If the soul does not encounter its mate, it wanders through the world seeking its mate, and eventually it has to be born into another body. If it does meet its partner soul, then love becomes one soul, and the lower love becomes higher love. Then both souls are elevated, both parts become whole, and a generous soul arises from them. Let us wish this pair that it happens to them!"

"Amen," the reply echoed throughout the hall.

▲▼▲▼▲▼

Following the blessing after the meal and the recitation of the seven blessings for the newlyweds, the ceremonial dance began.

Wedding bards stood on every table, pouring forth improvised rhymes, and summoned the groom to be the first for the dance.

The bride was led in with all of the female in-laws, the wives of the various rebbes, and as soon as the fourteen-year-old groom touched the edge of the kerchief whose other edge was in the hand of the bride and turned it one time, he was seized by a gang of Hasidim who began dancing with him, so that he might not, God forbid, dance too much with the bride and have improper thoughts . . .

It was quite different when they summoned the old Apter Rebbe himself to the dance.

At that, the dance was transformed into worship. The old Apter Rebbe first touched the kerchief that the bride held, did a few turns with the bride, and then he released it and began dancing facing her.

His old, worn-out feet barely moved at first, but with time they somehow became lighter, as if they were becoming separated from the ground.

The dozens of rebbes and hundreds of Hasidim watched devotedly as the old Apter Rebbe danced, but they didn't allow him to dance for long. He was gently surrounded and they danced back and forth before the bride a few more times in order to fulfill the commandment to make the bride happy.

Nor did the bride dance alone any longer. A group of rebbes' wives encircled her and danced with her, and the young bride, whose hair had just been shorn early in the evening and replaced by an elaborate headdress known as a *shterntikhl*, looked like a child dressed up as a grown woman, just like she had often played with her girlfriends in the various rebbes' courts of the day. In the middle of the dance the relatives led the old Apter Rebbe away, set him back on his chair, and fanned his sweating face with their fur hats.

When the ceremonial dance was over, the younger unmarried boys were quickly rushed home. Apparently the youngsters knew it wasn't proper for them to be there any longer, and they went away by themselves. But a few of the older ones, who really wanted to stay in the hall, were caught hiding under the benches.

"Vermin!" voices were heard. "Go on home! It's time for you to go to bed. It's not your time yet."

The crowd thinned out more and more, and even the married young men felt a bit embarrassed and eventually set off for their inns. The Hasidim began to sing the hymn Ein Kelohenu and drink a bit of liquor. The two rebbes' wives who served as the bride's chaperones came in, a sign that everything was ready. The male chaperones approached the thin groom and took him by the arms. The groom trembled violently, as though he was being led to the slaughter ... and he was brought home with song to go to bed.

The only ones who came along were the very old Hasidim.

And when the chaperones had led the groom into the house, the old Hasidim stationed themselves under the windows, and a Hasid who had already seen his eightieth year began quietly singing in a pleasant voice:

Day comes,
Day comes,
Day comes!
I praise God who searches the heart
Who created together the start of the morning
Attend to your soul
Jacinth, agate, and amethyst

They repeated over and over, "Day comes!" and "attend to your soul," so that the words wended their way into the sleeping houses and deep into every heart—for the old Hasidim knew very well what their singing at that moment meant, and they concentrated on their song with all their might.

The half moon, like a broken plate, was hiding somewhere behind the poplar trees, which stood like guards around the orchard outside of time, casting a mother-of-pearl shine into the sleeping marketplace, and the old Hasidim kept singing "attend to your soul," until the two mothers-in-law, the chaperones, came out in their nightgowns with honey cake and liquor, indicating with their hands that it was time to stop singing.

They drank with a wish of "Lechaim," quietly wished the chaperones "Mazel tov" and added a wish that the match would be successful. The mothers-in-law asked the old Hasidim to depart, for the children were already asleep.

11

The Trial

From early in the morning on Sunday the town was in a tizzy. All the Hasidim knew that the same evening, the "big night," during the feast at which the traditional Seven Blessings would be recited, the Rebbe Reb Yaakov Shimen Daytsh together with Reb Yosele Yartshever would accuse the Pshiskhe Hasidim in front of the old Apter Rebbe, and that he would demand that the Apter place the Rebbe Reb Bunim and his "sect" under a ban.

Many of the rebbes made their way out of Ostilye in time, in order to avoid being eyewitnesses to the excommunication of such a large congregation of Hasidim. Among those who escaped was the young Rebbe of Rizhin, Reb Yisroeltshe.[52] He had come during the day on Sunday to attend the feast on the "big night," but as soon as he heard about the preparations to place on trial a new path in Hasidism, which had begun to spread in Poland, he said: "Let my soul not come into their council! (Gen. 49:5). Who knows who they'll want to excommunicate next?" He ordered his fancy coach to be prepared, put the six horses in harness, and immediately rode away. The Rizhiner Hasidim say that on that occasion, while he was still a young man, he already hinted that a time would come when people would want to place his own way on trial, which actually happened years later during the great dispute between Sanz and Sadigura.

But more than eighty rebbes stayed in Ostilye all the same, including many great lights, such as the Rebbe Reb Sholem Rokeach of Belz;[53] the rebbe and kabbalist Reb Tsvi Hersh Ziditshover; and others. Indeed, everyone seated at the table at the feast for the "big night" were rebbes in their white coats, and around them in the big hall stood thousands of Hasidim, including the five from Pshiskhe.

---

52. R. Israel Friedman of Ruzhin (1796–1850), great-grandson of R. Dov Ber, the Great Maggid of Mezheritch, who was known for his regal lifestyle. R. Israel created one of the most impressive, flourishing dynasties in the history of Hasidism.

53. R. Shalom Rokeah of Belz (1783–1855), disciple of R. Jacob Isaac, the Seer of Lublin, and founder of the enduring Belz dynasty.

The secretaries and waiters brought out the food. Between one course and the next, jesters recited rhymes invented for the occasion.

At the end of the feast, when it came time to announce the wedding presents, the old Apter Rebbe said that he himself wanted to offer a Torah discourse instead of the groom. He focused on a difficult passage in the works of Maimonides, worked through a complex analysis, and then he found himself addressing a difficult question which he could not resolve.

"Who can resolve this difficult problem in the Mishnah for me?" the old Apter Rebbe called out.

The genius from Warsaw, Reb Itshe Meir, knew a way to resolve the problem, but he was afraid to call attention to himself. He grew pale and couldn't stay still. Reb Eliezer Ber Grobovitser, the spokesman for the five Hasidim, noticed this and said: "Now is the time to show them who we are; if you know a resolution, say it immediately."

The young genius from Warsaw didn't have the strength and courage to push his way through the packed crowd. He merely shouted: "That's a question that Tosafos asks in the tractate Kedushin, and Tosafos resolves the problem in the Mishnah!"

The young tremulous voice broke through the quiet in the hall. The old Apter Rebbe asked in amazement: "Who was that who responded? I'm delighted with that." "I'm delighted with that," he repeated a few times, but the Warsaw genius sank back among the great crowd of Hasidim and nobody knew who had given the answer.

When all of the wedding gifts had been announced, a group of actors from among the Galician Hasidic Cossacks appeared. They climbed up on the tables to perform "A Dispute Between a Hasid and a German Jew."

The play had been put together with the approval of Reb Yaakov Shimen Daytsh, as a way to begin the trial of the Rebbe Reb Bunem.

One of the Cossacks played a "blind German Jew" and imitated the voice of the Rebbe Reb Bunem, who became blind at the end of his days.

The play began with the dispute between the Hasid and the blind German. The blind German wanted to demonstrate that the most important aspect of prayer was the proper intention, not the performance itself. In his speech he bitterly teased all the other rebbes. But when the Hasid spoke, he demonstrated that the "blind German" was leading Jews away from Judaism with his approach.

And every time one of these disputes ended and the Hasid had bested the German, all of those in costume sang a song which ended with the words: "that German, the blind one / is ruining Jews."

All this time the five Pshiskhe Hasidim were scattered among the crowd, trembling with anger. Their blood seethed, but they didn't know what to do. Should they wait for the Rebbe Reb Shimen Daytsh to pronounce his charges, or should they respond now?

But suddenly, while the disguised Hasid began once again to mock the "blind German," a chandelier crashed down from the roof and barely missed striking the disguised Hasid's head.

The Hasid stood in astonishment for a moment, as if he had seen the finger of God in action. But Reb Shimen Daytsh shouted: "You shouldn't be afraid of anything! Satan won't frighten us off with tricks like that! We'll defeat them!"

At that the young genius from Warsaw couldn't restrain himself any longer; he jumped up on to the table, tore his shirt, and shouted: "You mock my Rebbe? You call our approach Satanic?"

All at once the entire hall grew quiet. The rebbes looked at the pale young man standing on the table before the Apter Rebbe in his torn shirt, with tears pouring from his eyes . . .

"Who is he and who is his rebbe?" came the question from all sides.

"Look into my heart and you'll see who my rebbe is!"

The old Apter Rebbe, who had been sitting engrossed in his own thoughts the whole time as if he had heard nothing of the play-acting, suddenly saw standing on the table before him the same young man who had given him a petition worthy of the Baal Shem on Friday, before the wedding ceremony. He asked him: "Who is your rebbe?"

"The Rebbe Reb Bunem of Pshiskhe!" proudly answered the genius from Warsaw.

"Are there other such Hasidim of the Rebbe Reb Bunem?" asked the old Apter Rebbe further.

At this the four other Pshiskhe Hasidim, Reb Fayvele Grister, Reb Zishe Shedlitser, Reb Eliezer Ber Grobovitser, and Reb Yisokherl Horovits, made their way forward. The pushed the actors aside. The

Rebbe Reb Shimen Daytsh and Reb Yosele Yartshever appeared at the other end of the tables, and quickly the lines were drawn.

The battle began.

All of the dishes were taken off the tables. All at once many candles were lit, all of a sudden the festive wedding atmosphere dissipated.

One thing baffled everyone: Where these Pshiskhe Hasidim had come from, and when they had arrived. But the Rebbe Reb Shimen Daytsh knew them well because he'd been keeping an eye on them throughout the Sabbath.

"Are there more disciples of your rebbe like you?" the old Apter Rebbe repeated.

"I'm the youngest and the least of all his disciples!" answered the Warsaw genius. "I don't even reach their ankles."

"Don't believe him!" responded the Rebbe Reb Shimen Daytsh. "They aren't even Torah scholars. All they know how to do is make fun of other rebbes!"

"This young man," spoke up Reb Eliezer Ber, "just mentioned the Tosafos concerning the difficult Mishnah the old Apter Rebbe asked about, and he didn't even want to say his name!"

At this moment the Kovler Rebbe, Reb Leybele, came to their aid just as he had promised. He declared: "The Rebbe Reb Bunem is holy and pure, and a master of the Holy Spirit. We must not promote such a libel on this congregation of God-fearing Jews, and if any of the young Hasidim make fun of other rebbes, the Rebbe Reb Bunem certainly doesn't know about it."

"Yet we must hear the charges of the other side, in order to fulfill the commandment to 'eradicate the evil from your midst,'" answered the old Apter Rebbe. "You may have forgotten the passage in the Jerusalem Talmud, Tractate Shabbat, at the end of Chapter Five, which talks about the cow belonging to the Tanna Rebbe Eliezer ben Azarya. She used to wear her leash between her horns on the Sabbath, which is forbidden, and this bothered the Sages greatly. The text actually says that it wasn't really his cow. It belonged to a neighbor, but since Rebbe Eliezer kept silent and didn't forbid it, they referred to it as his cow just as if it really belonged to him. The Talmud told us the whole story about the cow only to teach us that if someone is in a position to stop evildoing and he fails to, it's as if he committed the sin himself. So let's hear their charges," the old Apter Rebbe concluded.

At this, the Rebbe Reb Shimen Daytsh and Reb Yosele Yartshever read out a whole list of charges: the Rebbe Reb Bunem and his disciples distorted Judaism; they mocked all of the tzaddikim of the generation; they are lenient with regard to various forbidden things; they pray very early on Rosh Hashanah and make little feasts each day, then study speculative texts; demolish the established social order in every community; mock the miracles that rebbes perform. Reb Naftoli Hirsh of Ropshits, Reb Hershele of Ziditshov, Reb Moyshe of Kozhenits all loudly oppose their actions. "If they're not separated from the body of Israel," seethed the Rebbe Reb Shimen Daytsh, "then God forbid, it could lead to mass apostasy. That's why this whole sect has to be placed under a ban."

But Reb Eliezer Ber, the spokesman for the Pshiskhe Hasidim, didn't keep silent. He parried all of the charges of the Rebbe Reb Shimen Daytsh. He pointed out that the dispute had been going on since the time of the Seer and that they, Reb Shimen Daytsh and Reb Yosele Yartshever, had been parties to the dispute with their betrayals and false accusations against the Holy Jew. In his enthusiasm he forgot that he was standing in front of the old Apter Rebbe, and he related how the Pshiskhe Hasidim were persecuted everywhere, that they wanted to renew the Hasidism of the Baal Shem, and that they welcomed paupers and common folk. People who had been brought up to a high spiritual level at the time of the Baal Shem Tov and his disciples were in the present generation being pushed back into the anteroom. The rebbes take big contributions from them, and promise in return to do wonders on their behalf, yet the same rebbes do nothing to ameliorate their lowly spiritual state.

"That's exactly why we're persecuted," Reb Eliezer Ber concluded, "and that's why various libels are invented against us, and in some towns even Apter Hasidim persecute us."

The old Apter Rebbe listened to the charges from both sides. For a moment it seemed that he was about to issue a severe sentence against the Pshiskhe Hasidim, and yet a moment later it seemed that the scale was tipped to the other side, and the Pshiskhe Hasidim were going to win . . .

But when the old Apter Rebbe heard that his own Hasidim were persecuting the Pshiskhe Hasidim, he answered: "I didn't know anything about it!"

At that Reb Eliezer Ber Grobovitser showed that he really was a Pshiskhe Hasid, for he shouted: *"Rebbe, the cow is yours!"*[54]

All of the Hasidim were frightened as they heard these words. Reb Eliezer Ber sensed that people were crowding on him from all sides, ready to tear him apart like a fish. He jumped down from the table and out the window. He immediately returned to Pshiskhe, where the power of the old Apter Rebbe couldn't reach him. Hasidim relate that when he came to Pshiskhe, he became very sick. The Rebbe Reb Bunem said that he could do nothing to help Reb Eliezer Ber, who had forgotten the saying of the Sages: "Be careful of the coals of the Sages, lest you burn yourself . . ." and eight days later he died.

When the tumult quieted down, they could see that the old Apter Rebbe was deep in thought. All of the Hasidim waited in awe to find out what the old Apter Rebbe would say, what kind of sentence he would issue. They sensed that on his words depended the fate of the Pshiskhe Rebbe and his congregation of Hasidim. With the one word "guilty" the Pshiskhe Rebbe would be banished from the people of Israel, a disaster to be mourned for generations. And if the Apter Rebbe pronounced the single word "innocent," the Pshiskhe approach would be reunited with the people of Israel and Pshiskhe Hasidism would begin to grow.

But suddenly the old Apter Rebbe began instead to speak words of Torah.

"The Sages of Blessed Memory say, that the brothers of Joseph wanted to kill him because they saw with the spirit of prophecy that Jeroboam was destined to descend from him. That is, they wanted to judge him on account of his destiny, of what was to come later, and that is against God's Torah, which judges a person only for his current actions, not for those still in the future. That's why the Midrash says that they had strayed from the ways of the Most High . . .

---

54. Author's Note: These words had a twofold meaning. First, he wanted to remind the old Apter Rebbe of the story about Rebbe Eliezer ben Azarye's cow, which the Apter Rebbe had mentioned earlier; and second, there's a folk saying based on the following anecdote: Once a rabbi ruled that a cow could not be removed from a pit into which she had fallen on the Sabbath. But when they told him that the cow was his own, he immediately changed his decision and permitted the cow to be pulled out of the pit.

"Listen to what I'll tell you about the dispute between God and the people of Israel. God says: 'Return to me and I will return to you' (Malachi 3:7). In other words, the Jews should repent first; and the people of Israel say, 'Return us to you, Lord, and we will return' (Lamentations 5:21). The Jews don't have the strength to return until God himself redeems them from exile and sustains hem. And I'm on the side of the people of Israel; well, let's listen to what God will answer . . ."

And the old Apter Rebbe pricked up his ears, as if trying to catch the hidden tones of the air . . . It was so quiet for a few moments, that the flickering of the candles could be heard. The rebbes who were sitting at the tables waiting for the verdict trembled in fear, and then the Apter announced: "You want to know what the Most High answered? He's on our side!"

The old Apter Rebbe rested for a while again, and then addressed the rebbes, saying:

"Well, you agree with me too, that we can't judge them today. Their approach is a great one, it is the approach of 'return us and we will return.' And therefore, we will speak no evil of them. What do you say to that, Reb Yerakhmiel?" he suddenly turned to the son of the Holy Jew, who was also present at the wedding. "You know the Rebbe Reb Bunem well, he lives in your town, and he was a leading disciple of your holy father."

The four Pshiskhe Hasidim, who thought that they had already won, were frightened by the last question. They were afraid that the Rebbe Reb Yerakhmiel wouldn't have anything good to say about the Rebbe Reb Bunem because there was a certain amount of competition between the followers of the two rebbes.

But the Rebbe Reb Yerakhmiel answered the old Apter Rebbe that he had heard from his father, the Holy Jew, that the Rebbe Reb Bunem was the apple of his eye and that he had conveyed to Reb Bunem "his entire storehouse of Fear of Heaven."

"Well," said the old Apter Rebbe, "we don't have to listen to any more, we won't listen to any more tale-bearing. There are disputants and troublemakers, and if these people found themselves alone in a forest, they'd pick an argument with the trees.

"Kovler Rebbe! We agree with you. We won't cut off a living limb of the Jewish body, we won't banish a congregation of Jews, Hasidim and God-fearers and true, from the people of Israel . . . Let there be no more disputes, and let Jews live in peace!"

And immediately the Apter Rebbe ordered one of his Hasidim to sing a dance melody, and he himself began to dance with the rebbes.

More than eighty rebbes danced with the old Apter Rebbe on that occasion. The joy was boundless; the Pshiskhe Hasidim wept for joy and danced together with the Kovler Rebbe, and in the midst of the dance the Apter Rebbe grasped the Warsaw genius's belt and danced that way with him for a long time.

And while the rebbes and Hasidim were dancing in the hall, the Pshiskhe Hasidim surrounded the Kovler Rebbe and, together with Reb Yerakhmiel, they began dancing reverentially, singing the old Pshiskhe song:

Didn't pray, didn't study
As long as we didn't anger the Most High
Why do we have to worry about
What will happen tomorrow
Better let us correct
What we did wrong yesterday . . .

And they kept dancing like that until full daylight.

12

The Passing of the Rebbe Reb Bunem

The Rebbe of Pshiskhe Reb Bunem had gained a great victory at the wedding in Ostilye, and although he still had opponents among the rebbes, Pshiskhe Hasidism continued to spread throughout Poland.

Hasidic young men were attracted to Pshiskhe from every town and city in Poland. The Rebbe Bunem was extraordinarily attractive to the intellectuals. In every town and city they opened up Pshiskhe *shtiblech,* modest prayer rooms where these Hasidim met to pray and even more to study Hasidism. But just when it seemed that Pshiskhe Hasidism was about to conquer all of Poland, the Rebbe Reb Bunem became very sick.

And although the Rebbe Reb Bunem was by that time already sixty years old, had been blind for a number of years, and in very poor health, nevertheless this illness of the Rebbe's came unexpected.

After all, Reb Bunem was in the middle of the battle to spread Hasidism across Poland. He had just ended his dispute with the opponents of Hasidim, who had borne tales to the government claiming that the Hasidim were some sort of idolatrous sect, and attempting to have their synagogues shut down. In the course of that dispute the Hasidim were forced to publicly dispute their opponents in front of the well-known priest Staszic, and the Hasidim emerged thoroughly victorious.

The Rebbe Reb Bunem had just finished his memorandum about the economic situation of the Jews in Poland. The Polish autonomous government had chosen a special commission, and Reb Bunem was chosen as the member for the Sandomierz region.

Reb Bunem provided the Polish government with a comprehensive report in Polish concerning the difficult economic situation of the Jews, and indicated measures that needed to be taken to improve the situation.

The Rebbe Reb Bunem had served as rebbe for thirteen years, and precisely for that reason his sudden illness was unexpected by the Hasidim.

At the beginning of the Hebrew month of Elul in the year 1827, Reb Bunem was 65 years old. All of the devoted Hasidim gathered in Pshiskhe to be near the Rebbe's bed.

Among the hundreds of Hasidim gathered there were his great disciples: Reb Yitskhok of Vurke, Reb Mendele of Tomashov, Reb Mordkhe Yosef of Izhbitse, Reb Henekh of Aleksander, Reb Itshe Meirl of Warsaw, and many other prominent disciples.

The Rebbe Reb Bunem lay in bed for a few days in terrible weakness. He refused all of the medications he was offered.

"After all," he quietly said to his disciples as they stood by his bed, "I used to be a pharmacist myself, and I know what's fitting to heal a sick person . . . not these old wive's remedies."

And by now the Rebbe Reb Bunem's speech came in isolated sentences. Every word was fire, sharp as a slaughtering knife. The disciples stood by him and paid intense attention to every word, so that nothing would be lost.

Yet his illness grew worse from day to day. Only selected individuals, the very prominent disciples, were admitted to see him. Reb Bunem lay with his face toward the Hasidim, and he sensed that Reb Yitskhok Vurker was standing to one side. He ordered them to summon Reb Yitskhok closer and said to him in a weak voice:

"What are you so worried for? The most important task of a person is first to sink down, so that he can subsequently raise up the holy sparks that have fallen into the hands of the Other Side; and once that has been accomplished, one must attempt to climb higher and higher . . . And everything must be received with good cheer because it is the will of the Creator. If I were offered the chance to change places with our father Abraham," he said as he began a typical Hasidic lesson, "I wouldn't want to do it. Because it wouldn't change the fact that God still has only one Father Abraham and only one Blind Bunem—so what difference does it make which one of us is which? It's better for me to remain as God created me."

And suddenly he turned toward his disciples and said: "For many years I've been praying to the Master of the Universe that He remove the light from my eyes in order to open the eyes inside, so that I might see the hidden light, so that I might concentrate and take the measure of the Infinite . . ."

The Rebbe Reb Bunem extended his hand for a bit of water. Reb Itshe Meirl of Warsaw, who was standing closest, handed him a glass of water. Reb Bunem placed his fingers inside to wash, and then he spoke up: "I think that you were the one who gave it to me, Itshe Meirl? Well, I'll ask you about something that's bothering me now: 'Why was the confessional litany written as an acrostic?'"

"Because if it weren't for the alphabet," Reb Itshe Meirl answered with a smile, "we wouldn't know when to stop confessing... A person has so many sins to answer for."

"Right, right!" answered the Rebbe Reb Bunem, and a smile of pleasure appeared on his sallow face.

Among the Hasidim standing on the side was Reb Mendele Tomashover, a man of middling height, with a thick black beard and long brows, below which shone a fiery, piercing look. He stood the whole time engrossed in thought. He was persistently troubled by the same thought: How could he leave Reb Bunem in this condition, and travel to the wedding of his son Reb Dovidl, which was to take place the eleventh of Elul in Opatshno, where the bride's father Reb Hirsh Dishkes lived?

And in the midst of these thoughts a sigh tore itself from the depths of his heart.

"Who's sighing?" asked the Rebbe Reb Bunem. "Sadness! Forget it! Haven't we taught you that that's a bad character trait?"

Reb Bunem wanted to drive away the sorrow that had taken hold of his disciples, so he said: "If they lead me to Gehennom, do you know what I'm going to do, Mendele?"

Reb Mendele kept silent.

"I'll reply that they should bring with me the Rebbe of Lublin and the Holy Jew, because the Talmud says (Makkot 10a): 'When a disciple is exiled his master is exiled with him.' Well, Mendele, would you want to sit in such a Gehennom? What are you sorrowing for?" the Rebbe Reb Bunem asked again.

Reb Mendele couldn't contain himself any longer, and he said: "Tomorrow I have to marry off my son, and I don't want to leave the Rebbe."

"Is that it?" wondered Reb Bunem. "Go to the wedding right now, and don't disrupt a Jewish celebration. Don't be downcast. The verse says, 'Make fringes for yourself' (Deuteronomy 22:11). That means: You should instill greatness[55] in yourself, so that you don't become downcast . . . So travel in peace and have a joyous wedding.

The Rebbe Reb Bunem extended his trembling hand, and Reb Mendele had no choice but to take his leave.

But right after Reb Mendele left Pshiskhe, Reb Bunem's health took a severe turn for the worse.

There was a tumult in town. They sent for the Rebbe's son, Reb Avrom Moyshele, who had been sitting in his private room for a few days and didn't want to leave it. And even now, when he heard that his father was dangerously ill, he didn't want to leave the room:

"I want to have a father, like everybody else," he said. "I want to be a child. I don't want to go see him. I know what my father wants from me. He wants to pass on to me his spiritual attainments, but I want to keep him alive."

Meanwhile the situation grew continually worse. It was the evening of the twelfth of Elul. The Hasidim wandered through the rooms, saying Psalms. From time to time the bitter weeping of a Hasid could be heard.

Hundreds of candles burned in candelabras in the municipal study house and in the synagogue. Rachel, the women's secretary, gathered all the women in town and they burst into the synagogue. Reb Ayzikl, the community's teacher of young children, gathered all the children in town and went into the study house to recite Psalms with them.

A vigil was maintained at Reb Bunem's bedside all night. When the first rays of sun began to reach through the bars of the closed shutters, suddenly the quiet murmuring of the Rebbe Reb Bunem could be heard. The leading disciples, closely approaching the bed, heard him quietly saying: "Light, light! The light of my eyes was taken away, and I saw the brightnes of the 'hidden light.'"

They heard the Rebbe saying "Shema yisroel," and began to recite the prayer with him. When he reached the word "One," his holy soul departed . . .

It was the twelfth of Elul, 1827.

---

55. *Gedilin* "fringes" is read here as meaning *gadlus*, greatness.

A Fire Burns in Kotsk

From all the surrounding towns, wherever the news of the death of Reb Bunem reached, people came to the funeral, which took place in Pshiskhe that same evening.

And no later than the second day after the funeral the leading disciples began to think who should be named as the next Rebbe.

The Hasidim wanted to have someone to come to by Rosh Hashanah. They knew the extent of the enmity of other rebbes toward Pshiskhe, and they didn't want any splits among the Pshiskhe Hasidim. There were plans to name Reb Mendele Tomashover as rebbe, but some of the Hasidim thought that it would be better for the Pshiskhe Rebbe's son, Reb Avrom Moyshele, to be his replacement. They were afraid that the overly extreme approach of Reb Mendele Tomashover could further enflame the other rebbes' hostility toward them.

And neither those in favor of Reb Avrom Moyshele nor those in favor of Reb Mendele knew whether either one of them would even agree. Reb Avrom Moyshele was constantly cloistered in his private room, and he had always been a melancholy person. But occasionally, when he would experience a sudden intensity of feeling, he would stand up in the middle of the room and play his fiddle. Then the Hasidim would say that anyone who heard him play was aroused to repentance. And Reb Mendele Tomashover hadn't yet returned from his son's wedding.

Meanwhile they sat downcast in the Pshiskhe study house between the afternoon and evening prayers, carrying on sorrowful conversations.

A small group of Hasidim stood on one side conferring with Reb Mordkhe Yosef Izhbitser about what to do and whom to choose as a rebbe.

"Who could have foreseen," said Reb Velvel Apter, "that 'he' of blessed memory wouldn't bring the Messiah? And look how he's left us here, in the middle of the war."

"In each one of us there's a spark of the Messiah son of David. The tzaddik of the generation has the biggest share, and when you cling to him you can bring the Messiah," answered Reb Mordkhe Yosef.

"What are we by ourselves, without a leader? What is a human being—just dust and ashes. We need a rebbe to lead us. Without that, we're lost like sheep without a shepherd."

"The Rebbe of blessed memory used to say," said an old Hasid, "that every person must have two pockets. In one of them, the words 'for my sake the world was created' (Sanhedrin 5b); in the other, 'for I am but dust and ashes' (Genesis 18:27). So every individual needs to add a spark to the flame, and it will turn into a conflagration. But if you come with empty hands, how will the fire spread?"

So went the conversation among the leading Hasidim, and everyone was still waiting for Reb Mendele to arrive.

Suddenly the news reached the study house: Reb Mendele had returned to town.

A few Hasidim went out to meet him, and the first thing Reb Mendele did was to enter the room where the Rebbe Reb Bunem had died. He stayed there by himself for an hour and came out utterly transformed. As soon as he reopened the door of the study house, and the Hasidim began pressing toward him to greet him, he shouted: "What are you all running for?"

And then he turned to Reb Mordkhe Yosef:

"They think it's going to go on the same way, the Rebbe's going to do everything for them. From now on each person will have to have his own will, but he'll have to want so intensely that there won't be a single hair that doesn't desire..."

Reb Mendele Tomashover saw Reb Yitskhok Vurker among the crowd of Hasidim who had turned toward him:

"I know, Yitskhok, that you've got complaints against me because I'm so strict. But if you really love a Jew you have to see to it that he becomes great. You need to drag him out of bed by the hair and shout, 'Hear, O Israel!' And if each one is great, then you've got a holy congregation; but a lot of nothings aren't more than one big nothing..."

Reb Yitskhok Vurker sighed deeply and said, "It's three times now that I've had to attach myself anew, and now that I'm an old man, I have to go back to school... But I believe that strictness and anger doesn't accomplish anything. Only through goodness and love can one person become entwined with another and thus become a community. If one lags, the other encourages him; and when everyone has the same will and the same longing, they have the power to uproot evil at its source."

Reb Mendele Tomashover didn't answer. He left the study house and shouted:

"Let there be either a redeemed world, or a desert! And whoever isn't ready for the fight, let him stay here."

The most intensely devoted Hasidim, led by Reb Mordkhe Yosef, ran after him, and soon they had departed Pshiskhe for Tomashov.

Hundreds of Hasidim remained in the study house with Reb Yitskhok Vurker. They didn't know what to do, whom to choose as their rebbe now. They made their way toward the door to the room where Reb Avrom Moysheles sat secluded, aiming to bring him out and make him their rebbe.

Suddenly a window of the study house burst open and a Hasid shouted in, "A fire is burning in Tomashov, and you're still standing here thinking!"

And the hundreds of Hasidim stood there trembling . . .

13

A Fire Burns in Tomashov

The Hasidim who remained in the Pshiskhe study hall together with Reb Yitskhok Vurker after Reb Mendele Tomashover's departure approached the door of Reb Avrom Moyshele's room. They wanted to name him as their new rebbe.

Reb Avrom Moyshele was downcast by nature, always secluded in his private room. He seldom spoke to any Hasid, and his only pleasure was to play on his fiddle. Hasidim used to say that when you heard Reb Avrom Moyshele playing, it seemed as though the strings were weeping.

When Reb Yitskhok Vurker, the oldest Hasid, approached the door together with a few of the elders and opened it, they found Reb Avrom Moyshele standing by the window with the fiddle in his hand, playing such a sorrowful melody that no one dared approach closer, until Reb Yitskhok Vurker went up to him and said: "Reb Avrom Moyshele, Jews are gathered in the study hall, seeking a leader."

Reb Avrom Moyshele interrupted his playing as if a string had suddenly broken. He turned to the Hasidim with tears in his eyes:

"What do you want from me? If a Jew has no means of sustenance, one must pray. If there's a sick person in a Jew's family, one has to say something comforting. If he doesn't have any children, you have to give him hope. But what do you want from me? Let Yitskhok be the rebbe; he's more worthy than I am. I'm a broken shard. My father, may his memory shield us, took care of everyone, had everyone in mind—but not his son. He said that the son will have to work on his own. Well, you see how I turned out!"

Voices could be heard on all sides: "Be our Rebbe! Be our leader! Have pity on a congregation of Jews who are left like sheep without a shepherd and are yearning for an inspiring word!"

And Reb Yitskhok Vurker turned to Reb Avrom Moyshele: "Modesty is a fine character trait, but if the will of a Jewish congregation is that you should be their rebbe, that you should become their leader—then for the sake of the Jewish nation forget about your modesty. If the crowd calls you 'Rebbe,' then you are their rebbe. The power of the collective will sustain you to help you carry everything that you accept upon yourself."

Reb Avrom Moyshele stood perplexed, holding his fiddle, and said to himself: "Jews ask for mercy, can I refuse? What should I do? Master of the Universe, open my eyes so that I may see the right way!"

And Reb Avrom Moyshele began playing his fiddle again. At first the fiddle emitted sad, gloomy melodies, but the sadness gradually dissipated and the tones began to be more joyous. His face changed altogether and the melody was transformed into a paean to the Infinite.

The Hasidim stood to one side listening to the playing, and Reb Yitskhok Vurker said to them: "This was also the custom of his father, of blessed memory. They say that while he was still a pharmacist, with one hand he would prepare a prescription for a patient, and with the other hand he would play a cimbalo. According to the melody his hand played, he could tell whether the patient would recover or not. And now, too, Avrom Moyshele wants the melody to tell him what he should do."

Reb Avrom Moyshele kept playing for some time until he found himself playing a very lively tune. Still playing the tune, he strode into the study house and said to himself: "If it's the will of the congregation then it is also Your holy will, Master of the Universe! It is known and revealed before You that I'm not doing it for my own glory, nor in honor of my father of blessed memory, but to carry out Your will, Master of the entire world!" And as he played he came into the study house where hundreds of Hasidim were gathered.

Reb Yitskhok Vurker and the elderly Hasidim followed Reb Avrom Moyshele, and when the latter was in the middle of the study house Reb Yitskhok Vurker shouted: "Mazel tov, Rebbe, may the merit of your holy father, of blessed memory, protect us!"

"Mazel tov, mazel tov, may the merit of the *tzaddik* of our generation protect us!" came the reply from all corners.

"Amen, so may it be His will," responded Reb Avrom Moyshele.

Yidl the attendant immediately came in with a platter of honey cake and liquor, and began distributing it to the Hasidim. The old widow also came in. Reb Yitskhok Vurker ran to her and wished her "Mazel tov." Hasidim drank the liquor and toasted Reb Avrom Moyshele with 'Lechaim!' as one does for a rebbe. From the old widow's eyes flowed tears of joy. Reb Avrom Moyshele stood up again and began playing a happy tune, and the Hasidim, together with Reb Yitskhok Vurker, began dancing for joy.

Off to a side stood a few young Hasidim who had become Tomashov Hasidim. They shouted: "We need a rebbe, not a musician," and straightaway ran out of the study house. But Reb Yitskhok Vurker and the hundreds of remaining Hasidim kept dancing to express their great joy that Reb Avrom Moyshele had agreed to take his father's place.

Thus Reb Avrom Moyshele became the rebbe of the thousands of Pshiskhe Hasidim. But he felt that he was too weak to lead such a congregation, and he wanted Reb Mendele Tomashover to come to Pshiskhe at least for the first Rosh Hashanah to share the duties of the office with him. Reb Avrom Moyshele sent Reb Mendele a personal letter, in which he wrote: "Since I heard from you, when you were here, that you want to come here for Rosh Hashanah, but various impediments prevent you from doing so, I want to inform you that the anger is stilled. All enemies have become friends. Therefore if your desire remains as before, I beg you, come here. Perhaps through Menachem[56] I will be comforted as well."

Along with the Rebbe Reb Avrom Moyshele's signature, the letter was signed by a few of the most prominent Pshiskhe Hasidim as well.

But the Rebbe Reb Mendele Tomashover didn't want to go to Pshiskhe anymore. Instead he began to hold court himself in Tomashov.

However, both of the rebbes wanted Reb Itshe Meir, the genius from Warsaw who was later to become the Gerer Rebbe, to be their Hasid: the Rebbe Reb Avrom Moyshele because thousands of Hasidim from Warsaw and the surrounding region were waiting for word from Reb Itshe Meir, and Reb Mendele Tomashover because he sought a quorum of genuine and insightful men to help him bring the Messiah, and he counted Reb Itshe Meir among that minyan.

After long consideration, Reb Itshe Meir decided that first of all he would go to Pshiskhe to see how Hasidism was doing there, and then he would know who would be his rebbe.

---

56. The Kotsker Rebbe's name, from a Hebrew root meaning "one who comforts."

When Reb Itshe Meir entered the Pshiskhe study house, it was already some time after the evening prayers. Some of the Hasidim were pacing back and forth across the length of the study house, downcast because the old Rebbe was no longer with them and Reb Avrom Moyshele did not like to mix with people. Some of the Hasidim, elders, sat around a table near the huge oven, which took up half of the western wall. They poured liquor and wished "Lechaim!" to a certain Hasid who was observing the anniversary of a family member's death. They wished him: "May your father's soul rise in Heaven, and may you yourself be redeemed."

At the head of the table sat Reb Yitskhok Vurker, discussing points in Hasidism with the crowd. Among the Hasidim were some who had once gone to the Seer of Lublin and others who'd gone to the Holy Jew, and there were also a few Hasidim who had come clandestinely to recruit Hasidim for Tomashov.

And just as once upon a time, when the Holy Jew began to hold court while the Seer was still alive, Hasidim used to come to Lublin and enticed the devotees to come to Pshiskhe—so too now the Tomashov Hasidim did the same thing, although Reb Mendele Tomashover didn't know about it.

The ones these Tomashover Hasidim were after were the young men, the sharp minds who were capable of grasping the bold new Tomashov way.

The Hasidim sat talking about the Rebbe Reb Bunem, and one elderly Hasid called out: "The Rebbe Reb Bunem said that the reason the verse says, 'All of your deeds should be for the sake of Heaven' (Ethics of the Fathers, Ch. 1) is to let you know that even your 'for the sake of Heaven' should be for the sake of Heaven, that there must be no ulterior motive in all of the deeds a person carries out for the Master of the Universe."

"But how can one follow such a path?" replied another elderly Hasid. "It's very easy to go astray on that path!"

"Indeed, the Rebbe of blessed memory did say," replied the first Hasid, "that our path in the world is just like walking on the edge of a sword. On both sides lies the abyss, and the path of life is in the middle."

"It's hard to follow such a daring path," asserted a third Hasid. "We need a rebbe who can teach us how to walk on the edge of a sword."

"Reb Mendele Tomashover will teach you," spoke up one of the secret Tomashov Hasidim.

The eternal lamp burning near the lectern in the study hall flickered, throwing huge shadows on the walls. When Reb Itshe Meir came into the study house and approached the table, no one noticed him.

The Hasidic dialogue continued and one of the men present said: "Reb Mendele is mean. We want a rebbe we can pour out our hearts to, someone who wants to understand us, who can understand us."

"If so, Reb Mendele isn't for you because in Tomashov they rip out your veins!" spoke up Reb Hersh Tomashover, who was among those who had secretly come to Pshiskhe to recruit Hasidim for Tomashov.

Reb Yitskhok Vurker, who sat lost in thought the whole time, heard Reb Hersh Tomashover's last words, and said: "You don't accomplish anything with anger. Only through love of fellow Jews can the world be redeemed. Reb Mendele, however, puts everything on the tip of a knife: for him, it's all or nothing."

"In Tomashov they teach," answered Reb Hersh Tomashover once again, "that you must rip out falsehood altogether, and leave only pure truth."

"And I believe," cried Reb Yitskhok Vurker, "that each Jew, even if he isn't the biggest genius, can do worthwhile things if only he has the proper intent."

And Reb Yitskhok Vurker began relating a story to the Hasidim: "One time I was in Vurke studying with a group of Jews the Midrash on the verse, 'A man shall not aggrieve his fellow' (Leviticus 25:17), concerning the grave sin of deceiving someone. An agricultural broker heard this, went home to his wife, and said to her that she should stop adding water to the milk she sold in town because deception is forbidden. His wife heard him out and began bringing unadulterated milk to town. In a few days the Jews stopped buying milk from her. 'This milk is no good,' they said.

"The broker came to me complaining bitterly, and I answered: 'As we see, the world can't deal with the unadulterated truth. So add a little bit of water to the milk, and the Jews in town will start buying it again.' And so it was . . . The milk was 'good' again . . . And I say the same to you: 'You need to pour in a bit of water . . . if not, the world won't be able to stand it.'"

In the meantime the Rebbe Reb Avrom Moyshele came in. His skin had grown even paler lately. He sat down among the Hasidim, just as though he were one of them. A Jew from the country came in weeping bitterly that a plague had broken out among his cows. He had already lost ten cows, and he wanted to submit a petition to make sure that at least his last three cows would survive.

The Jew from the country wanted to go straight to Reb Yitskhok Vurker, who sat at the head of the table, and pour out his bitter heart, but Reb Yitskhok Vurker nodded to let him know that the Rebbe was sitting among the Hasidim. At first the country Jew didn't understand why Reb Yitskhok Vurker didn't want to take the note from him. It seemed to him that the Hasidim were mocking him. But when he saw that all the Hasidim had their eyes on Avrom Moyshele, he approached him, immediately handed him the note, and began sobbing out loud.

Reb Avrom Moyshele, who was easily swayed to sympathy, couldn't stand to hear a Jew weeping. He stood up from the table and said to him, "Do you know how to recite Psalms?"

"No," came the embarrassed reply. "I only know how to say, 'Hear, O Israel.'"

The Hasidim smiled at each other.

"Never laugh at a Jew," Reb Avrom Moyshele said to the Hasidim. "His 'Hear, O Israel' might sometimes accomplish more than your prayers. What should he do, since that's all he was taught? But a few Psalms could save him, and if you can't recite them yourself," he turned back to the country Jew, "I'll say them with you."

Reb Avrom Moyshele stood up and went into his private room with the country Jew. Soon those outside heard the country Jew's terrible weeping and the sorrowful recitation of Psalms by Reb Avrom Moyshele.

The Hasidim remained sitting in the study hall and listened to Reb Avrom Moyshele's weeping prayers, until Reb Yitskhok Vurker exclaimed: "Reb Avrom Moyshele has a heart that suffers along with the people of Israel, which is shattered by every moan that comes out of a Jewish mouth. He will bring down abundant prosperity into the world."

"If you want to keep earning a living and remain at the level of worms, you can stay here," replied Reb Hersh Tomashover, "but we want a rebbe who will open new heavens for us."

Meanwhile Reb Avrom Moyshele came in, his eyes red from weeping, accompanied by the country Jew. He assured the country Jew that in the merit of Reb Avrom Moyshele's father, the country Jew would certainly be helped and told him to go home "in health and peace."

Reb Avrom Moyshele sat back down among the Hasidim. He sensed that they were carrying on a heated discussion. He took the last bit of liquor remaining in the almost-empty bottle and said to the Hasidim:

"Well, why is everybody so sad? Why aren't you dancing?"

And immediately the Hasidim wove themselves into a circle, and the Rebbe Reb Avrom Moyshele went into the center, his head tipped far back, and began to sing:

"Whoever shelters / beneath my balcony / it's a sign / that he loved my old father."

Off to a side stood Reb Hersh Tomashover with a couple of young Tomashover Hasidim. Suddenly Reb Hersh saw Reb Itshe Meirl stretched out near the oven, lost in thought. He ran to him, and without even calling out "Shalom aleykhem!" he shouted, "Itshe Meirl! A fire is burning in Tomashov that's going to illuminate the world, and you came here instead?"

Reb Itshe Meirl aroused himself from his meditation and shouted: "There a fire is burning, and here they attend to sick cows!"

And the two Tomashov Hasidim immediately ran out of the study house along with Reb Itshe Meirl, leaving behind Reb Avrom Moyshele dancing with his Hasidim.

Reb Yitskhok Vurker recognized Reb Itshe Meirl's voice and quietly sighed, "Now Itshe Meirl has left us as well!"

14

Starting School All Over Again

Immediately after the few Tomashov Hasidim and Reb Itshe Meirl left the Pshiskhe study hall, they hired a large coach at the marketplace and ordered the driver to take them to Tomashov.

The horses galloped through the night, leaving the Pshiskhe marketplace for the open fields. In the distance they could hear the echoes of a song from the study house:

"Whoever shelters / beneath my balcony / it's a sign / that he loved my old father."

The new Tomashov Hasidim, excited to be on their way to see the Rebbe Reb Mendele, began singing the words they used to indicate his new approach:

"A fire is burning in Tomashov

"A new light is rising there . . ."

The words blended into one great stormy river of sound that was altogether different than the melody that could still be heard coming from the Pshiskhe study house.

And so they made their way through the Jewish communities, stopping at each town. Hearing the coach approaching, the various Pshiskhe Hasidim who were still doubtful whether they should become devotees of Reb Avrom Moyshe or Reb Mendele, likewise hired coaches and joined the long train of wagons headed toward Tomashov.

Only Reb Itshe Meirl, the genius from Warsaw, sat in the carriage for a while lost in thought. He knew that Reb Avrom Moyshele couldn't be his rebbe, but on the other hand he was afraid of Tomashov. He was afraid of the Rebbe Reb Avrom Moyshele's resentment. Reb Itshe Meirl know what a tzaddik's resentment might cost because in his youth he had abandoned the the Rebbe Reb Moyshele of Kozhenits and become a Pshiskhe Hasid. Since then he had had no luck raising children. One child had actually lived to age four. The child was a prodigy who had already memorized the Five Books. His wife had asked him to have pity on her only child and go to see the Rebbe Reb

Moyshele in Kozhenits, rather than going to Pshiskhe. But Reb Itshe Meirl refused to listen and kept spending the Sabbath in Pshiskhe. When he returned from Pshiskhe, he found the child mortally ill. A few days later the child died.

Reb Itshe Meirl knew quite well who had punished him. When his wife asked him why God punished them, Reb Itshe Meirl answered:

"So that others may be truly faithful, so that other people, God forbid, won't waiver in their faith! If, God forbid, a disaster like this befalls them, they will be able to comfort themselves by saying, 'Worse things happened to Itshe Meirl.'"

Reb Itshe Meirl sat in the carriage wondering whether his current journey might lead to a new episode of resentment at Reb Avrom Moyshele's hands.

Reb Hersh Tomashover noticed Reb Itshe Meirl's quiet sorrow, and leaned toward him.

"I don't know what you have to think about so hard. Everything depends on the will of the Almighty. We're drawing water from a new well."

"And what's wrong with the old well?" asked Reb Itshe Meirl.

"Because a well from which anyone can drink is ownerless, and something that has no owner cannot be sanctified. We want to pierce the heavens with our devotions! But the main thing is the proper intention . . ."

And Reb Hersh Tomashover reminded Reb Itshe Meirl about a time when the Rebbe Reb Bunem had been seriously ill. A fast was declared in Pshiskhe. A Jew came to town from the country, passed by a Jewish tavern, and ordered a glass of liquor. He was told that he shouldn't drink today because all the Jews were fasting so that Reb Bunem might grow well. The country Jew replied: "If so, then please Lord, heal the Rebbe immediately because I really want to drink a glass of liquor." And indeed, soon a few Hasidim ran out of the Rebbe's room and announced to the town that the Rebbe had suddenly improved, and everyone could resume eating . . . Afterward Reb Bunem himself said that he had gotten better on account of the country Jew, who had prayed with all his heart and with honest intent, since he really did want a glass of liquor . . . And from this we learn that the main thing is the intent, concluded Reb Hersh Tomashover.

A Fire Burns in Kotsk

"But we can also learn from this that liquor can fix many things," interjected a young Tomashov Hasid. "And indeed, we should go in to the Jewish tavern here, so that we can revive ourselves with a drop of alcohol."

The journey to Tomashov continued for a few days. At every town, another carriageful of Hasidim came along. And although the new Tomashov Hasidim didn't accept just anyone, still their numbers kept increasing. At night, when they reached the village that lies next to Tomashov, the Hasidim began joyfully singing again: "A fire is burning in Tomashov."

The peasants left their huts to see such a large crowd of Jews suddenly driving past. So the Hasidim began singing the same tune with Polish words: "A fire is burning in Tomashov." The peasants stared in astonishment at the Jewish town of Tomashov which lay deep in peaceful sleep, shrugged their shoulders, and went back into their huts.

With a gallop and a commotion the new Hasidim entered Tomashov. They passed by the huge wooden building that had just been put up for the Hasidim, and they immediately sensed that a new approach was being taught here, and that even though it was the continuation of Pshiskhe, it was something different.

The building, which stood next to the Rebbe Reb Mendele's house, was packed with Hasidim divided up into small groups discussing various matters in Hasidism. Among the Hasidim was Reb Ber Hasid. Instead of a skullcap he wore a cabbage leaf on his head, and a belt of straw around his waist.

The young Hasid, Reb Ber, immediately went up to Reb Itshe Meir, stuck out his hand and said, "Sholem-Aleykhem, Itshe Meir! When did you arrive?"

He didn't use the title "Reb," but simply the name "Itshe Meir." He didn't address him formally but familiarly, as though they had been in school together from the very beginning.

To one side stood a Hasid with his big skullcap drawn over his forehead. He drank one glass after another, and kept murmuring to himself, "Lechaim Belik!" On a bench near the oven sat a Hasid by himself, taking pulls out of a bottle and saying between one sip and another, "Lechaim God!"

Among the Hasidim there was one Jew whose appearance was remarkable. He had a very long, black beard, which was clean and carefully combed. He wore a high cloth cap and a short coat. He was Reb Shloyme Eiger, son of the genius Reb Akiva Eiger. He had come to Tomashov to search for his son, Reb Leybele Eiger, who had run away from home to stay in Tomashov.

Reb Shlomo Eiger went from one table to another, asking "Have you seen Leybele Eiger?" But the Hasidim paid him no heed. Instead they kept drinking or talking about Hasidism, until he met Reb Ber Hasid. He repeated the same question: "Have you ever seen Leybele Eiger?"

"I don't know whom you mean," answered Reb Ber Hasid, continuing to stride around the building lost in thought. But when he had gone a few paces, he ran back to Reb Shloyme Eiger and asked him, "Reb Jew, perhaps you mean Leybl, Shloyme Akiva's son? If that's whom you mean, he'll be coming in soon. We sent him for a bit of liquor."

The Hasidim in the building gradually learned that the Warsaw genius Reb Itshe Meirl had joined them. They all began to gather around him.

The Hasidim pressed toward the table where Reb Itshe Meirl sat. Reb Ber Hasid climbed onto the table displaying all his odd mannerisms, with his straw slippers on his feet, and he addressed the Warsaw genius: "Listen, Itshe Meirl! You need to offer us a drink! You've arrived at Tomashov!"

"You're right, Ber!" answered Reb Itshe Meirl, taking a few copper coins out of his pocket.

But suddenly there was a murmur among the Hasidim: "The Rebbe's coming." And everyone was overcome by sudden terror. Everyone headed toward the door to see the Rebbe as soon as possible.

The Rebbe Reb Mendele appeared in the door. He was slight, thin, with a black beard and a sharp glance. He wore a cotton jacket, even though it was quite warm outside.

All the Hasidim pressed toward him, but suddenly a wild shout came from his mouth: "Barbarians, what are you crowding me for? Who brought the mixed multitude here?"

And the Rebbe Reb Mendele strode purposefully through the building, as though he were looking for someone in particular. The Hasidim squeezed against the wall in terror. Then Reb Mendele spotted Reb Itshe Meirl. He ran up to him, seized his arm, and shouted in great joy: "Sholem-aleykhem, Reb Itshe Meirl! We've been waiting for you!"

And suddenly Reb Mendele's face looked different. He sat at the table and wouldn't let go of Reb Itshe Meirl's hand in his joy. Suddenly, too, he became kindly toward the Hasidim and stopped scolding them like he usually did.

Meanwhile, Reb Ber Hasid approached with a bottle of liquor, climbed onto the table, and placed it before Reb Itshe Meirl.

The Rebbe Reb Mendele thought for a while. Then he turned to Reb Itshe Meirl and said in a quiet voice:

"We were looking for you. We knew that you would come, but we were afraid that if you kept spending so much time studying, you wouldn't have any time to come!

"Itshe Meirl had his doubts about our approach," he said further. "He was seeking a goal, but he didn't understand the straightforward interpretation of the midrash."

And the Rebbe Reb Mendele, after meditating a bit more, suddenly began sharing his Torah.

The Hasidim, who had previously seemed to be a bit tipsy, suddenly sobered. They all approached the table. Some of them hung by their belts from the hooks that protruded from the walls of the building. All of them enthusiastically attended to the Rebbe's sharp, piercing words.

And the Rebbe Reb Mendele began:

"The verse says, 'A fool cannot reach the speaking of wisdom' (Proverbs 24:7). The Midrash in Ecclesiastes has three parables for this. The first compares it to a loaf of bread lying on a high shelf that no one can reach. Eventually a wise man came along and said, 'I will connect a ladder to a ladder, climb up and bring the bread down.' The second compares it to good, sweet water that was lying in a pit so deep that no one could reach it. Eventually a wise man came along and said, 'I will tie a rope to a rope, let a bucket down, and draw the water.' A third compares it to a king who hired workers to draw water in pails full of holes. The workers said to the king: 'How, O King, can we do it? What use will it be?' Until a wise man came along and said, 'What difference does it make, as long as I get paid?'

"The difference between these three sages," continued the Rebbe Reb Mendele, "is this. The first sage said, 'If the bread is on such a high shelf, someone must have placed it there, so we know that there's a way to get up there. So,' figured the sage, 'I'll try to figure out how to get up there as well.'

"The second sage went further and tried to find a way to reach the water in the pit, which no one before him had yet been able to do.

"But the third sage went further than either of them, for he agreed to draw water with pails full of holes. Because it's not what we little humans think is the way to do things that's the way to do things, and it's not what we think is the goal that's really the goal."

And the Rebbe Reb Mendele concluded: "The third sage was the wisest of them all. He opened up a new path ... But where do we find that kind of sage today?" He turned to Reb Itshe Meirl: "Tell me, where do we find them? True, many convince themselves that they are wise, but they forget the verse in Ecclesiastes (7:23), 'I said, "I shall become wise," but it was far from me.' The interpretation is that if a Jew convinces himself that 'I am wise,' it's a sign that 'wisdom is far from me.'

"Certainly, faith itself is a tremendous thing," shouted the Rebbe Reb Mendele, "but as the verse says (Psalm 37:3), 'dwell in the land and nourish yourself with faith ...' Jews, you have to have something in addition to faith. 'That he understands and knows Me' (Jeremiah 9:23). He has to recognize and comprehend My divinity!"

And the Rebbe Reb Mendele seized the lapel of Reb Itshe Meirl's coat and said to him, "I only need a minyan of Jews, and we could redeem the world!"

Then Reb Mendele took Reb Itshe Meirl by the hand and led him into his private room, where they spent a couple of hours together.

The Hasidim in the building waited for Itshe Meirl to come out and tell them what he and Reb Mendele had been discussing. Meanwhile, they reviewed the Rebbe's latest teaching, and Ber Hasid shouted that if anyone would give him enough money for a pot of mead, he would explain to that person the true meaning of the Rebbe's teaching. But when Reb Itshe Meirl came out of the Rebbe's private room, they saw that he was completely covered in sweat. When the Hasidim insisted that he tell them what the Rebbe had been discussing with him, he didn't want to reply at all. All he said to the elderly Reb Hersh Tomashover was, "We have to become schoolboys again! Oy, he rips your veins out! But there's nothing wrong with it. I've found my rebbe now, someone I can be completely devoted to. A fire is burning here!"

And in his great joy Reb Itshe Meirl began dancing with the Hasidim in the building. They began singing once again:

"A fire is burning in Tomashov

"A new light is rising there..."

Until suddenly a shout was heard: "Give me back my son!" It was none other than Reb Shloyme Eiger. "What is this place, a tavern?" he added for good measure.

The Hasidim stopped dancing. Reb Ber Hasid was ready to lay him out over the table and shake him down, but Reb Itshe Meirl indicated that they shouldn't bother him. He went to Reb Shloyme and asked him what he wanted.

Reb Shloyme Eiger was well acquainted with the Warsaw genius and asked in astonishment: "Even you, Reb Itshe Meirl, are here among them?"

"Yes, I'm here with them," answered Reb Itshe Meirl in a confident voice. "And you're altogether mistaken if you thank that this is, God forbid, a tavern. Do you know," he turned suddenly to Reb Shloyme, "why the Evil Inclination is called 'fool,' as the verse says: 'Better a poor and wise child than an old and foolish king' (Ecclesiastes 4:13)? Because in truth the Evil Inclination is extraordinarily wise, but he's only called a fool because he deals with fools..."

"Well said," called out Reb Ber Hasid. And before Reb Shloyme had time to respond, they formed a circle around him and began dancing with the same enthusiasm as before:

"A fire is burning in Tomashov

"A new light is rising there..."

Although Reb Itshe Meirl had already become a Tomashov Hasid, nevertheless when he returned to Warsaw from Tomashov, he could not get over his anguish for having shamed the Rebbe's son Reb Avrom Moyshele of Pshiskhe. He decided to desist from going to Tomashov for some time. The Rebbe Reb Mendele was aware of this, and he wrote him a letter:

Life and peace, to the honorable and singular individual in Israel, my soul's friend, the love of my heart, the insightful rabbi . . . our master Rabbi Yitskhok Meir may his light shine.

I cannot contain myself and remain silent, for I am in anguish after not having heard from you for three months.

My soul mourns greatly, and I feel alone even among dear friends, for they cannot comfort me in the depths of my most heartful meditations.

Out of all those who remain from those who were close to the Rebbe of sainted memory in Pshiskhe, only the young men who deeply desire to have their path through the darkness illuminated have remained faithful, and the rest are nothing.

But it is for you that my soul longs. Comfort me with a letter, for I am in pain and discernment is withheld from me.

I will not conceal the truth from you. There are times when I don't have money to pay postage, so I try to send letters only rarely.

The words of the lover of his soul, his soul friend, who wants to be comforted with all that is good eternally.

Menachem Mendel of Tomashov.[57]

The letter moved Reb Itshe Meirl profoundly. He wanted to retract his decision, but then another of his children died, and he thought it was another sign of resentment. So Reb Itshe Meirl decided to devote himself to the yeshiva he had founded in Warsaw.

The yeshiva attracted the most talented young men in Warsaw, continuing their studies with the support of their in-laws after they were married. The Warsaw genius had already converted a number of young men into Hasidim of the Pshiskhe school. Thus, for example, one of the new Hasidim was Reb Eliezer Hacohen, son of the respected Warsaw magnate Reb Volf Layptsiker, and son-in-law of the brilliant rabbi of Lissa Reb Yakov Lorberbaum (author of *Hakhavas Daas, Nesivos Hamishpat*, and other religious works). Reb Eliezer Hacohen, who was later to serve as rabbi in Makov, Pultusk, Plotsk, and Sokhatshov,

---

57. Author's note: The letter was in the possession of an elderly Kotsker Hasid in Jerusalem and was printed in the book *Maamar Eyney Hagolah*. It was written in the Holy Tongue.

grew into a great prodigy in the yeshiva headed by Reb Itshe Meirl. But his father wanted him to abandon Hasidism because in Warsaw people sensed that Reb Itshe Meirl was leading young men away from the proper path.

One time the Rabbi of Lissa himself came to Warsaw, and Reb Itshe Meirl visited him. They debated fine points in rabbinics for hours. Before the Rabbi of Lissa departed, his father-in-law, Reb Volf of Leipzig, came to see him and asked him to get his son to make three commitments: first, not to pray with the Pshiskhe Hasidim; second, not to make pilgrimages to Pshiskhe; and third, not to study at Reb Itshe Meirl's yeshiva. The Lissa Genius answered that he would undertake to extract the first two promises from Reb Eliezer Hacohen, but that he would not demand that the latter break off ties with Reb Itshe Meirl. On the contrary, the Rabbi of Lissa thought Reb Eliezer Hacohen did well to study with Reb Itshe Meirl and even more to make the latter his comrade, for in so doing he fulfilled the commandment to "acquire for yourself a comrade."

Yet the Rabbi of Lissa heard from a number of Warsaw Hasidim that Reb Itshe Meirl explicitly taught the young men that they didn't need to be precise about the set times for daily prayers if they didn't have the proper mental state in time. So the Lissa Rabbi wanted to find out whether Reb Itshe Meirl really did transgress the rules about when to pray.

Just then there was another great genius in Warsaw. The two geniuses were invited to the home of the Rabbi of Warsaw, author of the *Khemdas Shlomo,* and Reb Itshe Meirl was there as well.

The four scholars spent a long time discussing scholarly matters. Meanwhile, the Rabbi of Warsaw ordered refreshments to be brought in. Reb Itshe Meirl hadn't prayed yet, and he didn't know what to do. If he didn't eat anything, he would insult his company; on the other hand, if he told them he hadn't prayed yet, they would annoy him about transgressing the set times for prayer.

The Rabbi of Lissa evidently sensed that Reb Itshe Meirl hadn't yet prayed, and he wanted to see whether he would eat before he prayed. So the Rabbi of Lissa asked Reb Itshe Meirl why he wasn't eating anything. But Reb Itshe Meirl had an idea. He began a complicated discussion concerning the proper blessing for the jam that was placed on the table. A huge debate broke out among the several scholars, and Reb Itshe Meirl said that the rule he followed was corroborated in an old book written by one of the medieval commentators. But Reb Itshe Meirl knew very well that the book was not to be found in the library of the Warsaw Rabbi, and since all three scholars were very eager to see the book, Reb Itshe Meirl agreed to go right home and bring the book from his house. Reb Itshe Meirl went home, quickly said his prayers, then returned with the book, showed them his source, and was at last able to taste the refreshments.

But the opponents of Hasidism in Warsaw couldn't sit still while Reb Itshe Meirl took the best young men and turned them into Pshiskhe Hasidim. (Even though the Rebbe Reb Bunem had died, they were still called Pshiskhe Hasidim.) The communal judges and leaders in Warsaw were fed rumors that Reb Itshe Meirl denigrated all the leading scholars while he was instructing his disciples. They demanded the all of his students be removed from his tutelage.

The communal leaders of Warsaw decided to summon Reb Itshe Meirl to a trial, at which he would be asked to declare whether or not he mocked the leading scholars of the generation, especially the Vilna Gaon.

Reb Itshe Meirl prepared carefully before he went to the trial. He knew that the entire future of Pshiskhe Hasidism was at stake. The judges spent an entire day interrogating him. He denied all of the libels that had been invented against him, and when he heard one of the opponents testifying before the judges that he mocked the leading scholars of the generation, he wanted to tear his clothes as a sign of mourning and tears flowed from his eyes.

All of Hasidic Warsaw was on pins and needles that day. The Pshiskhe Hasidim knew that this was nothing but a prank arranged by the opponents in order to reduce Reb Itshe Meirl's influence on the young folk. At the same time they understood that if the ruling went against Reb Itshe Meirl, the other Hasidim in Warsaw would be confirmed in their own belief that Pshiskhe Hasidim was corrupting the youth—and the ruling pronounced by the opponents would be further evidence. So the Pshiskhe Hasidim stood in front of the Warsaw rabbinic courtroom, anxiously and impatiently waiting for the decision.

For his part Reb Itshe Meirl consistently denied all of the libels invented against him, modestly answered all of the judges' questions just like an ordinary litigant, and when the judges finally asked him whether it was true that he had insulted the Vilna Gaon, Reb Itshe Meirl answered: "You speak of the Vilna Gaon, and I know about the Vilna Gaon. By all means, let's see who has memorized more of the Vilna Gaon's insights into the Talmud."

And here Reb Itshe Meirl displayed his brilliance. He asked the judges to explain the meaning of one of the Vilna Gaon's notes on the Talmud, and he concluded: "If the honor of the Vilna Gaon is so important to you, then explain to me what it means!"

The judges and the anti-Hasidic community leaders spent hours trying to figure out the meaning, until Reb Itshe Meirl said with a smile: "If you had been at my lecture yesterday, you would have heard what it means, and you would no longer believe the false claims that I mock the Vilna Gaon."

Reb Itshe Meirl summoned one of his students, who immediately explained the Vilna Gaon's note.

After that the judges had no choice but to issue a ruling in favor of Reb Itshe Meirl.

The anti-Hasidim were upset about their loss, and they decided to secretly inscribe among the first columns of the Jewish chronicle of Warsaw, among the items for "eternal memory," that "The brilliant rabbi Our Master and Teacher Yitskhok Meirl of the city of Warsaw committed a misdeed, for from his mouth issued words of denigration against the honor of the Gaon Reb Eliahu of blessed memory of Vilna."

For many years this "eternal memory" item remained in the old chronicle of Warsaw without anyone knowing about it, until many years later when the community organizations decided to have the chronicle rewritten because the paper was crumbling and the handwriting was hard to discern.

They hired the Warsaw schoolteacher Sini Sapir, who was known as an excellent calligrapher, to copy out the chronicle.

The teacher Sini Sapir was actually a Kozhenitser Hasid, but he knew Reb Itshe Meirl well from the time they had both gone to the Kozhenitser Magid. So when he copied out the chronicle he did not include this particular "eternal memory."

When the communal leaders came to review the new chronicle to see whether it was correctly copied, they saw that the "eternal memory" had been omitted. They called a meeting and decided not to pay the copyist a single penny until he rewrote the whole thing, without omitting any item found in the original.

The teacher Sini Sapir told Reb Itshe Meirl what had been written about him in the chronicle and about his attempt to drop the false "eternal memory" from the new copy. And now they wanted to fine him for it.

When Reb Itshe Meirl heard what the communal leaders had done to him, he immediately gathered all of his disciples (who by now numbered a few hundred) and set off with them to the offices of the community. There he explained about the rabbinic trial he'd been through a few years ago, and about the ruling that had been issued. This time the communal leaders couldn't act brazenly in front of Reb Itshe Meirl. They also summoned the Warsaw judges, who confirmed everything Reb Itshe Meirl said. At that, the newly elected leaders agreed to leave out of the recopied chronicle the "eternal memory" against Reb Itshe Meirl.

And thus was removed the stain of scandal that the anti-Hasidim tried to attach to the young genius Reb Itshe Meirl and all of the Pshiskhe Hasidim.

Reb Itshe Meirl continued directing the yeshiva in Warsaw for a long time without going to see any rebbe. But after he'd been without a rebbe for a few months he began to miss Tomashov again. Around that time he received a visit from Reb Henekh of Aleksander, a leading Pshiskhe Hasid (and later the Rebbe of Ger after the death of Reb Itshe Meirl). He told Reb Itshe Meirl what was happening around Reb Mendele.

Reb Itshe Meirl told him that he, too, missed Tomashov and that the reason why he was asking what was happening around Reb Mendele was that he had himself sensed there that just as there was lightning and thunder when the Torah was given at Mt. Sinai, so too a new Torah was being given in Tomashov amidst thunder and lightning.

"Isn't it dangerous for the world?" asked Reb Henekh.

"What choice do we have? I saw a piece of true fire there, so I declared my loyalty."

"And perhaps they might choose someone else as the rebbe?" Reb Henekh asked further.

Reb Itshe Meirl knew that Reb Henekh had him in mind, for right after the death of Reb Simkhe Bunem the Pshiskhe Hasidim in Warsaw had wanted to name him as their rebbe, but he had refused.

"Believe me," answered Reb Itshe Meirl, "it wouldn't take much for me to have the loyalty of all the Pshiskhe Hasidim. But when a tzaddik has his own interests in mind, even a little bit, it can lead him, God forbid, straight into Gehennom!"

15

The Vurker Rebbe Goes to Tomashov

The numbers of the Tomashov Hasidim swelled in all the cities and towns of Poland.

Meanwhile the Rebbe Reb Avrom Moyshe, the son of the Pshiskhe Rebbe, died on the eighth day of Chanukah in the year 1828. He was just 32 years old.

The Pshiskhe Hasidim were certain that the next rebbe would be his loyal Hasid Reb Yitskhok Vurker. Throughout the two years the young Pshiskhe Rebbe had lived, Reb Yitskhok Vurker was the de facto leader. He was the one who dealt with the Hasidim on a day-to-day basis. Yet Reb Yitskhok Vurker said that first he had to go to see Reb Mendele, to talk things over with him. Perhaps he might yet be drawn to the Rebbe Reb Mendele's approach, and if so, he would become the latter's Hasid.

The older Pshiskhe Hasidim didn't want to agree to this, but Reb Yitskhok Vurker said to them: "The verse in Proverbs (13:23) says, 'Acquire truth and do not sell it.' This raises the question: If someone wants to buy truth, no one will be willing to sell it to him—so why does it say, 'do not sell it?' The proper interpretation is that as long as you sense that somewhere on the earth there's a drop of truth left, you shouldn't sell the truth you've gathered, but you should keep buying until you sense that there's no more truth left anywhere except in your possession. Only then are you permitted to begin selling your truth to others . . . So let's see whether there's still something worth buying in Tomashov."

And so Reb Yitskhok Vurker, along with a few of the more intense Pshiskhe Hasidim, set off for Tomashov.

When Reb Yitskhok Vurker arrived in Tomashov, he met Reb Henekh of Alexsander, Reb Yitskhok Meirl of Warsaw, Reb Hersh Tomashover, and many other veteran Pshiskhe Hasidim.

Reb Yitskhok Vurker was overjoyed to see all of them. He called out a warm "Sholem-aleykhem!" to Reb Itshe Meirl of Warsaw and said, "It's a real pleasure to be among familiar faces. What's new?"

"We're igniting a fire that will illuminate the world," answered Reb Itshe Meirl.

"God forbid you should get burned," said Reb Yitskhok Vurker.

Then Reb Yitskhok Vurker drew Reb Itshe Meirl and Reb Hersh Tomashover off to a side and began discussing with them the death of the Rebbe Reb Avrom Moyshele.

"We need to re-establish the school that the Rebbe Reb Bunem ran. All of the Hasidim who used to go there should come here to Tomashov, and everything will go smoothly."

"And who will be the rebbe?" asked Reb Itshe Meirl.

"I believe that he should remain the rebbe," replied Reb Yitskhok Vurker, indicating the door of the Rebbe Reb Mendele's private room.

"But he doesn't want a big crowd; he just wants talented individuals," answered Reb Hersh Tomashover.

"Doesn't matter. I'll talk to him, and maybe I'll convince him that he should bend toward the crowd a bit, so that everyone who comes can get what he needs. And what harm does it do to come down from his elevated state for the sake of the collective? Does he always have to be so far above them that they can't even touch him?"

"If you're looking for the real point of the truth, then everything has to be at that point," answered Reb Itshe Meirl. "I think you'll have a hard time convincing the Rebbe, but it can't hurt to try."

"We have a rule that we 'open with peace,'" responded Reb Yitskhok Vurker.

The conversation among the three men lasted a while, until suddenly the door burst open and in strode the Rebbe Reb Mendele, wearing a cotton jacket with a large skullcap on his head.

The Hasidim scattered to all sides in panic.

Reb Mendele immediately ran up to Reb Yitskhok Vurker, greeted him, and asked him: "Why are you so worried, Reb Yitskhok?"

"Our hearts are being torn in pieces! Our Rebbe's son, Reb Avrom Moyshe, has passed away."

"I know about it already," Reb Mendele answered sadly, "but if hearts can be torn to pieces," he turned to Reb Yitskhok Vurker, "why aren't they torn seeing the Divine Presence in exile, and people wandering around lost as if in a dungeon? The Jew was given a soul from right under the Throne of Glory, and he lets her stumble through the mud. Jews run to their rebbe to ask him to assure their livelihood!"

Reb Yitskhok Vurker, who always preferred to see the best in Jews, began arguing to the Rebbe Reb Mendele that Jews are preoccupied with earning a living, so it's enough if they manage to pray appropriately. "And what more can we demand of them?" he asked Reb Mendele.

"Do you know the meaning of the phrase from the Sabbath prayer service, 'Who chooses musical songs [shirey] of praise?'" suddenly shouted the Rebbe Reb Mendele. "It means, God chooses the leftovers [shirayim] from the songs, the remainder that can't find any words, that can't clothe itself, but sings inside the very depths of the soul. That's what God wants, that's the kind of prayer He's looking for."

"But there are Jews who aren't at that level, who are simple artisans, who need to work to earn a living," retorted Reb Yitkshok Vurker more warmly. "Should we tell them to stop praying?"

"We don't say anything, we don't give any advice. We just stoke the fire, so that anyone can go in search of the divine. They'll know how to break through, so that what must come will come."

"But the leader of the generation must have in mind everything and everyone, every detail, even what every Jew must do. That's what the Rebbe Elimelekh, the Seer, and other rebbes such as the Holy Jew and the Rebbe Reb Bunem taught us."

"But we won't busy ourselves with such things. We only pay attention to the things that clarify our own will. Chewing old straw and fetching water for horses is something I'll leave to others," said Reb Mendele.

"Yet our Sages advised us, 'Walk in the footsteps of the flock' (Song of Songs 1:8). We have to follow the ways of our ancestors," said Reb Yitskhok Vurker.

"You don't need rebbes to show you how to follow the old ways," answered Reb Mendele. "Whoever wants to be a rebbe has to blaze new, clear paths. But you also have to keep in mind the old ways not, God forbid, in order to abolish them, but to change them, so that you're encouraged to raise yourself higher and higher, until we can redeem ourselves from this world."

The Rebbe Reb Mendele spoke with passion. Great drops of sweat covered his brow. The Hasidim stood off to the side the whole time, afraid to approach. They knew that an intense discussion was underway between the Rebbe Reb Mendele and Reb Yitskhok Vurker. They prayed in their own hearts that Reb Yitskhok Vurker might win because they wanted a rebbe in whom they could confide, whom they could tell about the great poverty in their homes, rather than being constantly harassed and cursed for "having such things in mind," as Reb Mendele said.

And suddenly the Rebbe Reb Mendele stood up and said, "Believe me, Reb Yitskhok, I love the world as much as all of you. But I don't agree to compromise. My claim is that this world will truly be a world once it is purified. So you have to close your eyes to avoid getting caught up in the petty details, so that you can't see anything except the Messianic light . . . I know that not everyone can follow this path, and that's exactly why I'm looking only for those who understand me and want to follow my path!"

And Reb Mendele quickly stuck out his arm toward Reb Yitskhok Vurker, as if preparing to take his leave, and just as quickly ran into his private room. But he stood at the doorstep a while, and he heard Reb Yitskhok Vurker say to Reb Hersh Tomashover: "My heart cannot stand this!"

Reb Mendele shouted back: "If you want to redeem the world, you have to withstand everything!" and he banged the door shut.

The Hasidim, who had been standing off to the side the whole time, now approached Reb Yitskhok Vurker. They wanted Reb Yitskhok Vurker to stay with them because if the Rebbe continued to "flay them alive," Reb Yitskhok Vurker would be the one who would comfort them and soothe their aching hearts. And Reb Yitskhok Vurker turned to Reb Itshe Meirl:

"Is that what you call a leader of the generation? He wants to build the final redemption on the tears of the Jews? And I say that I exert all my efforts for the sake of the Jewish collective, and I pray to the Creator that all of the troubles that are supposed to befall all the Jews should fall on my head."

"And our Rebbe says," interrupted Reb Berl Hasid, still with a cabbage leaf on his head instead of a skullcap, with shoes made of straw on his feet and a belt made out of straw, with a bottle of liquor sticking out of his pocket, "that 'seek God where He can be found' (Isaiah 58:6) means: As hard as you look for God, that's how much you find Him. Therefore one must seek God constantly, without taking a break, you always have to be the seeker."

"But those words aren't meant for every Jew," answered Reb Yitskhok Vurker angrily. "If you listen to those words and you're not capable of fulfilling them they can do damage, rather than plowing your soul and turning it into a new creation. That path is only good for someone who understands, who sees the great fire burning behind every word. But in order to see that you have to have been through a world of sorrows, you have to have bathed in rivers of blood, so that you can feel with all your limbs what kind of worth the world has. But for the simple Jew that's no path at all. It can turn his head. He won't understand the true meaning of the words, and he can, God forbid, get lost. The trials that lie along that path are too great, too daring."

"And our Rebbe interprets the words, 'and you shall take for me a separation' (Exodus 25:2) to mean: You shall engage Me in separation from the world and from everything which has to do with the world."

"To be sure, it is a grand path," answered Reb Yitskhok Vurker, "but not for us."

And Reb Yitskhok Vurker started walking toward the door. The Pshiskhe Hasidim who had made the journey with him followed along. Several of the Tomashov Hasidim, those who couldn't comprehend the radical new approach, those who still longed for a rebbe who would give them advice, who would help them out in their times of trouble, pressed close to him.

Reb Yitskhok Vurker gathered larger and larger numbers around him, and when he was about to leave the door of the building, his Hasidim started pleading, "Become our Rebbe! Become our Rebbe!"

"I thought I'd be able to convince the Rebbe Reb Mendele to reestablish the old school. But he's determined to set out on daring paths, so instead I'll take away from him those who aren't fit for the new path, and let him see what he can accomplish!"

Suddenly the door across the room opened and the Rebbe Reb Mendele appeared. The most intense and devoted Tomashover Hasidim, those who had remained loyal to Reb Mendele, ran towards him. Voices could be heard from the other side of the door: "Mazel tov, Rebbe!"

"Take away the mixed multitude, and we'll be able to raise ourselves to a level where we can see the world as it really appears, and bring the Redemption closer!"

And suddenly Reb Mendele shut the door again. Reb Yitskhok Vurker rode back to his town and became rebbe there. He attracted the entire congregation of Pshiskhe Hasidim and some of Reb Mendele's Hasidim as well, especially those who couldn't follow the demanding new path of the Tomashover Rebbe.

16

The Hasidic Commune in Tomashov

When Reb Yitskhok Vurker became Rebbe, the only ones who stayed in Tomashov were the outstanding individuals, the dedicated minds, those who could separate themselves entirely from the world and engage the infinite.

With time, however, the crowd of Hasidim began to swell once again.

Hundreds of young men left their homes and went to Tomashov to study Hasidism.

In every Jewish town there were a few "living widows," who lived out their young lives in sorrow and had no choice but to seek out their own livelihoods so that they would have something to eat and be able to feed their children.

Among the young people who ran away to Tomashov there were also wealthy sons-in-law, recently married men still being supported by their in-laws, who wouldn't have to worry about earning a living for several years. They were tired of sitting in the local study house all day, swaying over a volume of the Talmud. They were attracted to Tomashov, where one could shed materiality and focus on Hasidism. And in addition, it was a place filled with a joyful sense of brotherhood.

Indeed, upon his first arrival in Tomashov every wealthy young man would surrender his bit of cash and the gold watch and chain he'd received from his father-in-law. With that he was accepted into the "brotherhood," which they also called the "Holy Society."

Yet not everyone was accepted into the brotherhood right away. One had to have achieved spiritual discipline, one had to be ready to sacrifice his entire being, to be a humble soul, and to share everything and everyone with all of the members of the brotherhood.

And in fact, there were two sorts of Hasidim in Tomashov. There were those who came to the Rebbe only for the Sabbath, sometimes staying for a week or two, and those who abandoned their wives and children for months on end and stayed in Tomashov.

These were the ones considered the true Tomashov Hasidim, the ones who were on fire. They regarded the "benchwarmers" with contempt, the ones who came to catch just enough Torah from the Rebbe to get by on, and thought that would keep them warm for quite some time.

At first the "true" Tomashov Hasidim lived on "refreshments." When a stranger arrived, they would first of all steal his prayer shawl and phylacteries. In order to redeem these articles, the stranger would have to provide refreshments. If Berl Hasid found out that the stranger was observing the anniversary of the death of a family member, the strange Hasid had to pay up for liquor again.

Occasionally one of these men would turn out to be stubborn. In that case they had no choice but to seize him, turn him upside down, and wait until the few silver coins in his pockets fell out.

But once that happened, the strange Tomashov Hasid would feel like a true outsider among the brotherhood. They would torment him until he would leave Tomashov. They would find out what inn he was staying at, and once that happened . . . he was certainly in no enviable position.

At night a Hasid would steal into the room where he was staying and fill his boots with water. Then Reb Hersh Tomashover would rush in shouting that the Rebbe was demanding to see the fellow. And then in the morning Khayem Borukh Strikover would start working on him. Khayem Borukh was a brilliant scholar, but he had a simple, coarse face that would fool you into thinking he could barely utter his prayers.

Khayem Borukh would approach the stranger and naively ask him the plain meaning of a statement in the Mishnah. The stranger thought he was dealing with an ignoramus, and tried to get rid of him as quickly as possible, but Khayem Borukh kept at him, asking one question after another, and among the naïve questions he would throw in a question pertaining to the commentary of the Maharsha, Rabbi Shmuel Edels.[58]

---

58. R. Samuel Eliezer ben Yehuda (1555–1631), renowned talmudic authority known as Maharsha—an acronym for "Our teacher, Rabbi Shmuel Edels."

Meanwhile a handful of Jews gathered around, looking on curiously at the strange Hasid's difficulty answering such a simple question. But Khayem Borukh didn't want to stop. He kept answering questions, adding various opinions of the medieval commentators. The Hasidim who were watching this doubled over in laughter, until the strange Hasid realized that his interlocutor wasn't such an ignoramus after all. And in the end, the strange Hasid stood in front of Khayem Borukh like a servant before his master, pleading with Khayem Borukh to explain the meaning of the statement. Only then would Khayem Borukh begin his verbal attack: "So now you see that even if we sit drinking days and nights on end, we still know more than somebody who's sitting and studying with a full belly. You want to know the meaning of the Mishnah—pay up for booze!"

Meanwhile the brotherhood grew, until they couldn't all live any more just on the "refreshments" they took from the strange Hasidim. Often the Hasidim would fast for days on end, without a spoonful of hot food passing their lips.

People grew very anxious. Reb Mordkhe Yosef Izhbitser saw that they would have to begin working in order to earn their livelihood, so that the communal kitchen wouldn't have to depend on refreshments from strangers, and they would be able to sustain themselves on their own earnings.

It just so happened that right then the Jewish community in Tomashov wanted to build themselves a new brick synagogue. The "real Hasidim" managed to get the job turned over to them. They brought in artisans from Warsaw, bricklayers and carpenters, and they themselves did the unskilled labor.

Berl Khosid, Reb Hersh Tomashover, and Reb Mordkhe Yosef Izhbitser were the supervisors. Every day they assigned a couple of dozen Hasidim from the brotherhood to work on the building. In the evening, when the workers brought their wages into the communal kitchen, they sent someone to buy potatoes and beans, and with the rest of the money they bought liquor.

During the period the synagogue was being built, the Holy Society lived in an entirely different fashion than the rest of the Tomashov Hasidim. Aside from the fact that they worked and ate together, shared everything they had, they also established a rule that they would equally share all of their good deeds and their sins.

Every evening after supper, the leading Hasidim of the Holy Society would get together. They would each tell the others what they had done in the course of the day. If it seemed to someone that he had even had an evil thought, everyone else would repent on his behalf.

Sometimes too, as they sat at supper late at night, the Rebbe Reb Mendele would come into the building. He would sit right down, wherever there was an empty spot, and that spot would become the head of the table.

The Rebbe grabbed hold of the Hasid who was sitting closest to him, and asked: "What did you do today?"

The Hasid, who was still wearing his work clothes, meekly answered: "I worked on the building of the synagogue."

The Rebbe tugged at the lapels of the Hasid's frock and said, "Fool, I'm not asking you what you did for your body, but what you did in order to bring the Redemption closer. A human being can't remain in one place—either he's ascending or he's descending. You need to climb higher every day, and if you don't you'll fall into Gehennom for good!"

The Hasidim stayed quiet, since no one knew how to answer. The Rebbe looked at them all with a wild, burning glance and spoke as if to himself but with passion:

"Why are there so many Hasidim? Who needs them? All we need is a minyan of Jews, just ten, not more, but they need to be the kind of Jews whose entire body is shot through with longing for Redemption. When the Torah was given, 'the mountain was burning to the heart of Heaven' (Deuteronomy 4:11). This means: The mountain was enflamed until the heart became heavenly. That's how we must set the world on fire until it becomes a single bright Heaven, only then will the world be a world."

The Hasidim were afraid to say a single word in reply. Yet Reb Hersh Tomashover gathered his courage and asked: "But Rebbe, how do we arrive at such a high spiritual level?"

"If you want to have a redeemed world, you have to close your eyes, so that all you see is the light of the Messiah!"

"And what should we do?" asked Berl Khosid, who by this time was rather tipsy.

"I don't mean you or you," the Rebbe indicated Berl Khosid and Reb Mordkhe Yosef Izhbitser, "but you see Zalmen Amshenover sitting over there? Do you hear how he sighs, how he shouts 'Oy' and 'Master of the whole world'? Do you really think that he's sighing because the Divine Presence is in exile? Maybe in some superficial sense that really is what he means, but I can tell you that I know better what's in his heart than he does. And I know that in the very essence of his heart, all he really cares about is his wife and children! He shouts 'Oy' because the world is in exile, and what he really means is that he's not at home with his wife and children. And that's how all of you here think . . . You can't get rid of all your material nature at once."

The Hasidim started looking toward the corner where Zalmen Amshenover sat, and Zalmen himself immediately got up and approached the Rebbe, his head lowered and his face clouded with tears.

The Hasidim spent hours afterward interpreting every word the Rebbe had said, precisely reviewing every motion the Rebbe had made, and it was only just before daybreak that they climbed up to the roof of the building, so that they could get a bit of rest before going to work again the next day.

The news that the Tomashov Hasidim were building a synagogue by themselves spread through the surrounding towns. In each town there were a few "living widows," whose husbands had been in Tomashov for quite some time. The protests grew more and more insistent, until one day a few dozen Jews from various towns gathered together, and traveled to Tomashov to retrieve their sons and sons-in-law. The young wives who had been abandoned went along as well.

There was a huge uproar in Tomashov that day. Many of the men didn't want to live with their wives altogether by that point. Tomashov had become a place of refuge for them. Some, on the other hand, had grown entirely unaccustomed to having the yoke of family around their necks.

But the Jews began threatening to send a libel off to the government. They had even brought along a document which they were ready to send if they didn't get their children back.

Many of the "true Hasidim" escaped to the nearby villages, while many others hid in attics, trying to ensure that they wouldn't have to go back home.

The Rebbe Reb Mendele himself had no idea what was going on in town. At one point he did in fact hear some shouting in the building. Reb Hersh Tomashover reassured him, saying that Jews had arrived seeking to consult with the Rebbe about various illnesses, but he wouldn't let them in.

The Rebbe was very pleased with this. In fact, the Jews sought to burst into the Rebbe's private room by force, but Reb Mordkhe Yosef Izhbitser and Reb Hersh Tomashover restrained them. They promised to convince the young men to go home.

For a couple of days the out-of-town Jews, their daughters, and their daughters-in-law continued to besiege the building. They were joined by the Vurker Hasidim who lived in Tomashov. And although Reb Hersh Tomashover and Reb Mordkhe Yosef Izhbitser did everything in their power to make sure that the Rebbe didn't hear about it, nevertheless he did learn what was going on. In order to avoid further disputes, the Rebbe Reb Mendele immediately left Tomashov and settled in Kotsk.

17

Court Intrigues at Kotsk

The Rebbe Reb Mendele thought that in Kotsk he would finally be free of his opponents and his own Hasidim. But the very fact of Kotsk's proximity to Warsaw resulted in a continuous increase in the ranks of his Hasidim. So Reb Mendele decided that from now on, he wouldn't have much to do with the simple Hasidim and would only engage with the elite.

Yet no matter how many times Reb Mendele Kotsker told his Hasidim not to harass him about performing miracles, there were always some among the Hasidim who would include various material petitions in their notes. This one had a sick wife, another one complained of his poor livelihood, and the Kotsker Rebbe couldn't stand this kind of petition.

"Itshe Meirl," the Kotsker once said in the course of a conversation with the genius from Warsaw, "is that what I worked for, so that I could become their magician? Just show them tricks, become their acrobat? They don't know that every miracle that happens to us is recorded in a book for the future, when Messiah will come. Then they'll open the book of miracles and it will become clear that every moment miracles happened in the world, that everything depends on miracles. But they don't realize that, and they don't want to see these everyday miracles!"

Moreover, the dispute between the Hasidim of Vurke and Kotsk became ever more heated. The Vurker Rebbe and the Kotsker Rebbe got along with each other and the Vurker would even come to spend a Sabbath in Kotsk every year. But that did nothing to discourage the growing rift between the two Hasidic camps.

One time when Reb Yitskhok Vurker came to spend a Sabbath in Kotsk, he and the Kotsker Rebbe had a heated discussion.

The Vurker Rebbe became more and more insistent on his approach to Hasidism, which focused on love for fellow Jews after the manner of Reb Levi Yitskhok of Berditshev. He couldn't agree to the approach of Reb Mendele Kotsker, for whom everything had to be as sharp as a slaughtering knife.

"Do you know, Reb Mendele, a rebbe has to be like a coachman. The coachman rides from Kotsk to Warsaw. But the way of the world is that when he encounters somebody who's just going from one inn to another, he lets that one climb in as well. The coachman just stops at the inn for a while to let that passenger off, cracks his whip, and drives on. It's the same with a rebbe," concluded Reb Yitskhok Vurker. "True, he can't forget to drive until he reaches his final destination, but he needs to be able to pick up different sorts of Jews along the way as well..."

But Reb Mendele was concentrating on himself, and he answered: "A Jew first has to be able to say 'the God of my father and I will exalt Him' (Exodus 15:2). The Jew must realize with his own intellect that this is 'the God of my father,' so that he can say 'this is my God.' No one can help him in that."

Old Hasidim relate that during that conversation Kotsker Hasidim stood by the windows of the study house, mockingly shouting "Black Yitskhok!"

The Kotsker Hasidim took no notice of the fact that the two rebbes got along with each other. For them it was enough that the Vurker Rebbe wasn't becoming a disciple of the Kotsker Rebbe and didn't follow the latter's approach, to convince them to denigrate and mock him.

One time the Kotsker Rebbe's wife Glike became very ill. The Kotsker sent her to Warsaw, where she stayed with the Vurker Rebbe for more than six weeks. The Kotsker Rebbe also came to spend a Sabbath in Vurke. Hasidim relate that on Saturday evening after havdalah, the Vurker Rebbe said to the Kotsker Rebbe:

"This Sabbath Kotsker Hasidim were together with Vurke Hasidim and they didn't fight. It's a sign that eventually there will be peace."

"That's bad, very bad," sighed the Kotsker Rebbe in response. "I'm afraid that the drop of truth my Hasidim managed to achieve will be drowned in the sea of falsehood."

But the Kotsker's fear was premature because the disputes between the Vurker and Kotsker Hasidim were only beginning to develop. The

Kotsker Hasidim had maintained their decorum that Sabbath only because they didn't want to start up with the Vurke Hasidim in Vurke while the Kotsker Rebbe was visiting there. As soon as the Kotsker left Vurke, a fistfight broke out in a tavern outside of town between Hasidim of the two camps. At that occasion the Kotsker Rebbe grabbed hold of a Vurke Hasid and asked him, 'What is greatness in your opinion? Do you think your heart is pure? Do you know why, when the words 'Thou shalt be wholehearted with the Lord thy God' (Deuteronomy 18:13) appear in the Torah, the first letter of that sentence is extraordinarily large? It's to indicate that every Jew can enter into the world 'wholehearted,' except for someone who's arrogant. He can't go in because he thinks he's even bigger!"

▲▼▲▼▲▼

After a few weeks of illness, the wife of the Kotsker Rebbe passed away and he was left a widower.

Various matches were proposed. But black clouds began to gather in the skies of Kotsk. The Kotsker Rebbe certainly would not have remarried but for the fact that his courtiers decided that the Rebbe could not remain single. Reb Itshe Meirl was particularly insistent that the Rebbe take his sister-in-law, Reb Moyshe Khalfan's daughter, as a wife.

But the Kotsker Rebbe knew nothing about the plans the courtiers were making behind his back. He sat for days on end in his private room. When he would come into the study house for the afternoon prayers, he sat in a sea of gloom, and the Hasidim could see that he was troubled by dark thoughts. His moral teachings became so bitter that the leading Hasidim were afraid that the simpler Hasidim might hear about them, and they drove away the young men from the Rebbe.

"What is the meaning of, 'And Jacob loved Rachel' (Genesis 29:18)," the Kotsker once opened his discourse. "Jacob loved Rachel. Did he love Rachel? He loved *himself*. If I say that I love pike, does that mean that I love the fish? I love myself. So why is the Torah telling me that Jacob loved Rachel? I'm the one I love, and I do everything for myself!"

He drew the thought out further: "So what is the meaning of 'and you shall love the Lord your God?' (Deuteronomy 6:8). If you love God, is it God that you love, or once again just yourself? And what's the difference between 'and Jacob loved Rachel' and 'you shall love the Lord your God?' What's the difference between love between fellow humans and love between humans and God?"

All of these critical thoughts made their way into the Kotsker Rebbe's mind and began to bore deeper and deeper.

The courtiers wanted to draw the Rebbe away from such heavy thoughts. They sensed that these kinds of ideas would lead the Rebbe to become a hermit. They hoped that by seeing to it that the Rebbe married Reb Itshe Meirl's sister-in-law, who happened to have the reputation of being extraordinarily intelligent, they would encourage him to engage with his Hasidim again.

But not all of the prominent Hasidim agreed to the Kotsker Rebbe's becoming Reb Itshe Meirl's brother-in-law. They did want the Rebbe to remarry but not with Reb Itshe Meirl's sister-in-law. They didn't want Reb Itshe Meirl to have too much influence at Kotsk.

Intrigues began. Reb Mordkhe Yosef Izhbitser began to rebel against Reb Itshe Meirl. He sought ways to make the Kotsker Rebbe his own relative. He proposed a match between the Rebbe and a widowed cousin of his.

But as far as the Kotsker Rebbe himself was concerned, it didn't matter much who became his wife. He was spending most of his time in higher worlds. The courtiers didn't allow the Kotsker Rebbe to become a relative of Reb Mordkhe Yosef Izhbitser. And at one nighttime meeting of the courtiers, when Reb Mordkhe Yosef announced that he planned to propose that the Rebbe marry his widowed cousin, Reb Hersh Tomashover, the Kotsker Rebbe's "bodyguard," responsed: "Our Rebbe is the equivalent of a High Priest, and a High Priest is forbidden to marry a widow!"

At the same meeting elderly Hasidim related that when Reb Moyshe Khalfan's wife and her daughter Khaye had gone to see the Rebbe Reb Bunem, the Reb Bunem had read their note and said: "I've seen to Khaye's future already. All seven heavens are open before her! She will have a husband who is a tzaddik and a scholar, as well as good children."

The Hasidim were certain that the Pshiskhe Rebbe had the Kotsker Rebbe in mind.

Gradually two parties formed among the leading Hasidim at Kotsk: The Izhbitsers, led by Reb Mordkhe Yosef; and the Warsaw group, lead by Reb Itshe Meirl. By this point, seeing that the Kotsker Rebbe was progressively distancing himself from his Hasidim, Reb Mordkhe Yosef Izhbitser had started giving a regular class in Midrash to a group of Hasidim, while Reb Itshe Meirl taught Talmud.

The quiet competition in the court of Kotsk reached a point where Reb Itshe Meirl appealed to the Vurker Rebbe to intervene on his behalf and convince the Kotsker Rebbe to marry Reb Itshe Meirl's sister-in-law.

And then the Kotsker Rebbe received a letter from the Vurker Rebbe. The latter wrote:

"Life, peace, and all good things to the honored, holy and famous rabbi, etc., our Master Menachem Mendel may his light shine and may he live.

"I was overjoyed to hear the good news about his health and the health of his family. May God increase his strength, so that he may grow stronger in joy and confidence in the merit of the prayers of our holy rebbes. I have conveyed my advice, which I think is for the best, that the bearer of this letter should travel to Warsaw and conclude the pertinent matter, which is most appropriate and convenient in all respects, as the bearer will explain orally. May God aid him so that he can conclude the match with good luck, and may much good come to him and to all that are attached to him."

This is followed by a postscript containing a greeting to the Kotsker Rebbe from Reb Dovidl, the future Kotsker Rebbe, and a greeting to all his friends and relatives. He requests that good wine be provided in his name for the Sabbath, and that he be remembered favorably.

It appears that the bearer of the letter was Reb Hersh Tomashover, and it seems that the letter tipped the scale. When Reb Mordkhe Yosef Izhbitser's loyalists saw that the Kotsker Rebbe had received a letter from the Vurker Rebbe, they recruited the Kotsker Rebbe's son, Reb Dovidl, to influence his father not to marry again at all. But by this point no one could further influence the Kotsker Rebbe. As soon as he received the letter from his good friend, the Vurker Rebbe, he ordered Reb Hersh Tomashover immediately to travel to Warsaw to meet the bride, make sure she had no defects and arrange the wedding date.

And thus Reb Itshe Meirl managed to defeat Reb Mordkhe Yosef Izhbitser.

A Fire Burns in Kotsk

The leading Kotsker Hasidim arranged an elaborate party for Saturday evening to celebrate. Liquor was cheap, a quart for sixpence. Moreover Shmuel Nashelsker was in Kotsk for the Sabbath, and he agreed to bear all the costs of the party.

And they really made a party like King Solomon in his time, celebrating throughout the night.

When the Hasidim were already quite high, Reb Hersh Tomashover called out, "Once upon a time the Rebbe asked a Hasid why it is that we drink liquor to accompany the fulfillment of every commandment.

"And a Hasid answered, 'Because before we drink liquor we say the blessing, "Who creates everything with his speech."'[59]

"The Rebbe asked again, 'Can you drink plain water?'

"And the Hasid didn't have a response to that.

"'The answer is,' concluded the Rebbe, 'that if you always remember that everything comes from God, you deserve a drink of liquor.'"

And Reb Shmuel Nashelsker opened his purse once again and sent for more liquor.

Not until just before daybreak did the Hasidim see Reb Hersh Tomashover off on his way to examine the Rebbe's prospective bride.

---

59. The last words of the standard blessing before eating (or drinking) anything not covered by one of the more specific blessings for food.

18

The Kotsker Rebbe Forgets to Go to His Own Wedding Ceremony

Reb Hersh Tomashover arrived at Warsaw on his mission from the Kotsker Rebbe to examine the bride, Reb Itshe Meirl's sister-in-law, to make sure that she didn't have any defects and that she was worthy to be the Rebbe's wife.

The news that the Kotsker Rebbe had spent the past few years secluded from society had also reached the bride.

"I want to have a husband like everybody else and raise a new generation. If I want to get assistance from a rebbe, I'll send my husband to consult with him. I want to have a child, too!" she wept bitterly.

Her sister, Reb Itshe Meirl's wife, managed to get her to hold off on giving an answer until Reb Itshe Meirl's wife had time to go to Kotsk and talk personally with the Rebbe. She promised to find out whether he only wanted to marry again in order to fulfill the saying in the Talmud: "Every Jew who does not have a wife is not a man" (Yevamos 73a), or whether he meant to be a real husband . . .

Reb Itshe Meirl's wife set off for Kotsk together with her husband, and although women had never been allowed in to consult with the Kotsker Rebbe, the secretary Reb Hersh Tomashover made an exception in her case.

Reb Itshe Meirl's wife told the Rebbe that her sister agreed to the match, "but since there's a rumor that the Rebbe renounced all corporeal things once the Rebbe had fathered his son Reb Dovidl, the bride wants the Rebbe first to promise her that she will have a child."

The Kotsker Rebbe didn't answer her at all. The whole time Reb Itshe Meirl's wife was in the room he stood with his face to the wall. Then he began scurrying around the room, his eyes covered by his hand, deep in thought. Suddenly he stopped next to his secretary, Reb Hersh Tomashover, and angrily murmured to him, "Let her go to see a sorcerer, and then she'll know whether she'll have a child. What's she bothering me for?" he began angrily complaining to Reb Hersh Tomashover. "Why don't people leave me alone, why does everybody keep shoving me into materiality?"

But Reb Hersh the Secretary was entirely unimpressed by these statements, and he told Reb Itshe Meirl's wife, "If the Rebbe doesn't say 'no,' then it's good: with God's help, they will have children!"

The Kotsker Rebbe didn't even hear Reb Hersh's answer to her. He lapsed back into his thoughts and strode back and forth across the room.

Reb Itshe Meirl's wife burst into tears of joy when she heard the answer Reb Hersh the Secretary gave her.

When the Kotsker Rebbe heard her crying, he added: "Tears of joy . . . a very great thing . . . I promise you that I myself will lead the children to the marriage canopy."

The terms of the marriage were quickly settled on, and a few weeks later the date for the wedding was set.

From every corner of Poland people assembled for the Kotsker Rebbe's wedding. All of the leading Hasidim, all of the true disciples were there. Mordkhe Yosef Izhbitser came as well, even though he personally didn't want the Rebbe to marry Reb Itshe Meirl's sister-in-law. Only the Kotsker Rebbe's son set off for a nearby city because he didn't want to attend the wedding of his father.

The thousands of Hasidim who assembled at the wedding had begun drinking and celebrating a few days earlier.

The wealthy Temerl of Warsaw sent along with the Hasidim a few barrels of wine.

All of the inns in Kotsk were jammed full of Hasidim. Everywhere little feasts were organized. Reb Henekh of Aleksander was staying at one of the hotels, and he organized his own feast. The liquor flowed freely. As they were drinking in came a rich man from Warsaw, Reb Sholem Fridman. Reb Henekh of Aleksander approached him and demanded that he pay for refreshments. But the rich man was stingy, and he only offered sixpence. The Hasidim began shouting that they should execute sentence on the rich man in accordance with the rule that "we force him to say, 'I'm willing.'" But Reb Sholem didn't let it come to that. He took back the sixpence, and replaced it with a silver coin from his pocket, and with that they sent for more liquor.

When the rich man from Warsaw found out that the person who had demanded refreshments from him was none other than Reb Henekh of Aleksander, he was mortified that he had haggled with Reb Henekh and given him such a small coin. He ran back to the inn where Reb Henekh was staying and began begging them to take more from him.

But Reb Henekh didn't want to take any more of that man's money, and he told his Hasidim the following story:

"The Holy Jew, as is well known, spent some time together with Reb Dovid Lelever, wandering from town to town incognito and collecting money so that poor girls could get married.

"Once they arrived at a village where a Jewish leaseholder lived, and they asked him for a donation. The leaseholder was rich but stingy. He looked at the Holy Jew and shrugged, 'To you I'm not going to give anything more than a three-penny coin because a Jew like you is healthy and can go to work. But the other one will get a nice donation from me.'

"The two disguised travelers suffered greatly from the rich man's insults, and they didn't want to take his charity. After they departed the stingy leaseholder happened to find out from a rural Jew who was sitting at the inn who these travelers were—that the Jew whom he had told to go to work was the 'Holy Jew.' He ran after them and invited them to return to his house. He wanted to conciliate them and give them generous donations. He turned to the 'Holy Jew' and pleaded to be forgiven.

"The Holy Jew responded: 'When you didn't know who I was, you didn't have me in mind. So I've got nothing against you. But that "ordinary Jew" whom you insulted, that Jew doesn't forgive you . . . You embarrassed a "Jew" you didn't know, and that "Jew" isn't here now—so who can forgive you?'

"From that moment on the leaseholder never refused alms to any Jew. Whenever a Jew came through begging, he would give a generous donation and ask for forgiveness . . . They say as well, that before he died, the leaseholder adjured his sons to do the same, to give every pauper a generous donation and to ask forgiveness of every pauper."

And Reb Henekh of Aleksander said further: "With regard to that story, our Rebbe, may he live, said: 'This teaches us that in every Jew there are two "Jews": one is simple, materialistic, the common working Jew. But there's also another "Jew," a spiritual Jew, the "Divine-image Jew," the little dot of Jewishness,[60] what becomes excited when matters of Torah are discussed. The spiritual Jew you don't see. The first little Jew goes into the street, does business, travels to fairs, is obsessed with deals, gives donations—all that is the first "little Jew."

"'The other "little Jew" sits in the Holy of Holies and studies, loves the Creator, wants to serve God, and when it senses that its surrounded by its own kind of people, it comes outside and can be seen. Then the room grows brighter. The "light of the Infinite" is manifest. That's the meaning of the verse "and God made humans in His image, in the image of God He made humanity" (Genesis 1:27). First came "his own image," then "in the image of God." That is the true Jew.'"

And Reb Henekh concluded: "So when I saw that Reb Sholem Fridman's 'second little Jew' didn't want to reveal itself even when it found itself in familiar company, why should I take the contribution from an ordinary person? If it's just to provide liquor, we can do that ourselves!"

And the Hasidim began drinking again.

They kept on celebrating like this until the day of the wedding, and that's when the real celebration began.

Very early in the morning the Hasidim got through their prayers and began drinking liquor.

The wedding canopy was set up in the midst of the large courtyard. The four poles were placed into the ground, and the Hasidim danced around the canopy.

On the porch of the Kotsker Rebbe's house stood Reb Itshe Meirl with a few leading Hasidim, singing happy melodies. But suddenly the door burst open and the groom, the Kotsker Rebbe, appeared in a simple cotton jacket, with a large skullcap on his head which reached below his ears. He drew his eyebrows close together as he contemplated the crowd and his voice thundered out: "What are you so happy about?"

In the blink of an eye, the thousands of Hasidim dancing around the courtyard became stock still. The Kotsker Rebbe approced closer to the porch and said angrily,

---

60. The Hebrew letter *yud* (pronounced "*yid*" in the Polish Yiddish dialect), a homonym of the word that means "Jew," is a mere short stroke of a pen. See note 12.

"'For you did not serve the Lord your God with joy and with a good heart' (Deuteronomy 28:47), it is written in the holy Torah at the end of the passage of admonition. This is hard to understand: Do such curses really come just for failure to serve God joyfully? Rather, it's not enough that 'you failed to serve the Lord your God,' but on top of that you were joyful and your heart was content when you cast off the yoke of Torah, with your wanton behavior. And for that, the curses in the admonition aren't enough!"

And when the Kotsker Rebbe saw Reb Itshe Meirl standing and trembling uncontrollably, he shouted: "Itshe Meirl! Why did you drag this mixed multitude to me?"

And with that he immediately returned to his private room.

The dead silence pervaded the entire courtyard; the Hasidim stood with their heads bowed and their brows furrowed. Sighs could be heard on all sides.

But Reb Itshe Meirl didn't lose his composure. He turned to the crowd of Hasidim and said, "The angels and seraphs are rejoicing today because our Rebbe is getting married. Shouldn't we rejoice as well?"

And he resumed tossing bottles of wine among the crowd. This had its effect. Most of the Hasidim grabbed the bottles of wine and resumed their dancing. But the elite individuals retreated into corners and thought about the Rebbe's latest utterance . . .

The Hasidim continued dancing until late at night. The wedding jester had already toasted the bride, the bridesmaids had already danced prior to settling the bride in her seat, and Reb Itshe Meirl's wife had already arrived along with a group of the female in-laws to complain to her husband that the groom had not yet arrived to the bride's veiling ceremony.

Reb Itshe Meirl didn't know what to say in reply, but to reassure them he claimed that the Rebbe would probably emerge soon from his private room.

"It's terrible to see how mortified the bride is. In addition, she no longer has the strength to keep fasting, and she keeps passing out," complained the bride's sister, Reb Itshe Meirl's wife, to her husband. "Go in to him, talk to him, get him to come outside."

But Reb Itshe Meirl didn't want to enter the Kotsker Rebbe's room. He understood that the Rebbe was certainly deep in contemplation, and he didn't want to interrupt him. In addition, he was afraid that the Rebbe might once again express the angry thoughts that had lately been consuming him. His brother-in-law, the bride's brother, a simple merchant from Warsaw, got involved at this point, saying that he would go in to the Rebbe's room.

At that point, Reb Itshe Meirl decided to go in himself.

But as soon as the Warsaw merchant went into the Rebbe's room, he was overcome with such terror that he could barely stammer the single word, "In-law!"

The Kotsker Rebbe stood by the bookcase with his back facing the intruder. One of his feet was leaning on a chair, and in his hand he held a large edition of the commentary of the Rif published in the town of Duerenport, quite heavy and bound in wooden covers.

The Warsaw merchant called out again, "In-law!"

The Kotsker Rebbe twisted to face him and with a piercing, sidelong glance shouted out: "How am I related to you?"

The Warsaw merchant was so frightened by these few words that he barely managed to run out of the Rebbe's room, and he was embarrassed to tell Reb Itshe Meirl what the Rebbe's reply to him had been.

Reb Itshe Meirl easily discerned what the exchange had been like. But his wife still stood before him, weeping and repeating that it was a shameful insult to keep the bride waiting for the groom to come in to the veiling. So Reb Itshe Meirl wrapped his belt tight around his gown, set his fur hat squarely on his head, and entered the Rebbe's private room with slow, quiet steps, as if he were treading on glass. And thus he quietly approached the Kotsker Rebbe, who was still standing at the same place as when Reb Itshe Meirl's brother-in-law had run out.

But the Rebbe immediately sensed that someone had entered his room and quickly turned around. Spotting Reb Itshe Meirl, he greeted him joyfully:

"It's good that you came. I've been looking for a resolution to this difficult passage in the Rif's commentary for a couple of hours."

Reb Itshe Meirl began to discuss the intricacies of the topic with the Kotsker Rebbe. Both of them displayed their broad knowledge and their sharp insight, and both of them forgot that it was time for the ceremony and everyone was waiting outside.

The crowd in the courtyard grew more and more impatient. Messengers came running to tell Reb Hersh Tomashover that the bride wouldn't stop weeping and complaining of the great embarrassment the groom caused her by his failure to come to the veiling and his evident unwillingness to go through the ceremony. So Reb Hersh Tomashover and a few of the leading Hasidim went to see the Rebbe, intending to remind him that "it's time to go to the veiling."

But the Rebbe angrily said to him, "Don't bother me. Don't you see that I'm in the middle of studying?"

But Reb Hersh Tomashover refused to be brushed off so easily and said: "The bride is weeping!"

At this Reb Itshe Meirl remembered why he had come to see the Rebbe, and he too began echoing Reb Hersh Tomashover.

The Kotsker Rebbe, who all this time had been wearing an ordinary cotton jacket, allowed himself to be convinced. He finally ordered that his new silk clothes be brought in. He became quite joyful, turning to Reb Itshe Meirl and saying:

"The Talmud says in Tractate Kidushin (Folio 49b) that when someone says to a woman, 'You are betrothed to me on condition that I am a tzaddik,' the rule is that even if he is completely wicked, the betrothal is valid. For if he reflects and feels penitence in his heart, he will certainly be a tzaddik. That's correct, if someone just says 'a tzaddik.' But when a woman thinks that the person who's betrothing her is a rebbe, and he knows that in truth he isn't one, the betrothal shouldn't be valid because penitence will never make him a rebbe!"

All of the leading Hasidim who stood in the Rebbe's private room were pleased that the Rebbe's mood had improved, and they were eager to hear how Reb Itshe Meirl would respond.

Reb Itshe Meirl spoke up: "A rebbe means someone who has Hasidim. The bride considers the Rebbe a rebbe because everyone else considers him a rebbe, and thus it's no use for the Rebbe to insist that he's not a rebbe. For we will just continue to shout that you are!"

The Kotsker Rebbe smiled at Reb Itshe Meirl's answer. Then he put on the silken clothes and went to the veiling.

After the ceremony the bride and groom were led into a room for their prescribed time alone together. The Hasidim stood around the room, dancing enthusiastically. Suddenly the Kotsker Rebbe could be heard reciting Psalms in a terrible, loud voice.

Reb Itshe Meirl and his wife, along with the attendants and a few of the Hasidim, entered the room. They saw the bride lying in a faint, and the Kotsker Rebbe striding around lost in thought, as if he had no idea what was happening in the room.

The bride was led out and, with difficulty, revived. Later she said that the Rebbe had been so lost in thought that she fainted in terror: "I want a husband, and I'm afraid to be alone in the room with the Rebbe!" she wept.

Reb Hersh the secretary and Reb Itshe Meirl reassured her that the Rebbe would be a good husband for her. Eventually the bride was convinced to go to the wedding feast.

19

The Kotsker Rebbe and the Polish Uprising of 1830

The ranks of the Kotsker Hasidim continued to grow throughout all the towns and cities of Poland, and in Warsaw itself.

The archives of Warsaw contain a petition from Reb Itshe Meirl himself for permission to open a Hasidic prayer room on Grzybowska Street, which at that time was the new Jewish quarter.

Kotsk Hasidism continued to flourish. The Kotsker Rebbe himself grew progressively more distant from his Hasidim, even though he had remarried. Yet there were drastic changes in the country that forced the spiritual leaders of the Hasidim to take sides. These changes would decide the fate of the Polish people, as well as the roughly 372,000 Jews then living in Russian Poland.

It was the night of November 29, 1830, when great tongues of fire in Solec and Nowolipie Streets illuminated Warsaw, and the streets were suddenly filled with various ranks of Polish soldiers and students from the officer training school.

Jews, too, supported the Polish November Rebellion.

The Jews didn't enjoy a very good situation in the independent duchy of Warsaw. The heroic acts of Berek Joselowicz[61] and his comrades during the Kosciuszko Rebellion didn't do much to improve the attitude of the Poles toward the Jews. But nevertheless, and even in the face of the false predictions of some Poles that the Jews would disrupt the rebellion—such as that of Mochnacki, who writes that "when the population contains very many different elements; when, among 120,000 residents, there are 80,000 Jews, nearly two thirds of the overall population, then in the current situation that is not a

---

61. Col. Berek Joselewicz (1764–1809), Jewish colonel of the Polish Army during the Kościuszko Uprising (1794), Poland's last stand before being completely partitioned. He was killed in the Battle of Kock in 1809 by Austrian troops during the Napoleonic Wars.

A Fire Burns in Kotsk

significant asset, but perhaps even a deficit—" despite all the negative opinions expressed by some Poles, the Jews immediately entered on the side of the rebellion with the greatest enthusiasm.

The first to join in support of the rebellion were the Jewish academicians, including the students of the modern rabbinical seminary. Quite a few Jews also entered the Academic Guard.

The Academic Guard fought heroically and were the first to arrive at the most dangerous battle positions.

The author Sini Hernish, together with Yosef Joselowicz (a son of Berek's) began organizing a Jewish regiment, following the example and organizational form of Berek Joselowicz's regiment. These Jews appealed to the dictator Chlopicki to allow them to organize. This petition, signed personally by Hernish, was composed in a thoroughly patriotic tone. Hernish promises in the communication to recruit troops for the regiment from among the "finest families" of the Jews, so that they would serve as examples for the masses of the Jews.

Chlopicki replied to this petition that if the Jews helped the Poles to gain their liberation, they would then be able to demand rights equal to all the other citizens of the country—and that could not be permitted. In addition, it simply was not appropriate for Jewish blood to mix with noble Polish blood on the battlefield.

Some of those in the Polish rebellion did want Jews to take an active part in the rebellion, but the war minister Morawski declared that Jews were forbidden from being mustered into Polish military service.

That was the general attitude of the Polish leadership toward the Jews in the early days of the rebellion. But when it was learned that the Tsar had sent out a large army under the leadership of General Paskiewicz,[62] it was no longer quite so easy to refuse Jewish assistance.

A separate Jewish military unit was established, consisting of a cavalry squadron and an infantry regiment, which were to be supported by Jews.

These units were filled by Polish and foreign Jews with military experience.

62. Russian general (1782–1856) who led the suppression of the Polish uprising and then served as the Czar's viceroy in the Kingdom of Poland.

The Warsaw Jewish community organization was also drawn into the events.

The military staff of the Polish rebels wanted to determine whether the community authorities had authorized Yosef and Hernish to organize Jewish military units.

This put the community organization into a dilemma. They were afraid that if the Jews failed to acquit themselves heroically on the battlefield, the entire Jewish population would suffer embarrassment.

The organization answered somewhat diplomatically that it was against "separation" and believed it would be better for "the Jews to fight together with the Poles under one flag, which would bring about feelings of unity rather than separating residents of various faiths."

At the same time as the Jewish military unit was organized by Yosef Berkovitsh,[63] the head of the National Guard, Antoni Ostrowski,[64] who was thoroughly progressive and opposed religious prejudice, also busied himself with the establishment of Jewish military units.

The first thing he thought of doing was to raise money to fund the rebellion among the Jewish capitalists.

Among the richest Jews in Warsaw at the time were a number of Kotsker Hasidim, including Reb Moshe Khalfan, the father-in-law of Reb Itshe Meirl, the greatest Kotsker Hasid in Warsaw. Reb Moshe Khalfan lived on Med Street, where he had his bank.

One time, on a Sunday morning, when Reb Itshe Meirl and a few devoted Kotsker Hasidim were sitting with his father-in-law Reb Moshe Khalfan, the lame gentile servant Jan came running into the room saying that a general had arrived riding on a horse and asked to see the master.

Reb Moshe Khalfan, who was sitting and enjoying a little meal with the Kotsker Hasidim, was at first terrified and didn't know what to do. But before he had time to put on his new frock and his high fur hat, General Ostrowski's adjutant had come in, announced that General Ostrowski wanted to visit the gentleman "Moshko Khalfan," and asked whether the gentleman was at home.

---

63. The unit formed by Yosef Berkovitsh consisted of Jews who were willing to shave their beards. He was the son of Colonel Berek Joselewicz.

64. See introduction, p. xviii.

A Fire Burns in Kotsk

Reb Moshe Khalfan wasn't much of a formal speaker by nature and in addition he didn't know much Polish. On the other hand his son-in-law, Reb Itshe Meirl, did know how to speak and write Polish. (As described in the volume *Meir eynei hagola*, the Pshiskhe Rebbe Reb Bunem had taught him Polish and German, as well as how to write prescriptions. It is also possible that before his wedding, Reb Itshe Meirl had to take an exam in Polish language. According to Polish law at that time, no Jewish man could marry before the age of thirty. The only exceptions were those who could pass an exam in either the Polish or the German language, and they could marry when they were quite young. The Kotsker Rebbe Reb Mendele had passed such an exam in Lemberg, after which he had received permission to marry.)

Reb Itshe Meirl asked the other Kotsker Hasidim to go out through a side door. He went down the front steps by himself and invited General Ostrowski into the house.

General Ostrowski's heavy military boots trod the wooden steps that led to the wealthy Hasidic home of Reb Moshe Khalfan.

The house was richly appointed. Along the walls were rows of sacred texts. On one side stood a heavy commode, covered with brass, on iron wheels so that it could easily be moved from place to place. The commode was also used as a fireproof safe, and hidden in it was nearly all of Reb Moshe Khalfan's wealth: golden ducats, pearls, diamonds, items held as collateral, and dowries that poor brides had entrusted to him.

At the eastern wall stood a large, glass-covered display case containing various precious items: golden and silver kiddush goblets, spiceboxes, Hanukkah lamps, silver matzah platters, menorahs, Torah crowns and pointers, ivory tobacco boxes, and mother-of-pearl knives for cutting the challah on the Sabbath.

On the wall next to the display case hung a large silver amulet, which had been beaten and engraved by a great Jewish artist in Amsterdam.

On the table stood a large silver jar filled with tobacco and various ivory tobacco boxes.

On the walls hung various carved pipes.

When the general came in, Reb Moshe Khalfan bowed deeply to him. He removed his large fur hat and remained standing in a large satin skullcap, which reached to his ears.

Reb Itshe Meirl pulled up a richly upholstered armchair.

General Ostrowski cheerfully sat down on the chair. Right away Reb Moshe Khalfan humbly brought over a large pipe with an expensive amber mouthpiece and offered the general a pipeful of tobacco. Then he ordered his Jewish servant, the tall Juzep, to bring up from the cellar a pot of double mead, which had been bottled at the time of the Kosciuszko Rebellion.

Large silver kiddush goblets were brought out, and the general was treated to the precious mead.

When the general had drunk a few cups of mead and smoked an entire pipeful of tobacco, Reb Moshe Khalfan asked General Ostrowski in a humble tone how he could serve him.

General Ostrowski smoothed his mustache, looked from side to side, glanced at the display case and the iron chest on wheels, and began quietly, but with confidence in his voice: "You should realize, Moshke, that the rebellion which we Poles have undertaken against the Russian oppressors is on the verge of complete victory. I've always appreciated the services the Jews have provided for the Polish people, and just today I've gotten the approval of the Council of Ministers to have a certain number of Jews accepted into the National Guard. But we now need help from the Jews in the small towns. We need to do reconnaissance to establish where the enemy positions are. Since I've learned that the small-town Jews belong to a sect called the 'Hasidim,' and that you belong to them as well, I want the leader of the sect, the rabbi who lives in Kotsk, to order his followers to support our rebellion. And I want you yourself to know that right now we're suffering from a severe shortage of funds. We know that you, Moshke, possess a great deal of capital, and we want you to lend us a hundred thousand rubles." Reb Moshe's eyebrows flew up at the last words, just as if he'd been bitten by a snake.

"What did the General say?" he replied, as if he didn't believe his ears. "A hundred thousand rubles?"

"Yes, yes, one hundred thousand," the General repeated. "That's not so much for you, Moshke. You've got lots more than that lying in one corner, ha ha ha!" He laughed so hard that he began coughing.

Reb Moshe Khalfan also smiled so that the General wouldn't be upset, but he couldn't speak further. He stood with his mouth hanging open as if his tongue had been removed.

"Well, don't you understand yet?" the General asked in a more insistent tone. "You still haven't digested my words? So let this young man translate into his Yiddish what I just said," pointing to Reb Itshe Meirl. "He's probably your son, and he doubtless knows more Polish than you."

"No, he's my son-in-law," Reb Moshe Khalfan answered proudly.

"Your son-in-law? Oh, I like him! Well, why don't you explain to your father-in-law what I'm demanding?" he said to Reb Itshe Meirl.

"My father-in-law, I believe, understood everything," answered Reb Itshe Meirl. "But I think that such things cannot be decided so quickly. And it seems to me that my father-in-law would rather put off the decision. He would probably prefer to go to Kotsk, talk it over with the Rebbe, and give his answer in a day or two."

"I like that! That's a horse of a different color!" the General cried. "Alright, let it be a day or two from now. But I want you to come see me in the General Staff, with a clear answer."

And when the General was about to leave Reb Moshe Khalfan's room, he turned backward and said: "You see, Moshke, I forgot to tell you the most important thing: As collateral for the loan, we will write over to you the headquarters of the Warsaw magistrate, the great theater and the military buildings on Przejazd. But see to it that you provide the loan, and that your rabbi in Kotsk calls on his followers to support our rebellion!"

That same evening Reb Itshe Meirl summoned a council at the home of his father-in-law to consider whether the Hasidim should provide money for the Polish Rebellion, and whether they should ask the Kotsker Rebbe to announce that his Hasidim should support the rebellion as well.

20

The Council at Moshe Khalfan's House

The discussion at the council wasn't only about money, although the sum demanded was extraordinary for the time. The main question was: can the Jews risk open conflict with the Russian government? The Jews of Poland were afraid that even if the Polish rebellion were successful, the Rusian government would subsequently take its revenge on the Jews living in Russia.

The Rebbe Reb Yitskhok Vurker came to Warsaw the same day, and he was invited to the council. Reb Yitskhok Vurker had always been an intercessor on behalf of any Jew who was tormented and persecuted. Now he came spreading the alarm that a large number of the Polish rebels were treating the Jews in the provinces brutally, repeatedly hanging innocent Jews on mere suspicion of being hired Russian spies.

In addition to the Vurker Rebbe and the leaders from Warsaw who had come to the council, there was also a special messenger from the court of Kotsk.

The president of the council was Reb Itshe Meirl, although the Vurker Rebbe was much older. The Vurker Rebbe was altogether downcast after all the suffering he had seen among the Jews in the provinces.

The Hasidic Jews gathered at the council were accomplished not only in rabbinics and Hasidism, but also well aware of what was going on in the wider world.

Reb Itshe Meirl told the gathering that even in the camp of the Polish rebels there was no unity concerning the revolution. The Polish aristocracy, who set the tone for the social life of Poland, weren't interested in the rebellion at all. The most salient expression of their dissatisfaction had been a legal protest in the Polish Sejm. The Polish noblemen were attached to the official positions and bureaucratic posts they had received from the Russian government, and the Polish noblemen also knew that the revolution endangered their privileges and fortunes. History had provided them with more than one warning of the risk they ran.

"Now," Reb Itshe Meirl turned to the gathering, "the question is, what should we do? Our experiences in the past were bitter. The Jews didn't benefit from the independent Duchy of Warsaw. The Jews were constantly persecuted, and they had to withstand all sorts of harassment from Polish government officials. So we need to carefully consider what we should do."

Immediately after Reb Itshe Meirl concluded his speech, one of the trustees of the Warsaw Jewish community who knew a great deal about history and was also a fervent Vurke Hasid, as well as having frequent dealings in government circles, said:

"Gentlemen! Why should we put a healthy body into a sick bed? We've seen how the Jews were 'rewarded' for the heroic acts of Berek Joselowicz and his comrades during the Kosciuszko Rebellion and in other struggles. Even now you can visit his abandoned grave near Kotsk, where all the Gentiles consider it a good deed to desecrate his grave. It didn't do much to improve their attitude toward us Jews."

And the Hasidic trustee began saying favorable things about the Tsarist representatives in Poland.

"But Nikolai Novosiltsev,"[65] responded one of the others present, "only responds to the petitions of the Jews to spite the Poles, and only in return for big bribes."

"Why do we care about his motivations," said the trustee, "as long as the burden of exile is eased a bit? What more can we expect in our bitter exile?"

An old Pshiskhe Hasid called out, "Have you already forgotten that the Russian government three years ago issued a decree that Jews should be conscripted into the military, while before then we could buy our way out?"

---

65. Senator Nikolai Novosiltsev (ca. 1768–1838), imperial commissioner in the Kingdom of Poland, a post designed to reconcile the interests of the kingdom with those of the Empire. Novosiltsev seemed to see a potential for Jewish loyalty to the tsar and was very receptive to "gifts"; thus he helped postpone Jewish conscription and residential restrictions, among other things.

"But you have to keep in mind," said Reb Itshe Meirl, "that the Enlighteners and students in the Rabbinical seminary in Warsaw are in any case already participating in the rebellion. If the Poles win, the Jewish contribution to the victory will be attributed solely to them. If the Enlighteners get credit for the victory, it will strengthen the opponents of Hasidism."

Voices were heard insisting, "The Rebbe Reb Shneur Zalmen of Liady, may his merit protect us, the 'Rav,' said that we should always support the Russian Empire."

The discussion grew ever more heated; everyone spoke at once, trying to drown out his fellows.

Reb Moshe Khalfan, who was sitting on an upholstered armchair, dressed in a flowered frock and slippers with just a skullcap on his head, smoking a long pipe, asked everyone to speak more quietly because he was afraid that people outside might learn about the council. Although General Ostrowski knew that such a council would be held, Reb Moshe Khalfan was afraid that Polish rebels might burst in and disrupt the meeting.

But if it was difficult for Reb Moshe Khalfan to quiet the assembly down, everything did suddenly become quiet when Reb Yitskhok Vurker suddenly stood up and shouted: "Jews! You don't know what's going on in the small towns!"

The Vurker Rebbe looked altogether downcast. His face was even darker than usual, and with tears in his eyes he continued: "Innocent Jews are being hung, and you're sitting here chatting about things that have nothing to do with the heart of the matter. The forces under the command of Majors Puszet and Szon are treating Jews brutally. Everyone is suspected of spying for Russia, and they hang them without the least investigation or trial. Thus, for example, a Jew was hung last week in Pyatetshne, wearing his tallit and tefillin, the way the soldiers caught him. They said that while he was praying and motioning with his hands, he was giving signs to the enemy. And you're sitting here speaking empty words, discussing whether or not we should give money to the rebels!"

As long as the Vurker Rebbe spoke, a sorrowful quiet reigned; everyone listened in discouragement to the Vurker Rebbe's words.

Indeed, the situation of the Jews in the provinces at that time was catastrophic. Not all the commanders were as good as General

Ostrowski. The leaders of the rebellion would slaughter dozens of people in the most brutal fashion. Dozens of quiet, innocent Jews were slaughtered in the Agustov region, for example, and if any officer dared to defend the Jews, he was threatened with severe punishment.

The Jews suffered most of all because they were both sides' scapegoats. If the Russians suffered a defeat somewhere, then in the nearest town they would take out their fury on the Jews, accusing them of espionage.

The Polish rebels did the same thing; and since a certain number of towns changed hands several times, each victorious army decided that its first task was to deal with the Jews.

A chronicler of those times relates that every time a new military unit entered a town, executions would be carried out right in the marketplace. The Polish rebels issued corporal punishment to every Jew who fell under the slightest suspicion of giving aid to the Russians; and the Russians for their part beat the Jews with their whips, assuming that all the Jews were assisting the Polish rebellion.

There were exceptional cases when the Polish military officers managed to prevent pogroms against Jews in the areas they conquered. This happened, for example, in Lublin, thanks to Jan Czynski, son of a convert, who protected the Jews. But there weren't many Czynskis.

The military commanders were mostly recruited from the ranks of the Polish nobility, and their typical representative was General Skrzynecki, who had been the commander in chief for a short time. He was a reactionary and fanatical clericalist. At the crucial moment when the fate of the entire rebellion depended on the rebels in Lithuania, he refused to place his trust in the talented and energetic General Elwinski, merely because the latter was of Jewish descent. This contributed greatly to the collapse of the rebellion.

And the Rebbe Reb Yitskhok Vurker talked about all of these Jewish troubles resulting from the rebellion.

Those assembled had by now forgotten the ostensible reason for their meeting, and instead of considering whether to lend money to the Polish rebels, they began discussing the catastrophic situation of the Jews. Several Jews among the gathering complained that even in Warsaw many Jews had already lost their entire fortunes, right at the beginning of the revolt; commerce had died completely; Jews had lost their livelihood; all the roads were blocked; and peasants didn't come into the city at all.

The representatives of the official Jewish community complained that their organization was likewise short on revenue, and in addition they still had to meet the burden of the kosher food tax that was still in force.

And now a new burden had been placed on them—the new military recruit tax, and the obligation to provide 1,547 pelts, not to mention the absolutely necessary "voluntary" donations and levies demanded by the leaders of the revolt. And if that wasn't enough, the community had taken on another burden—to pay 150 guldens for every Jewish volunteer in the Polish military.

It seemed that nothing would come of the council. There were voices calling for Reb Itshe Meirl to go to General Ostrowski and ask him to order the Polish officers to behave more humanely toward the Jews in the countryside.

But Reb Itshe Meirl argued that he couldn't appear before General Ostrowski if he didn't at least bring the loan of 100,000 rubles, not to mention the proclamation the general demanded from the Kotsker Rebbe calling on every Jew to support the rebellion.

"If so, then we should lend him the money, if only to save Jewish lives," said Reb Yitskhok Vurker.

"Yes, the money should be lent to him," several voices agreed.

Reb Moshe Khalfan interjected: "It's easy for you to say we should lend him the money! But I've been sitting here almost all night long, and you haven't even begun to think where so much money could come from."

"Don't worry, the money will be there," called the Vurke Rebbe. "I think that our host is still capable of borrowing that much money."

"Certainly I'm capable of borrowing that sum, although it's not often I see that much money these days; but I want to know how I can be certain that I'll get the money back."

His son-in-law, Reb Itshe Meirl, stood up and declared, "I myself have heard from General Ostrowski that the Polish government will offer buildings as collateral—that they will sign over the courthouse, the theater building, and the barracks on Przejazd Street."

"Well, what are you afraid of then?" the Vurke Rebbe asked Reb Moshe Khalfan. "If they don't pay, then you'll get all those buildings, and we'll celebrate the Sabbath in one of them," he added in jest.

A few hours after midnight the assembly dispersed, after everyone had drunk a few glasses of mead.

It was unanimously decided that Reb Moshe Khalfan should lend the money demanded by General Ostrowski, but not until Reb Itshe Meirl had consulted with the Kotsker Rebbe concerning the "proclamation" the general demanded of the Rebbe.

21

Reb Itshe Meirl Is Arrested as a Spy

The road to Kotsk was dangerous. On every side Polish revolutionary military units were on the march.

Reb Itshe Meirl, who had set off for Kotsk on his own to consult with the Rebbe, sat on the sled wrapped in a great sheepskin coat. He had to provide the various military patrols along the way with an explanation of his destination. Every several miles the sled was stopped by mounted Polish patrols which thoroughly checked the sled and began investigating who Reb Itshe Meirl was and where he was headed so early in the morning.

Each time Reb Itshe Meirl placed himself at great risk because of the Polish military's suspicion that all Jews were spies. Each time he managed to wriggle out of their hands, until he was close to Kotsk. Close to the grave of Yosef Berkovitsh the sled was suddenly stopped by a patrol that didn't want to hear any excuses. The patrol strictly ordered the Polish coachman to drive the wagon directly to the Polish command center, not far from Kotsk.

Reb Itshe Meirl did everything he could to show that he was a citizen of Warsaw, and that he was on his way to Kotsk so early in the morning because he desperately needed to consult the Rebbe. His arguments were unavailing, and soon the sled was surrounded by four horsemen who didn't let Reb Itshe Meirl out of their sight and made sure he didn't escape. The short and sharp answers that Reb Itshe Meirl had given them convinced them they had a "live one" on their hands. And they were even more certain when he mentioned the name of General Antony Ostrowski—because otherwise why would this little Jew be talking about General Ostroswki?

"Stop giving us this story about General Ostrowski, you lousy Jew, or else I'll knock your chin off!" shouted the eldest member of the patrol. "You'd do better to tell us where the commander of the Russian forces is, and how many of our battalions you've already betrayed!"

Reb Itshe Meirl wanted to tell the soldiers that the Jews of Warsaw had volunteered and were fighting hand in hand with the Polish revolutionaries on some of the fronts, but one of the horsemen stuck his bayonet so far inside the sled that he nearly cut through Reb Itshe Meirl's sheepskin coat.

"You were told to keep your mouth shut!" he raged. "You suck Polish blood, you eat Polish bread, and you betray us! You good-for-nothing, if we win and get our free Poland, then we'll reckon with you! There won't be enough trees to hang you on. First we'll beat the Russians, and then you'll see what a party we'll have!"

Reb Itshe Meirl realized that the more he talked to the soldiers the worse off he would be. He stopped arguing with them altogether and began to think about how he could get the information about his predicament both to the Kotsker Rebbe and to his father-in-law in Warsaw. All the same, he tried one more time:

"You should know that you're going to regret not letting me go to Kotsk. Tomorrow evening I have to be back in Warsaw to see General Ostrowski, and I—"

The soldiers didn't let him finish his sentence, and one of them rode close to the sled and cracked his whip over Reb Itshe Meirl's head. Reb Itshe Meirl only avoided the lash by quickly ducking his head into his big coat, and the soldier muttered: "Stop mentioning the name of our leader, General Ostrowski, you son of a bitch, and if not we'll carry out your sentence right here."

Reb Itshe Meir said nothing further to them. He burrowed into his coat and listened to the conversation among the soldiers crowded near the sled, which by now was traveling down a side road that led to the command post.

"I think they'll take care of him today!"

"Sure, you think they're going to play with him?"

"They're so good at disguising themselves, these little Jews, and creeping over to the Russians."

"Just this week we caught a Jew disguised as an old lady, trying to go join them. We caught him and we hung him."

"In the old lady's clothes?"

"No, we caught him before he put the old lady's clothes on."

"It's great that we're clearing them out so quickly."

"But what use is it, when they keep multiplying? Every Jew—a spy."

"Just yesterday in the town nearby we found two Jews who were spying. One of them was standing on a porch in a white shawl with leather straps on his arm and head. He was gesturing to the enemy, and he had the nerve to claim that he was praying. Hey, you, listen!" he turned to Reb Itshe Meir, "I'll bet you too have a white shawl with black boxes and leather straps to give signals to our enemy. You'd better admit it yourself, or things will go worse for you."

"Leave him alone for now. We'll get the information out of him at the command post."

Reb Itshe Meir heard their entire conversation, and his blood froze in his veins.

As soon as the sled rode into the military camp in a field not far from Kotsk, he was surrounded by little groups of soldiers who shouted: "You caught another spy? Another Jew? Ay, we're going to celebrate today!"

Reb Itshe Meirl didn't lose his composure. He asked them to take him straight to the camp commandant so that he could explain the situation.

But the soldiers were in no hurry to introduce him to the commandant. They took him into a peasant hut and placed two soldiers as a guard at the door.

Later a few soldiers came in with their rifles pointing at him, and ordered him to go with them. They took Reb Itshe Meirl to a small house that had been freshly whitewashed.

In one of the rooms sat a Polish officer who ordered them first of all to thoroughly search Reb Itshe Meirl. Meanwhile the officer asked where he came from, why he was going to Kotsk and, most of all, why he was telling them this story about General Ostrowski.

As they searched they found in one of Reb Itshe Meirl's pockets a package of manuscripts—a major responsum, part of his text *Khidushey HaRim*,[66] which he was then getting ready to publish. He had just recently written the responsum regarding a case of an abandoned wife, and as long as he was going to be seeing the Kotsker Rebbe, he wanted to show him the responsum to get the latter's approval of Reb Itshe Meirl's permission to remarry.

---

66. That is, Novellae of Reb Yitskhok Meir.

A Fire Burns in Kotsk

But when the soldiers came upon this "find," they joyfully brought it to the officer as if waiting to see what their reward would be for catching the dangerous spy with the goods.

The officer looked at the package of writings as if he had dug up buried treasure. He turned the papers over and over, and finally turned to Reb Itshe Meirl:

"Well, what's this? What do you have to say about this?"

The officer kept looking at the manuscripts as though they contained all of the secret military orders that would have fallen into the enemy's hands, if it weren't that he and his faithful soldiers were keeping an eye on all the roads, smelling out what the Jewish spies were up to.

"Nu, what's this?" the officer asked again.

Reb Itshe Meirl stood utterly perplexed. He began stammering, lacking words to explain in Polish about the abandoned woman whom he'd permitted to remarry.

"They are religious writings," answered Reb Itshe Meirl after some time.

"Really, that's what they are, not secret documents? If so, why did you write it in secret code, so we can't read it?"

"It's written in the holy script."

"If so, read me what it says there," the officer ordered.

"You won't understand it," answered Reb Itshe Meirl with a smile.

And indeed, what would the Polish officer have understood if Reb Itshe Meirl had read aloud to him his analysis of the legal ramifications of there being only a single witness to a husband's death?

But the Polish officer wasn't interested in excuses, and he shouted: "What do you mean, we won't understand? Dirty little Jew! Probably you're afraid to read it. We'll find somebody on our own who can read it through, and I pity you if we find out that it's not just religious writings as you're claiming!"

Reb Itshe Meirl couldn't stop trembling. Meanwhile various peasants were brought in, all of whom had been arrested on the roads on suspicion of espionage.

Reb Itshe Meirl looked through the window and in the gray light of early morning he saw a sled entering the courtyard. Out of it came a Jew who seemed to Reb Itshe Meirl to be half Jew, half soldier. He wore a gray fur-lined coat and a high military hat. When he took off the coat and left it on the sled, he suddenly took on the appearance of a Jewish pauper who wanders through the countryside begging alms.

Reb Itshe Meirl couldn't understand how the poor Jew with the carrot-red beard moved around the camp freely, running from one house to another, as if he were running the place.

Suddenly the door opened up, and to Reb Itshe Meirl's great wonder the red-hearded Jew walked straight up to the officer, who approached him with a cheerful shout: "Oh, Berko, when did you arrive? What did you bring along?"

"Lots of good things," said Berko, rubbing his hands.

"Well, okay, soon I'll get rid of these few spies, and then we'll talk," the officer said, continuing to slap Berko on his back.

Berko approached the table and spotted a package of writings in the Holy Tongue there.

"And what's this?" Berko asked the officer, as if he wanted to know all the secrets.

"Those are secret writings by a Jewish spy we caught today. We're waiting for you to read them over. The spy is over there," the officer added, pointing to Reb Itshe Meirl.

Berko turned toward Reb Itshe Meirl and the latter suddenly recognized a very familiar face. Berko came closer to Reb Itshe Meirl. He suddenly shouted, wringing his hands: "Who do I see here? Reb Itshe Meirl, what are you doing here?"

And even before Reb Itshe Meirl had time to answer, he began running around the room like a mouse in a trap. He ran toward the officer, then toward Reb Itshe Meir and back, grabbed the package of writings, immediately gave it to Reb Itshe Meirl and ordered that he be immediately brought back to the sled.

The officer watched Berko in wonderment and finally asked him, "What are you doing, Berko? Sure you're not making a mistake? We have to be very careful!"

"It's not your business," Berko yelled as if addressing a small child. "Don't mix in!"

And he addressed the soldiers in a loud voice: "Who had the nerve to harass this holy man? Whoever it was, the Devil take you! It's a good thing I happened to stop by today! Probably Heaven meant for me to have the merit of saving this holy saint!" he concluded, turning toward Reb Itshe Meirl.

And conducting Reb Itshe Meirl to the sled, Berko said, "Doubtless you're on your way to Kotsk. I'll accompany you, and it will give me the opportunity to submit a note."

Reb Itshe Meirl walked in a daze, as if he didn't believe what his eyes had just seen. In one second he had been rescued from certain death. He kept looking at Berko, as if he were the Prophet Elijah in disguise.

"Why are you looking at me like that?" asked Berko while Reb Itshe Meirl was climbing into the sled. "Don't you recognize me? I'm Berl Khayem's from Kuzmir! I'm secretly with the Polish rebels, and that's why I go around in these clothes. I often sneak over to the Russian side, find out the necessary information, and then pass it back to our camp. But I don't take any money for it—I do it out of loyalty to Poland and hatred of the Russians."

Throughout the journey, until the sled reached Kotsk, Berl kept telling Reb Itshe Meirl about all the Jews from the various towns who had volunteered as spies for Poland.

The sled was stopped a few more times by Polish military patrols, but each time, as soon as Berl Khayem's showed them a certain paper, the soldiers saluted him respectfully and immediately departed.

As soon as the sled arrived at the court of Kotsk, Reb Itshe Meirl went in and secluded himself with the Rebbe Reb Mendele.

It took a few hours until Reb Itshe Meirl left Reb Mendele's private room, and he immediately summoned the coachman to harness the horses and quickly drive back to Warsaw. He didn't want to see any of the Hasidim who were hanging around in the Kotsk study hall.

Berl Khayem's from Kuzmir went to Warsaw with Reb Itshe Meirl. As soon as the latter arrived in Warsaw, he rode to the house of his father-in-law, who awaited him at the doorstep. Reb Itshe Meirl shouted from the sled: "He said yes! He said we should give it! I'll tell you everything . . ." and he immediately went into his father-in-law's house, chilled to the bone.

22

The Kotsker Rebbe Issues a Call to Support the Polish Rebellion

The very evening Reb Itshe Meirl returned from Warsaw, he and his father-in-law Reb Moshe Khalfan went to see General Ostrowski. General Ostrowski had his headquarters at the barracks on Przejazd.

Reb Itshe Meirl and Reb Moshe Khalfan put on their silken Sabbath clothes and placed their high fur hats on their heads. They rode in Reb Moshe Khalfan's sled. Next to them rode two Jews belonging to the National Guard established by General Ostrowski. The two Jewish guardsmen served as a sort of honor guard sent by General Ostrowski, to protect them on the way and at the same time to accord them due respect.

Reb Itshe Meirl and Reb Moshe Khalfan didn't have to wait long in the corridor of the old barracks.

As soon as General Ostrowski found out that the two Jews he had sent for had arrived, he immediately ordered them to be ushered in.

The room in which General Ostrowski sat was old. The thick stone walls were decorated with various antique weapons, large maps, portraits of old Polish nationalist fighters. On the wall behind the chair where the General sat hung a large silk national flag embroidered in gold.

This was the flag of the Jewish city guard which had the Tetragrammaton inscribed in the middle of the Polish eagle. (Until the Second World War the flag was located in the collection of Dr. N. Davidson of Warsaw.)

General Ostrowski was happy to see Reb Moshe Khalfan and Reb Itshe Meirl. He invited them to sit and ordered the servant to bring in the old national Polish drink: a pot of double mead. Then he poured out large silver goblets for them.

Once General Ostrowski himself had downed a couple of large goblets, his tongue loosened a bit. He began praising the Jewish people, swearing every few minutes "I love the Jews," and insisted he was confident that Moshko Khalfan would lend the hundred thousand rubles.

"Well, Moshko, I didn't make a mistake, did I?" he addressed Reb Moshe Khalfan with a mischievous smile.

But it was Reb Itshe Meirl who actually answered him, saying, "My father-in-law has decided to assist the Polish rebellion and will lend the sum requested by the General."

The General became even more cheerful and began walking around the room saying: "You see, I knew we could get money from you Jews."

Reb Itshe Meirl suddenly sensed the full weight of the General's contempt for the Jews, and he answered, "We're not giving the money only because the General requested it, but because we Jews are interested in the revolt just the same as the Polish people themselves. True, people have always turned to Jews for money, but this time we're giving more than money, we're giving our lives."

"Yes, I know about it," General Ostrowski answered, sobering up a bit in response to Reb Itshe Meirl's sharp words. "I know about the heroism of the Jews!"

"You know about it, yet you don't want to acknowledge our sacrifices," continued Reb Itshe Meirl. "In all the towns innocent Jews are being hung on suspicion of espionage. Jewish life is cheap in the countryside. Every Polish soldier feels free to do what whatever he wants to a Jew; and if we're providing men and money for the Polish rebellion, the least we want in exchange is not to be treated as traitors."

"But this is impossible," General Ostrowski said in a more agitated tone. "By all means, give me facts—where and when were Jews abused?"

"Why should I provide lots of examples?" Reb Itshe Meirl boldly answered. "It happened to me personally. Just two days ago, when I left here for Kotsk, I was stopped on the way by Polish soldiers. They arrested me and took me to a military camp. They were on the verge of hanging me, but coincidentally a Jew who serves as a volunteer in the Polish army happened to recognize me and told them to free me."

"What is the name of that Jew?" asked General Ostrowski. "And why were you detained? What kind of suspicious matter did they find on you?"

"I don't know why I was detained. The only reason for suspicion was that I was traveling freely on the roads, even though I'm a Jew. They found religious writings in my possession, and they wanted to treat them as secret military documents. I don't know what the Jew's name is in your army, but we call him Berl Khayem's, and he's from Kuzmir."

"Oh," cried the general, slapping his hand on the table. "I think that's Berko. Wait a while. It seems that just today I got a report about the 'As I love God,' and it's starting to get interesting."

The general got up from his chair, strode to the fireproof cabinet in his spurred boots, took out a folder containing secret documents, and began ruffling through them until he stopped at a piece of paper that had a large, wax seal on its obverse. He began quietly reading, but soon he set the documents down on a table, quickly approached Reb Itshe Meirl and cheerfully called out:

"Aha! You're the Itzik Meirl who was detained on the road. You're the one that happened to, and you're the son-in-law of Moshe Khalfan. Why didn't you tell me about it?" he said, suddenly addressing Reb Itshe Meirl's father-n-law. "Why didn't you tell me what a wonderful son-in-law you have, and how much the Jews respect him? I was just looking at the report about your arrest," he turned back toward Reb Itshe Meirl. "Berko came to see me earlier and told me everything. The soldiers have already been punished. I'm delighted that you happen to be with me now because in any case I was thinking of sending for you so that we could have a chat. But let's postpone that until later. First things first. So, Moshe Khalfan, you're going to lend the money to the current Polish government? As collateral we will sign over to you the buildings in Warsaw, as already promised. Again, those are the theater, the council house, and the barracks on Przejazd." And with that General Ostrowski took out from the fireproof chest a contract written on sheets of parchment that had been prepared earlier.

Reb Moshe Khalfan slowly and precisely read through the contract and signed it. Then General Ostrowski signed and sealed the contract with his signet ring.

Next General Ostrowski took the contract, rolled it up as a scroll and placed it in a carved wooden sheath. Then, with a celebratory gesture, he handed it to Reb Moshe Khalfan.

Reb Moshe Khalfan took the contract and placed it in his capacious chest pocket. Then he asked the general to detail two reliable officers to deliver the chest with the golden ducats.

Reb Moshe Khalfan and Reb Itshe Meirl had already stood up to go, but the general asked Reb Itshe Meirl to stay with him for a few more minutes.

When Reb Moshe Khalfan had left, General Ostrowski reminded Reb Itshe Meirl of his second request—that the Kotsker Rebbe and Reb Itshe Meirl should both sign an appeal to the Jews to volunteer for the Jewish guard and to support the rebellion in any way they could.

The general also told Reb Itshe Meirl about the difficult struggle he had had convincing the Polish government to allow a certain category of Jews into the Polish guard. This category consisted of Jews who owned houses or considerable other property, and among them especially those who were prepared to shave their beards. His new goal was to create a national guard with the same status as the general guard, but which would also have the privilege of wearing beards, so that pious Jews would be able to volunteer.

Hasidim relate that the Kotsker Rebbe and Reb Itshe Meirl actually did issue an appeal to the Jewish population of Poland to volunteer for the Polish national guard.

Elderly Hasidim explain that the reason the appeal hasn't been found to this day is that after the rebellion failed, the Hasidim themselves destroyed all of the announcements, so that the Russian government wouldn't know about it.

More than 800 Jews were recruited for this new guard unit. The rest were assigned to the local security patrols, and both groups came through with shining colors.

The best evidence for this is what General Ostrowski himself relates about the guard. He writes, "When one's eye fell on these impoverished, nearly naked, terrified people, who looked as if though the authorities had always persecuted them, there was no choice but to give aid to this, obviously the most persecuted segment of the population of our country."

And further: "Everywhere the Jews fought like true heroes. Although they seemed to be timid, nevertheless they never held back fighting at the front line together with the Polish military."

Unfortunately, the self-sacrifice of the Jews was of no avail. The Jews' voluntary service in the Polish army couldn't quell the Polish guardsmen's persecution of the Jews, even after General Ostrowski issued a direct order to the army, consistent with Reb Itshe Meirl's request, that in this critical moment for the fatherland it was necessary to stop the pogroms against the Jewish population.

The upshot came on May 30, 1831, when the Sejm passed a law expelling the Jews from the army, and simultaneously imposing on them payment of a certain amount for being released from army service.

On September 8, 1831, following a major battle, the Russian General Paskiewicz took Warsaw.

All the leaders of the rebellion managed to escape abroad in time. Likewise, the Kotsker Rebbe, along with Reb Itshe Meirl, was obligated to escape to Lemberg.

According to Hasidic legend, a certain Hasid betrayed them, motivated by the enmity of the Galician Hasidim toward the Kotsker approach.

By chance Reb Itshe Meirl managed to escape prison. He quickly went to see the chief rabbi of Lemberg at the time, Reb Yakov Orenshteyn, author of the volume *Yeshues Yankev*, and immediately began discussing scholarly matters with him.

The Rabbi of Lemberg was astonished by Reb Itshe Meirl's sharp insights, and asked him who he was and where he came from. Reb Itshe Meirl answered that he was a student of the Rebbe who was currently imprisoned in the Lemberg jail. The Rabbi of Lemberg said to him that he hadn't heard much about the Kotsker Rebbe, so he wanted to know who the Kotsker Rebbe's grandfather was.

Reb Itshe Meirl answered that a grandfather isn't always the most important thing, and he cited a verse from the Torah to support his claim. "A man who is a leader of his father's household" (Numbers 1:4)—this means: someone whose authority does not derive from ancestral merit, not through inherited wealth, but someone who is worthy in his own right to have the lineage begin with him.

The Rabbi of Lemberg continued his scholarly discussion with Reb Itshe Meirl, and he was so taken with the latter's intellect that he immediately intervened with the government to get the Kotsker Rebbe released from prison.

A Fire Burns in Kotsk

▲▼▲▼▼

After the Russian government had thoroughly suppressed the rebellion, the Reb Mendele and Reb Itshe Meirl returned to Poland. They changed their last names, so that if the government got ahold of one of the proclamations in support of the rebellion they could not be held accountable.

The Kotsker Rebbe changed his last name from Halpern to Morgenstern, and Reb Itshe Meirl changed his last name from Rotenberg to Alter.

Since that time all the descendants of the Kotsker Rebbe have retained the name Morgenstern and the descendants of Reb Itshe Meirl, Alter.

The Kotsker Rebbe once again settled in Kotsk, and Reb Itshe Meirl in Warsaw.

23

The Battle Between Maskilim and Hasidim in Warsaw

Reb Itshe Meirl reopened his yeshiva in Warsaw and recruited Hasidim for Kotsk, but suddenly there broke out an intense struggle between the Hasidim and the Maskilim, the Jewish Enlighteners, sparked by the visit of the "Minister," Moses Montefiore,[67] to Warsaw.

The Maskilim were preparing a memorandum for Montefiore concerning the introduction of secular subjects into the traditional Jewish schools and about general reform of the educational system.

The Hasidim, under the leadership of the Vurker Rebbe, the Kotsker Rebbe and Reb Itshe Meirl, publicly opposed all reforms, for in their opinion these would certainly have led to assimilation, leaving the path open to conversion itself.

But in order to better understand the bitter opposition of the Hasidim to reforms or any kind of change whatsoever in Jewish life, it is necessary to become better acquainted with the cultural and economic situation of the Jews in Poland at that time.

Following the November rebellion in 1830, relations between Jews and Poles hardly improved. Even before the firing stopped the struggles began in Warsaw concerning such "vital" matters as, for example, the buildings located on the corners opening to those streets where Jews were not allowed to live. (Jews were forbidden to live on many of Warsaw's streets at that time. The Jews were concentrated on and around Grzybow Street.) Should the houses be considered as fronting on the street where the Jews were forbidden to live, or should the permissive view be taken in cases where the entrance leads to a "permitted" street but windows face on a "forbidden" street?

---

67. Moses Montefiore (1784–1885), British philanthropist who personally appealed to the tsar in 1846 to alleviate restrictions on Jews in the Pale of Settlement and Kingdom of Poland. Montefiore was, nevertheless, a modernizer who favored Jewish educational and sartorial reform.

A Fire Burns in Kotsk

The Jews of Warsaw were obligated to diligently study the city plan, in order to determine which streets Jews were permitted to live on and which not.

And in 1832 the government declared that those Jews who lived in corner buildings had to arrange to have their entrance only on the "permitted" streets. On the other hand, they didn't place any particular restrictions on the stores in those buildings.

Then a group of Jews calling themselves "Deputation of the Jews of the Kingdom of Poland" addressed an appeal to Viceroy Iwan Paskiewicz to expand their civil rights.

Paskiewicz was actually sympathetic to the Jewish request, and forwarded it to Tsar Nikolai with the observation that the Jewish population had to receive attention, since they were the least loyal to the "legitimate government" of all the residents of Poland—but nothing came of it.

Instead, a few years later the Jews came to receive equal treatment with the overall population regarding the heavy burden of military service. Initially, due to the sorry state of the government budget in Poland, a minor regulation was introduced requiring Jews to continue paying the recruitment tax in addition to their actual service, but that law never went on the books. But the introduction of general military service caused great consternation among the religious Jews, because the draft age was set as low as twelve. The Hasidim and other religious Jews were afraid that if their children were taken from them so young, they would be torn away completely from Jewishness, and when they completed their military service they would be culturally lost and alienated from Jewish ways.

Reb Itshe Meirl and a group of Hasidic activists from Warsaw therefore appealed to Paskiewicz to take the particular conditions of Jewish life into account, and not to draft any young Jewish children. Thanks to the intervention of these Hasidic activists, led by Reb Itshe Meirl, the draft age for Jews was raised to 20. In this manner the Hasidic Jews of Warsaw managed to avert the application in Poland of the cantonist system which poisoned the lives of the Jews of Russia.

The Jews had to continue paying the special "kosher tax" on the pretext that the Jews were still not citizens, although they were serving in the military.

Moses Montefiore was deeply involved in the effort to improve the situation of the Jews in Poland and throughout the Russian Empire. Starting on the first of March, 1846, Montefiore visited St. Petersburg, Vilna, and finally Warsaw.

The Minister Moses Montefiore wrote a special memorandum to the government in which he described the catastrophic living conditions of the Jews in Poland.

He pointed to a range of cities where the Jews were entirely banned. In other cities, Jews were only allowed to live on certain streets. They were banned from the frontier corridor. The Jewish artisans were strictly limited in their range of activity because they could not hire journeymen or day laborers. Nor could they apprentice to Christian masters, so that they might themselves be recognized as masters one day. The tax on kosher meat and poultry was another burden on the population. They also had to pay a fee before entering Warsaw.

In many respects the Jews were effectively outlaws. For example, a Jew could not appear in court as witness against a Christian.

In government circles, in Russia as in Poland, attempts were made to smear the Jews. It was said that they avoided productive labor, engaging in petty commerce instead, being disinclined to any agricultural work; that they didn't want to engage in crafts, preferring to deal in contraband; that their clothing set them apart from the Christian population; and that in general they were a dark, backward mass.

Montefiore pointed out in his memorandum to the contrary: that there was a greater percentage of artisans among the Jewish population than among the general population, and that the Jews undertook the most difficult occupations. He specified among other things that among the Jews there were many bricklayers, smiths, and others engaged in heavy crafts and that the number of Jews ready to engage in productive labor would certainly have been much higher if they had not been subject to unjustifiable restrictions at every turn. The best evidence of this, wrote Montefiore, was that when Alexander I's government had demanded that Jews undertake agricultural labor, they eagerly responded. The results were unimpressive only because the government had placed terrible obstacles in their way.

As far as distinctive clothing went, wrote Montefiore, the Polish government itself had forced the Jews to wear it three hundred years earlier. In any case, simply on account of the fact that the wearing of distinctive clothing had no basis in the Jewish religion, the Jews themselves would gradually become unaccustomed to it.

Yet Montefiore wanted to become personally acquainted with the larger Jewish settlements of Poland, and thus he visited Vilna and Warsaw.

And when the Jews of Warsaw learned that Montefiore was going to visit their city, they prepared to greet him with highest honors. This was the subject of a quiet competition between the Maskilim and the Hasidim. Each side wanted to win Montefiore over. The Maskilim worked on ways to please the "Minister," while the Hasidim knew that he was a pious Jew, even though he didn't know anything about Hasidism yet. The Hasidim composed a paean in honor of his arrival.

In those times the Hasidim regarded the Maskilim as missionaries who wanted to destroy Judaism, because under the conditions of those times it should have been clear that any attempt to spread modern culture among the Jewish masses would necessarily denigrate the sacredness of Judaism. Therefore it was important to avoid every effort at change, even those aimed at customs and superstitions that have nothing to do with true Jewish faith, in the belief that the Enlightenment itself will cause many backward customs to die. Perhaps this was a longer road, but it was a safer one.

But the Maskilic intelligentsia were looking for some easy victories, and they began to get friendly with the government, although they understood well that the government was not friendly to Jews, and that the Jewish moral revival that the Maskilim constantly preached was something the government didn't understand as anything but a way to uproot Judaism altogether, or better, as a way to lead the Jews to the dominant religion.

And indeed, the desire of the ruling circles to turn the Jews into Catholics began to become clear.

A Bible Society was even founded in Warsaw, with the goal of spreading Christianity among the Jews. Respected missionaries to the Jews were brought from London and given special privileges and rights.

The Jewish converts were welcomed with open arms into the highest Polish society and shown particular respect. These converts married into the leading Polish nobility, and then were themselves adorned with various noble titles. It is enough to mention the daughters of the famous Yehudis Yakubovitsh who, after their conversions, married members of the top Polish and French aristocracy.

And many Jewish Maskilim were unashamed to admit quite freely that their notion of assimilation meant complete Polonization of the Jews, including conversion. It is thus no wonder that all of their efforts elicited mistrust among the broad Jewish masses, and most of all among the Hasidim. This was even more true since, under their influence, even those institutions which may well have been useful and necessary for the Jewish population took on a character that betrayed their original goal—such as the rabbinical seminary, which raised a generation of assimilationists who alienated the Jews and detested the Jewish religion.

So the Hasidim were distraught when they heard that the "Minister" was coming to Warsaw and that the Maskilim were preparing to present him with a petition.

And since Montefiore was seeing so many government representatives in Warsaw, the Maskilim announced that they wanted to discuss with him the situation of the Jews in Poland.

But the Hasidim were busy, too.

Reb Itshe Meirl called a meeting at the home of his father-in-law, Reb Moshe Khalfan, to consider the next steps. The meeting was attended by the Vurker Rebbe and by a special representative of the Kotsker court. All night they sat discussing whether to come out in complete opposition to the Maskilim, or to talk to him first, since the "Minister" might not understand what Hasidism is.

The Vurker Rebbe, who always emphasized the good points of the Jews, held that they should first go see the "Minister." At the meeting he said to the Hasidim, "I'm struggling again with the verse in the Passover Haggadah: 'If He had brought us to Mount Sinai and not given us the Torah, it would have been enough for us.' If we hadn't gotten the Torah, what good would it have been for us to be brought to Mt. Sinai? The importance of Mt. Sinai, in addition to being the place where the Torah was received, is that it was the first place where the Jews were unified, as it is written, 'Israel camped there across from the mountain' (Exodus 19:2). All of them as one! That was a significant thing in itself, that alone was 'enough.'

"But on account of our many sins," the Vurker Rebbe concluded, "there is no longer unity among Jews, especially among those who have run away, who don't want to be considered members of the Jewish collective any longer, and whose numbers increase from day to day. So the question returns, in what sense was that 'enough?'"

And the meeting determined that the Vurker Rebbe and Reb Itshe Meirl should visit Moses Montefiore and explain to him what Hasidism was, and convince him not to promote the reform of the Jewish schools in Poland.

24

"Minister" Montefiore and the Vurker Rebbe

Before Itshe Meirl and the Vurker Rebbe went to visit Moses Montefiore, Reb Itshe Meirl went to see the Maskil Matisyahu Rosen. He asked him not to convince Montefiore to reform the Jewish schools. But he got nowhere. Indeed, Matisyahu Rosen explained to Reb Itshe Meirl that the Maskilin were the true Jews, and that only they had the right to speak in the name of the people.

After Reb Itshe Meirl's visit to the Maskil Rosen, Reb Itshe Meirl wrote a letter about the matter to the magnate Reb Avrom Yanover.

Here's what Reb Itshe Meirl wrote in his letter: "Given that he considers himself a saint, even though he violates the entire Torah, and he wants others as well to be 'saints' like he is, what is there for me to say? Woe to us that such has transpired in our days. And it's not enough for them that they transgress the Torah in public and there's nothing you can say to them, but anyone who mentions the name 'Jew' in public and who holds fast to God's Torah is like a thorn in their eyes."

Montefiore had heard long before that there was a sect called the Hasidim in Poland, and that it enjoyed the loyalty of most of the Jewish masses, especially the poorer sectors. But he had no notion what Hasidism was.

He knew his history: Hasidism had arisen after the Frankist movement. Consistent with the vague rumors circulating about Hasidism in Western Europe, Montefiore supposed that the Hasidim were some sort of secret mystic sect, led by "tzaddikim" who were false prophets or charlatans, and who exploited the benighted, backward elements for their own worldly purposes.

And when the two Warsaw Maskilim, the magnates Matisyahu Rosen and Epstein visited Montefiore and described the situation of the Jews of Poland to him, they told him about the sect of Hasidim.

"I'm very interested in seeing the representatives of this sect," said Montefiore during their conversation. "Everything I hear from you is

A Fire Burns in Kotsk

very interesting, but I'd like to speak with them myself, and to meet their leaders face to face. Are they actually interesting characters?" he asked the two Maskilim, and he immediately added: "Perhaps you can explain to me who the founder of the sect was, and whether they are really apostates against the holy Torah?"

"The founder of the sect," said Rosen in a contemptuous tone, beginning to lecture Montefiore on the history of Hasidism, "was a certain Jew from the country named Yisroel Mezhbuzher, who made his living treating women's illnesses with herbal remedies. He was uneducated, but he had a certain charisma and attracted a group of similar ignoramuses, common people. He started calling them 'Hasidim' and he gave himself the 'modest' title of Baal Shem Tov (the Good Master of Names) or Besht as they say today. Since then there have arisen a number of leaders, or maybe we should say misleaders, who call themselves 'tzaddikim' or 'rebbes.' All of them, may we be spared!, are big ignoramuses and what they teach their disciples is nothing but superstition."

"And yet yesterday we met a Polish count," responded Montefiore, "who occupies a very respected role in the government, and when we started talking about the Jews, he told me that his father had told him that somewhere in a small town—I think he mentioned the name 'Koznits' or 'Kozenets,' lived a tzaddik, a leader of that very same sect. The count's father frequently went to see him in order to get his advice on various matters. Whatever the tzaddik told him to do, he did because the tzaddik was something of a prophet, according to the count."

"That was a rabbi who was called the 'Kozhenitser Preacher,'" answered the Maskil Epstein in an aggrieved tone. "He happened to be well-learned and he was very smart, and that's how he managed to deceive the Polish noblemen. Counts and princes really did go to see him, and in various ways he fooled them into believing the various pieces of advice he gave them about business deals, something he had no knowledge of himself."

"And who is this 'wonder rabbi' of Kotsk, whom a Polish count described to me yesterday as a very interesting person?"

"A sadly confused soul," Epstein answered quickly. "He's gathered a crowd around him, and he carries on in his bizarre way with them."

"I'd be very interested to see them. When will I have a day free?" he asked, suddenly turning to his secretary, Dr. Levi. "I would like to go to Kotsk and speak to this 'wonder rabbi.' I will immediately be able to determine what sort of person he is."

The two Maskilim became extremely anxious. They were afraid that the Kotsker Rebbe with his sharp turn of phrase might make a good impression on the Minister. They waited with their mouths half-open for Dr. Levi's answer.

But Dr. Levi himself was something of a Maskil, and he already was somewhat prejudiced against all of these Hasidim and rebbes. So Dr. Levi took out his diary and began reading: Tomorrow such-and-such count is coming, in the evening we're visiting institutions, then a visit from the city president.

He listed a long series of appointments and concluded: "It seems to me that we won't have any time to stop at Kotsk."

"It's a shame, a shame," answered Montefiore, taking out his ivory tobacco box and slowly lifting it toward his nose. He passed the tobacco box by his nostrils, back and forth, and stood up, then walked toward the window lost in thought.

Suddenly Montefiore called out, "Dr. Levi! Look at that tumult out on the street. Are they beating Jews, God forbid! Send a messenger straight to the governor to find out what happened," Montefiore added in terror.

Levi and the two Maskilim ran toward the window and saw a black human mass crowding around a coach, which moved forward very slowly. In the coach sat three Jews, two in the front and the third facing them. Hundreds of adult Jews and youngsters hung near the coach. Among them were dozens of policemen who were brutally driving the huge crowd.

It was the Vurker Rebbe and Reb Itshe Meirl coming to see Montefiore. All those in Warsaw who had once been Pshiskhe Hasidim and now were loyal to Vurke or Kotsk were in the street to see the Vurker Rebbe.

The Hasidim ran after the coach and hung close to the wheels, while policemen ran around among them, beating them constantly because an order had been issued banning Jewish demonstrations while Montefiore was in town. The policemen kept beating the crowd and trying to get them to disperse, but the Hasidim paid them no attention, as if they didn't feel the blows that rained down on them. Their eyes were fixed on the coach in which the Vurker Rebbe was sitting.

By the time the coach approached the house where Montefiore was staying, the two Maskilim recognized the Vurker Rebbe and Reb Itshe Meirl, and they reassured Montefiore.

"Those are two leaders of the Hasidim, two 'tzaddikim,' and that's what the Hasidim look like. They make us look bad in the eyes of the Christian population, they chase after the rebbes like a tribe of primitives."

"But they must be extraordinary personalities if they can attract so many people to themselves, rushing after them so enthusiastically. Those people don't even feel the policemen hitting them, and indeed why are the police hitting them?" asked Montefiore. "The task of the police is to keep the peace, not to beat well-behaved citizens. This is a barbaric country with barbaric ways," Montefiore concluded more to himself. And he addressed Dr. Levy: "If the 'tzaddikim' have come to see me, let them right in."

In front of the house where Montefiore was living stood various noble coaches. From time to time a countess would step out, on her way to visit Montefiore's wife Judith. Attendants with white wigs and gloves stood by the coaches, opening the golden doors and leading and countesses and other ladies of the court.

The Vurker Rebbe and Reb Itshe Meirl were almost propelled into the house by the huge crowd of Hasidim, but only the two people who had been sitting in the coach were allowed into the house, and the huge crowd of Hasidim stayed outside.

A number of Jews from Warsaw and the surrounding towns were gathered in the foyer of Montefiore's house. They had come to pour out their bitter hearts to the Jewish "Minister," and Dr. Levy had one answer for all of them: "Your 'Minister' Montefiore isn't at home!" When the secretary saw the Vurker Rebbe, he asked him to wait a bit, quietly letting him know that he would soon be admitted.

It hurt the Vurker Rebbe to see the other Jews being deceived, and he smiled bitterly.

"Now," said the Vurker Rebbe to the secretary Dr. Levy, "I understood the saying in the Talmud, 'Hospitality is greater than welcoming the Divine Presence' (Shabbat 127b). When our leader Moses encountered the Divine Presence, it is written 'and Moses hid his face' (Exodus 3:6). He only hid his face—but when rich men see a poor beggar coming, they hide themselves altogether!"

Dr. Levy got the point, reluctantly smiled, and quickly disappeared into the room where Montefiore sat.

"Let them enter!" Montefiore ordered Dr. Levy.

The two Maskilim apparently wanted to stay in the room while the Hasidic delegation met with Montefiore, but Dr. Levy indicated to them that they should go into the next room. Montefiore never wanted others present when he met with guests. The two Maskilim went to the next room, planning to wait until the rebbes departed, so that they could refute their claims.

Dr. Levy conducted three Jews into the room, announced: "These are the Rebbes," and went out.

Montefiore, seeing these Jews with their long silk clothing, rose out of respect and asked them to sit.

In front of him sat the Vurker Rebbe, small, thin, with a dark face, an even darker, thick beard, shot through with threads of silver hair, and with thick brows, dressed in a high fur hat with a broad satin belt wrapped around his silken gown. Next to him sat his secretary Moyshe, a tall Jew with a strict, angry face, with a bristly red beard and two long arms ready to start swinging if anyone dared to impugn the honor of the Rebbe. At his right sat Reb Itshe Meirl, whose bearing elicited respect from all who saw him.

"Are you all rebbes?" asked Montefiore, after they had all sat down.

"No!" answered Reb Itshe Meirl. "Only this Jew," he indicated the Vurker, "is a rebbe, and the second is his secretary, and I am barely a Hasid."

The impression Montefiore got from them was entirely different from everything he'd been led to believe until now. It couldn't be that these were just charlatans who deceived backward people. "No," he thought to himself, "they must be deep thinkers. Eyes and faces like that don't belong to swindlers."

"How can I help you?" he asked.

"We heard about your greatness and about your commitment to Jewish welfare," began the Vurker Rebbe. "We heard about your visit to Russia to meet with the Tsar, to intercede on behalf of the Jewish people, and we prayed to God that you, great Minister, might win over the Tsar and all the ministers who surround him. And therefore we came to ask you to reverse the decree about reforming our schools, which have been the sole basis of our continued existence until now."

"What?" Montefiore asked crossly. "Do you really want the people to continue being excluded from knowledge, so that you can keep them in the dark and propagate your sectarian teachings, this Hasidism that is against the Torah?"

"On the contrary," Reb Itshe Meirl responded calmly, "we want to avoid these reforms so that the Jews will be able to continue observing the Torah and all its commandments, just as our ancestors kept them."

"We do try to observe the Torah," modestly responded the Vurker Rebbe.

"And do you know how to study the traditional texts at least?" asked Montefiore further.

"We try to know how," answered the Vurker Rebbe.

And with that, the Vurker Rebbe and Reb Itshe Meirl began to articulate their claims to Montefiore. Montefiore had great difficulty understanding their Yiddish, and eventually he asked Dr. Levy to come in and interpret. The Vurker Rebbe finished their conversation by saying, "We do not want to keep the Jews in exile. On the contrary, we want them to sense that the Divine Presence and the entire collective are in exile. As our Rebbe Reb Bunem of Pshiskhe explained the verse: 'And I brought you forth from the sufferings of Egypt' (Exodus 6:6). The worst thing is when you stop feeling the exile, when you become accustomed to being subservient and overly humble. 'And I brought you forth from tolerating Egypt—'[68] if you're already at the stage where you can put up with exile and it doesn't bother you any more, then it's too late for waiting, that's when God said it's high time to get you out of there!"

Dr. Levy interpreted this homily for the "Minister," whose eyes lit up with joy.

---

68. The Hebrew verb *lisbol* means both "to suffer" and "to tolerate."

And Montefiore said to Dr. Levy, "Call in the two guests who were here earlier. Let them hear the things that are being said here, and let's hear their answers."

At first Reb Itshe Meirl was afraid when he saw the two Maskilim, but he immediately calmed down and they began arguing in front of Montefiore. The latter didn't attend to the whole dispute between the Vurker Rebbe and Reb Itshe Meirl on one hand and the Maskilim on the other. Instead he watched the Vurker Rebbe's gestures. He saw in front of him a person who lived in another world, a mystical, esoteric world that was alien to Montefiore—but the Rebbe gained Montefiore's respect.

And when the Maskilim kept insisting that the Hasidim denigrated Torah scholars, the Vurker Rebbe answered: "There are two important mountains. Mt. Sinai, where the Jews received the Torah, and Mt. Moriah, where Abraham led Isaac to the altar. A question presents itself: Why was the Holy Temple built on Mt. Moriah, and not on Mt. Sinai, where the Torah was given? And the answer is: The place where a Jew is prepared to stretch out his neck before the Almighty is much more significant in the eyes of the Divine than the place where the Torah was given. Torah and scholarship are certainly good, but the main thing is willingness to sacrifice all for Judaism!"

Montefiore was delighted by the Vurker Rebbe's homily, and when he took his leave, it seemed that the Vurker Rebbe had won the day, and that Montefiore was convinced by the Hasidim.

But Hasidism was still alien to him. He himself could make no sense of the dispute between the Hasidim and the Maskilim. When Montefiore submitted his memorandum on "The Condition of Jewish Education in Russia and Poland," he did not take the pleas of the Hasidic delegation into account at all.

25

The Kotsker Rebbe after His Second Marriage

After the marriage of the Kotsker Rebbe to Reb Itshe Meirl's sister-in-law the Kotsker Rebbe grew more familiar with his Hasidim. Leading Kotsker Hasidim themselves didn't understand what had caused the change, and instead they just shrugged their shoulders.

For the Pshiskhe Hasidim Kotsk became a Paradise. The Rebbe became more cheerful. He allowed people to speak to him while they were handing him a note, and in general he grew more calm. He didn't harass his Hasidim as he used to. He also began to come into the study house, chatting with the Hasidim, repeating a clever saying of his Rebbe Reb Bunem of Pshiskhe, and from time to time a smile would even appear on his anxious face.

The Hasidim thought they had gotten their old Rebbe back. Some of the Hasidim even dared to ask him for advice about material matters.

It began with Ayzikl Amshinover, who was a Kotsker Hasid but no great scholar. One time he came and handed the Rebbe a note. As was the custom in Kotsk, he wrote, "For spiritual healing and fear of Heaven." And when the Rebbe gave him his blessing, Ayzik stood a moment longer. The Rebbe asked him, "Ayzik, why are you so downcast?" Ayzik stood in terror, and he was afraid to answer, but suddenly he burst into tears, covered his face with his kerchief, and told the Rebbe that his wife had been suffering from a leg disease for weeks, and he was incapable of running a business himself. She used to go to the fairs while he sat in the synagogue, and now she was in bed all the time with swollen feet, and he was left without a penny for food.

As soon as Ayzik had finished telling the Rebbe about his troubles, he regretted it because he knew that the Rebbe never wanted to hear that kind of request. He thought that the Rebbe would dismiss him immediately. But all the Hasidim who happened to be in the Rebbe's reception room were astonished to hear the Rebbe ask Ayzik to repeat his wife's name and the name of the disease, and when the Rebbe began to sigh: "Your wife is sick, a sick woman in the house, such troubles!" And the Rebbe finally wished Ayzik that this wife might be healed.

Quickly the rumor spread through the Kotsk court that the Rebbe would hear supplications about material matters. Hasidim began asking the Rebbe for advice—this one about livelihood, this one about children. The Rebbe calmly heard them all out, responded to each and wished him whatever he needed.

People at the court began saying to each other that Reb Itshe Meirl had foreseen all of this, and that's why he had insisted in the match with his sister-in-law and pushed so hard for the wedding to be celebrated quickly. They said that the Kotsker Rebbe had suffered greatly with his first wife. He who always insisted on the highest standards, he who wanted only elite Hasidim, couldn't tolerate his wife, who was a simple rabbi's wife, who didn't understand him at all, but instead kept distracting him with her petty domestic concerns. In addition she was cross, and always wanted to demonstrate that she was running the show, that she could accomplish what his top Hasidim couldn't. She routinely made his days bitter. And the people at the court related that while the Kotsker Rebbe was still a disciple of the Rebbe Reb Bunem, he had once spent three straight years at Pshiskhe. They remembered that when he came home, his wife didn't want to let him into the house, shouting, "Go back where you've been until now."

On that occasion the Kotsker Rebbe had to go to his comrade, the future Hasid Reb Mordkhe Yosef Izhbitser, and ask him to convince his wife to let him back into the house, without causing a scandal in town. But his wife wouldn't let him cross the threshold of his house for four weeks, and he had to stay with Reb Mordkhe Yosef.

Only four weeks later, when his wife was ready for him to come home and be a husband like all husbands, did the Kotsker Rebbe finally leave town. He quickly began to long to see his Rebbe, and he and Reb Mordkhe Yosef went to Pshiskhe. They really meant to spend just a couple of days with the Rebbe, but as it turned out they didn't leave Pshiskhe for four months.

And the people at court said to each other that the Rebbe's second wife was good-natured and had great respect for the Rebbe. She didn't do anything without first checking with her brother-in-law, Reb Itshe Meirl.

The Rebbe's wife was also very intelligent, and she knew how to run the court. She introduced a new arrangement: since her husband, the Kotsker Rebbe, never took contributions, his young wife sat in the front room and collected contributions for the maintenance of the court. She would slip the coins into her apron and then bind it in little bundles. The Hasidim even said that the Rebbe himself didn't know about it, but even if he had, he wouldn't have said anything because everything his wife did was acceptable to him.

And indeed, lately the court had been crowded with Jewish agricultural brokers and wealthy rural Jews who came to the Rebbe to celebrate and to ask for cures for their sick wives and children. The news had spread throughout the region that the Kotsker Rebbe was receiving common people and brokers, and that he had become altogether empathetic. It was even said that it was not uncommon for him to see a Jew weeping and to weep along, and once he said to a Hasid that a Jew, even if he is a Hasid, is obligated to help his wife earn their living!

Those who were constantly with the Rebbe, the "constant benchwarmers," as the village Jews called them, the ones who spent months on end with the Rebbe and only went home for a few weeks a year to see their wives and children, began to live it up. They kept taking "contributions" from the brokers and the rich village Jews. The common people were happy to give them coins, since the resident Hasidim were willing to be their friends.

On one occasion a new recruit came, a wealthy son-in-law who wanted to become one of the Rebbe's regulars. First they took his gold watch and chain, turned him upside down and emptied his pockets on the table, and only then was he considered one of the regulars. He lived from the communal fund kept by Reb Hersh Tomashover, and ate from the kitchen that had been set up by the study house.

Reb Itshe Meirl was also in the study house, engrossed in study. From time to time he would approach the table where the regulars sat, hear one of their witticisms, have a drink with them, and then return to his studies. Since he had become the Rebbe's brother-in-law the Hasidim treated him with more respect, although the Kotsker way had always been to belittle one's own ego and that of others.

And once when Reb Itshe Meirl was walking around the study house with Reb Mordkhe Yosef Izhbitser discussing Hasidism, they approached the table where Reb Hersh Tomashover sat with a group of Hasidim.

They sat on the side, familiarly addressed an old Pshiskhe Hasid: "You, move over!" and took a bit of the liquor that Reb Hersh Tomashover was passing out from a bottle wrapped in a kerchief. That kept everyone from seeing how much was left in the bottle and also was thought to help assure that the blessings in the liquor would accrue to the drinkers. And Reb Hersh Tomashover explained to the regulars the significance of drinking liquor.

"I'm going to tell you a story," said Reb Hersh Tomashover. "Once we were sitting in the study house in Pshiskhe—our Rebbe may he be preserved; 'Black Yitskhok' (the Vurker Rebbe); and I. We were drinking a few drops of liquor. Suddenly an elderly village Jew came in and pushed his way to the Rebbe's door. Our Rebbe may he live asked him: 'Mr. Jew, what's your hurry? Probably you've got a cow in your barn who has trouble giving birth?'

"'No!' answered the village Jew, and he told us a story that he just wanted to ask the Rebbe for advice, that since he was an old Jew his children wouldn't let him work in the fields anymore, and he didn't know what to do all day.

"Our Rebbe spoke up: 'That's not something you have to go to the Rebbe about. We can give you good advice. Buy yourself a Bible with Yiddish translation, and study it all day.'

"The Jew contributed a valuable coin that he had prepared to give to the Rebbe, and we sent for more liquor.

"A few weeks ago," Reb Hersh Tomashover continued, "after people all through the area found out that Reb Mendele was receiving simple Jews, I suddenly saw an elderly village Jew pushing his way to the door, trying to get to see the Rebbe. I looked at him carefully and saw that it was the same village Jew who had come to Pshiskhe. I asked him: 'What happened this time? Have you learned the entire Bible?'

"No," he answered me, "I only came to thank the Rebbe because only later did I realize why he told me to study the Bible. It came in very handy.'

"And the elderly village Jew told us that one time a grandchild of his had fallen sick, and everything thought that the child was dying. Suddenly the old man remembered the story of Elisha the Prophet, and he did the same thing: He lay across the child's body, spread his hands on his hands, his feet on his feet and his face on his face, and 'What can I tell you?' the village Jew concluded. 'My grandchild became healthy again! That's why I wanted to thank the Rebbe for his good advice.'"

Reb Itshe Meirl, who had also heard the story, spoke up: "We see once again that the main thing is always to have the right intentions. It may well be that the simple village Jew rose momentarily to the level of a prophet."

"If so," responded Reb Hersh Tomashover, "if the main thing is really just the right intent, then a glass of liquor can also bring us to the right intent."

"But they have to be rich," responded a young regular, "both the liquor and the intent."

"Rich, to be sure," smiled Reb Hersh Tomashover, "and let's drink to that."

The regulars enjoyed Reb Hersh Tomashover's witticism, and they all took a drink of the liquor. Then they danced a bit, and when they sat back down at the table, Reb Hersh Tomashover called to Reb Yakov Moshe Kutner: "Give us a few rubles for liquor."

Reb Yakov Moshe was wealthy and learned, but he was a stingy moneylender. He resisted giving the money right away. Reb Hersh Tomashover said to him, "Now I can understand the simple meaning of the verse, 'Do not lend your money at interest' (Leviticus 25:37). What does the word translated as interest, *neshekh*, mean? That you shouldn't bite. What does the Torah mean with this reference to biting? Why did the Torah use a metaphor of biting to refer to interest?

"In order to understand the verse, I'll tell you a story:

"When the Jews were leaving Egypt, they borrowed from the Egyptians many silver and golden items. But not every Jew managed to borrow these things. There was a certain learned Jew who had borrowed much from the Egyptians, and when the Jews were already in the desert this Jew set up a gold shop where he sold precious rings, earrings, and goblets. And many Jews who needed these things had to get them from him.

"But there was no money to pay for things in the desert, and when somebody wanted a pair of earrings for his wife, or a ring, he came to the Jew who kept the store. But the Jew didn't want to just lend everything out, so he came upon a plan to make everybody sign a loan document, in which he promised to pay for the item with interest once they reached the Land of Israel.

"The lender did a great deal of business handing out precious items in exchange for this written promise to pay later with interest.

"But when our teacher Moses received the Torah at Mt. Sinai and conveyed it to the Jews, Moses knew all the Jews in the desert very well. When Moses reached the verse, 'Do not lend your silver at interest,' the lender shouted, 'I'm not going to lend anything from now on!'

"Then the lender started pestering Moses—after all, he was a learned Jew, and he knew about the way to make loans at interest permissible under Jewish law. He wanted to demonstrate to Moses that this formula could be used.

"Moses said to him: 'Come here and I'll explain to you the verse, "Don't give out your silver for biting."[69] Even if you avail yourself of a way to lend at interest in accordance with Jewish law, you shouldn't be so greedy that the borrower has to work while you sit and study and go to see a rebbe,'" concluded Reb Hersh Tomashover, "'and bite into what's already prepared for you.'"

Reb Yakov Moshe was ready to take his purse out and pay for the liquor, but one of the regulars, the son of a rich man from Warsaw, beat him to it, coming up with several rubles so that they could send for more liquor.

Reb Itshe Meirl, who had been sitting at the table the whole time next to Reb Mordkhe Yosef Izhbitser, called to Reb Mordkhe Yosef while the latter was getting up: "The old times are coming back like in Pshiskhe. Now, I think, you'll agree that the Rebbe's path is the right one!"

"No," angrily retorted Reb Mordkhe Yosef, "by no means! I couldn't agree when the Rebbe wanted to seclude himself from his Hasidim and follow his own elite path, and I don't agree now, when the Rebbe opened his door again. Now, he's opened them to village Jews, brokers,

---

69. The Hebrew words for interest—*neshekh*—and biting—*neshikhe*—are closely similar.

moneylenders, so that his wife can pour money into her apron. I thought that the Rebbe would come down to the level of his Hasidim in order to raise them up to his . . ."

"Ay, Mordkhe Yosef, Mordkhe Yosef," answered Reb Itshe Meirl. "It's never good enough for you."

"Good enough?" shouted Reb Mordhe Yosef. "Do you remember how the Rebbe used to say: 'Good enough? Never—it has to be all or nothing.' Lately the Rebbe's turning into too much of a housewife . . ."

And they parted in anger.

26

The Izhbitser Rebbe in Kotsk

When the Kotsker Rebbe's young wife was well into her pregnancy, she became steadily more nervous and capricious. The least agitation would cause her to go into spasms, until it was necessary to summon from Warsaw her sister, Reb Itshe Meirl's wife, who stayed until after the child was born.

The court of Kotsk began to prepare for the birth of the child. Village Jews brought hens, geese, and turkeys, and the entire courtyard was suddenly filled with the noise of live poultry.

The Hasidim, who had become somewhat riotous lately, couldn't sit idly by watching the poultry wandering around the yard. Bunem Nashelsker kept shouting to Reb Yekhiel Meir of Gostinin[70] that he couldn't concentrate on his studies because he sensed that the lost souls trapped inside the birds[71] were begging for release. "They're simply pleading, 'kill me!'" Bunem Nashelsker argued with Reb Yekhiel Meirl and the regulars. But the regulars were afraid to start up with the Rebbe's wife, and they kept looking greedily at the rooms where the birds were kept.

Until finally, one Saturday evening before the ritual celebration of the departure of the Sabbath, a couple of the younger regulars led by Bunem Nashelsker stole into the poultry room and swiped the fattest turkeys, binding their long beaks with red kerchiefs, their wings with silken belts. Then they scurried off to the slaughterer with the birds.

The slaughterer was in the middle of saying the prayers for the conclusion of the Sabbath when the young Hasidim burst into his house, demanding that he slaughter the turkeys. But the slaughterer of Kotsk was a stickler. He stubbornly insisted that he wouldn't slaughter the birds until he knew where they came from.

---

70. R. Yehiel Meir Lifshitz of Gostinin (1816–1888), known as a miracle-working tzaddik.

71. Transmigration of souls (*gilgul neshamot*) was an important doctrine in Hasidism with roots in Lurianic kabbalah, claiming that a soul may have to be reborn several times to atone for sins or to fulfill all 613 commandments. The souls of those guilty of graver sins transmigrated into animals, plants, and even stones.

A Fire Burns in Kotsk

"A village Jew brought them for the Saturday night celebration," shouted one of the regulars, thinking that would take care of the matter. But the slaughterer knew all the village Jews in the area around Kotsk because he did the kosher slaughter for them as well. So he didn't let them get away with this vague claim. A village Jew? The slaughterer wanted to know what his name was and which village he lived in.

"Zayvl Mukhsnik," someone responded.

At this, however, the slaughterer of Kotsk burst out laughing and muttered: "Really, such fat turkeys grew up at Zayvl's place overnight . . ." For the slaughterer knew what was in every village Jew's barn and poultry shed.

The regulars had no choice but to admit that they had taken the turkeys from the poultry shed in the courtyard.

The slaughterer got up from the table, took out a couple of slaughtering knives sheathed in leather and wood from his chest pocket, and began preparing the knives. He poured a few drops of water onto a whetstone, and the regulars thought that as soon as the knives were ready, he would slaughter the birds. But while the slaughterer was calmly checking the knives with his fingernail, he spoke up straightforwardly: "I won't slaughter the birds. They are stolen, and it is forbidden to recite a blessing over them."

The regulars began to argue with the slaughterer, claiming that there had been no theft. They told him the birds were flying around the courtyard, stretching out their necks and pleading, 'Come on, slaughter us!' What were we to do?" explained Bunem Nashelsker.

But the slaughterer was stubborn. He looked at his reflection in the polished knife and said, "I won't recite the blessing for slaughter over these birds. They are stolen."

The young regulars stood there perplexed. They had been expecting a nice feast, and now they were being blocked from slaughtering the turkeys.

"On account of a blessing an entire congregation of Jews should be deprived of a Saturday night feast?" a few of the regulars challenged the slaughterer. "What are you, a Litvak or a Hasid?"

But the slaughterer wouldn't budge.

Eventually one of the regulars had an idea. He rushed into the anteroom, climbed up a ladder and went to the poultry cage in the attic. He seized a big rooster, brought it down to the slaughterer and shouted: "Here, now you can do your slaughtering! Now you can make a kosher blessing—the bird belongs to you."

The slaughterer had to comply, and the regulars had a rich Saturday night.

But the Rebbe's pregnant young wife soon found out about the theft. They tried to convince her, too, that a village Jew had brought turkeys for Saturday night and the birds were quickly brought into the regulars' kitchen. But the Rebbe's wife wasn't reassured. She told the cook to go into the poultry shed to see what was there. And of course the cook ran out in alarm tugging at her cheeks and crying: "Woe is me! The turkey cage is empty."

And the young wife, weeping, ran straight into the Rebbe's room shouting that the Hasidim had stolen her best turkeys.

At that moment the Kotsker Rebbe was sitting engrossed in a passage written by Judah Loeb of Prague. He was terrified by her shouts. He thought that it wasn't his wife but her sister who was shouting, and that most likely his wife was having a difficult labor. But when he saw who was making the wild ruckus and what the big deal was, he yelled: "What do you want from me? Am I supposed to guard your turkeys?"

That was enough. The Rebbe's wife started trembling violently. Her sister soon ran in and she was led off to her room in a faint.

A wailing began and it carried from house to house because everyone was afraid lest the Rebbe's wife go into premature labor, God forbid.

And later, when Reb Itshe Meirl came into the Rebbe's room, he found the Rebbe pacing back and forth, downcast, his fur hat in his hand, rubbing his large skullcap back and forth over his head with the other.

The Kotsker Rebbe came up to Reb Itshe Meirl and recited a Biblical verse: "'And she opened the ark and she saw him, the child, and behold!, a lad crying; and she took pity on him and she said, this one is of the Hebrew children' (Exodus 2:6). If you first open up and only then do you hear the crying, it's a sign of Jewishness. A Jew should weep in his heart, not out loud."

All at once Reb Itshe Meirl saw before him the old Kotsker, with his sharp aphorisms, walking around the room and speaking mostly to himself: "I've been trapped! On one side I have turkeys, and on the other side I give blessings to heal sick cows. And I thought that I could find four hundred men, go to the forest with them, eat manna and see the power of the Divine kingdom . . . To redeem the kingdom of God . . ."

He stopped and asked Reb Itshe Meirl: "What are they celebrating there? What's the big Saturday night party?"

And the Kotsker Rebbe hurried to the door, entered the study house and rushed to the table.

The regulars were busy over big platters of roast turkey. One regular had grabbed a leg, and when the Rebbe entered, the regular stood frozen in astonishment, with the turkey leg in his hand.

The Kotsker Rebbe looked around on every side. Wherever his glance fell, he saw Jews sitting with pieces of turkey shoulder or leg in their hands.

And the Kotsker Rebbe shouted: "What great celebration do you deserve tonight? When God cursed the serpent, he said: 'you shall crawl on your belly and you shall eat the dust' (Genesis 3:14). The Talmud comments, 'and his nourishment shall be with him.' How was that a curse for the serpent, to see that wherever he went he would have food? Here's what it means. God says to the serpent, 'Gobble as much as you want, I don't even want to hear your sighs!' And that's the worst possible curse."

And with that the Kotsker Rebbe went back into his private room.

Since that night the Rebbe had spent a few weeks secluded in his private room, and wouldn't let anyone in to see him.

Every day the Rebbe's young wife would complain to her brother-in-law that the Rebbe had fallen back into depression. He wouldn't speak to anyone. He brushed off his Hasidim, and he didn't even pay any attention to her, who had once been able to convince him of anything.

And now Reb Itshe Meirl acknowledged for the first time that arranging for the Kotsker Rebbe to remarry hadn't worked. His apparent calm and good cheer right after the marriage had been like the calm before a storm, which was sure to break out sooner or later, perhaps with more violence than before.

Reb Itshe Meirl was especially worried about Reb Mordkhe Yosef, the future Izhbitser Rebbe, who continued to campaign quietly against the Kotsker Rebbe and to oppose his individualistic approach.

Reb Itshe Meirl and other courtiers sought every means possible to assure that the news about the current situation didn't spread beyond the Rebbe's room.

The courtiers even figured out a way to keep the Rebbe apart from his Hasidim and admit no one except selected individuals. But how were they to deal with Mordkhe Yosef? How were they to make sure that he knew nothing about what was going on in the Rebbe's room? And would the Rebbe agree to it in any case? Mordkhe Yosef was one of the few whom the Rebbe regularly saw.

And Reb Itshe Meirl's downcast appearance as he made his way around the study house aroused the suspicion of the young Hasidim.

Eventually, one Saturday night an elderly Pshiskhe Hasid approached him and accosted him: "Listen, you, Itshe Meirl! Something's the matter with you. If I still had the strength of my early years and the comrades I used to have, we'd turn you upside down for your sadness. But since I'm here by myself while you've grown into the 'Polish genius,' it will be enough for us to fine you the price of a pot of mead."

Reb Itshe Meirl immediately paid the fine, and the mead was sent for. It was relief for him to know that there was an old Pshiskhe Hasid in Kotsk. It somehow seemed to him that if such people were still to be found in Kotsk, everything might still be made right. And yet he was crestfallen when he remembered the early times in Tomashov, when they broke away from Pshiskhe after the death of the Rebbe Reb Bunem, when Reb Mordkhe Yosef was among the first to gather fuel for the fire. Everything looked bright back then. And now the Rebbe had broken away from them, like a lava flow, himself climbing higher and higher, leaving his Hasidim behind.

Reb Itshe Meirl considered who his fellow Hasidim were now, and his sorrow became even greater.

But the regulars didn't notice this. Like thirsty men they rushed toward the mead, totally forgetting the Rebbe's words at the previous Saturday night party. They drank one glass after another, until the old Pshiskhe Hasid himself became tipsy. He approached Reb Itshe Meirl, placed a friendly hand on his back, and holding a glass of mead in his other hand, he said to him with eyes full of sadness, "You're evidently still a young man, dear Itshe Meirl! You haven't lived through what I've lived through. What else can I say?" He began to weep, while the glass of mead trembled in his hand. "What else can I say? I was there at the beginning, when the school was first being established, when the Holy Jew of blessed memory first broke away from Lublin and began propagating the new approach . . . We thought then that Messiah was standing so close, that all we had to do was stick our hands out. And now I've been chastised for the third time. What else can I say?"

"Did everything really go smoothly then?" asked Reb Itshe Meirl. "Weren't there any moments of sorrow?"

"Sorrow? Every Jew has his ups and downs, and even more so the collective. But a drop of liquor would drive all the clouds away," laughed the old Pshiskhe Hasid, draining his glass of mead.

The old Pshiskhe Hasid's words actually encouraged Reb Itshe Meirl. But later, he looked around the large study house that the rich Hasidim had built, and he saw small groups of Hasidim sitting in every corner looking depressed, while individual Hasidim wandered around lost in thought smoking long pipes. One question hung over every head: When will the Rebbe start seeing us? The old Pshiskhe Hasid's words of comfort rang hollow now, and Reb Itshe Meirl's face betrayed his loneliness. For several weeks now the Rebbe had refused to see anyone or to let anyone take his leave. So the whole crowd who had come to see the Rebbe weeks earlier remained stuck there.[72]

The Hasidim gathered at the Rebbe's door, and the secretary Reb Hersh Tomashover kept meeting them with the same response: "The Rebbe isn't saying goodbye to anyone today!"

Reb Mordkhe Yosef Izhbitser tried to go in as well. He had come for the Sabbath and had remained a few extra days with all the other Hasidim. But he too received the same answer: "The Rebbe is in solitude and won't say goodbye to anyone today!"

Eventually, late one night, when Reb Mordhe Yosef was sitting in the study house with his devotees talking about the Rebbe's new ways, he got up and went to the secretary's room to try to get in to see the

---

72. It was accepted in Hasidic circles that no one would depart from a rebbe's court without first taking his leave.

Rebbe. He thought the Rebbe would see him if he insisted. After all, he and the Kotsker Rebbe were old friends, from the times of Pshiskhe and Tomashov, when they were both still young. But Reb Hersh Tomashover blocked the doorway, saying "You won't get anywhere; he doesn't want to say goodbye."

"And what will happen to the Hasidim? It's heartbreaking to see them pining away here."

"You know something?" answered Reb Hersh Tomashover. "Just now, when I was about to lie down to sleep, he suddenly opened the door, stood with a burning candle in his hand dressed in a coarse shirt, stared at me for a long time, and said, pointing to his heart, 'Hersh, my dear! It hurts here, and "they" keep tormenting me with their petty worries...'"

But Reb Mordkhe Yosef didn't want to listen to everything Reb Hersh Tomashover had to say to him, and instead returned to the study house: "He's the only one hurting? We're all hurting!"

And from that moment on, Reb Mordkhe Yosef began gathering his own Hasidim right in Kotsk.

27

The Contentious Conversation

Some time passed. A pervasive sense of loneliness permeated the court of Kotsk once again. Everyone was downcast. They didn't sing like they once did. They didn't even spend time in solitary contemplation as was the practice in Kotsk. Village Jews stopped coming. If you can't get to see the Rebbe, if you can't act like a Hasid—what's the point of going to Kotsk? The village people weren't interested in just giving gratuitous handouts to the regulars so they could make their little feasts.

Devoted Kotsker Hasidim told astonishing things about the Rebbe: that he didn't even want to see those in his inner circle anymore; and that when Hersh Tomashover wanted to bring the leftovers of the Rebbe's meal to the Hasidim, the Rebbe wouldn't let him. Instead he opened the window of his private room, which opened onto a low roof, and threw the remainders to the birds . . .

And Reb Mordkhe Yosef Izhbitser gathered more and more Hasidim. He began preaching to them, to show them what to do, and to behave as their rebbe.

"I can't stand to see a congregation of Hasidim abandoned," Reb Mordkhe Yosef argued. "We have a seraph who refuses to descend from his lofty heights for one second, but we don't have a rebbe!"

Wives began to come from various cities and towns to pick up their husbands, and Reb Mordkhe Yosef shouted: "It's time for school to be over!"

"Go home!" shouted Mordkhe Yosef one day, as he burst into the study house. "You sit here stuffing yourself with these little feasts, and your wives should be working to support you? They should have all the responsibility for your family's livelihood? What about the commandment to raise children? When did you fulfill the commandment to teach them Torah? You've been staring over there," he pointed to the Kotsker Rebbe's private room, "but he doesn't want to have you. He completely forgot the verse, 'the ladder was based on the earth and its top reached Heaven.' You can only lean your head on Heaven when your feet are on the ground, when you don't try to free yourself from all materiality at once."

And the simple village Jews, for whom the straightforward approach of Reb Mordkhe Yosef was still too intense, clung to Reb Yekhiel Meir of Gostinin, who reassured them.

When a village Jew came with a heart full of care and wanted to see the Rebbe, Reb Yekhiel Meir would say to him that "you need to take a drink even before you get to the inn," that is, before he went to see the Rebbe he should say a Psalm. So Reb Yekhiel Meir would go over to a corner of the study house with a small group of village Jews and start reciting Psalms with them.

A wailing arose in the study house as though they were praying for someone who was mortally ill, until a couple of the more fanatical Kotsker Hasidim ran in and complained loudly: "What is this, the ladies' section?" They would drive Reb Yekhiel Meir of Gostinin into the anteroom. But all of the Hasidim respected Reb Yekhiel Meirl's modesty and goodness. And none of the leading Kotskers bothered him.

It is said, however that one time when Reb Yekhiel Meirl was sitting with a group of village Jews, a Hasid from his town came in. The Hasid told him that Reb Yekhiel Meir's wife had been sentenced to three months in prison because a Jewish clerk in her store had once had his thumb on the scale when he sold goods to a Russian officer. The officer noticed what was happening, reweighed the goods and saw that he'd been cheated. He accused Reb Yekhiel Meir's wife, even though she wasn't the one who'd cheated the officer.

Reb Yekhiel Meirl heard what the Hasid had to say and called: "Certainly she should serve her time; if you cheat, you have to be punished!"

"But it wasn't your wife who gave the false weight," the Hasid tried to explain, "it was her clerk."

"And is she supposed to go rat on a fellow Jew?"

And so the Hasidim split into three camps. The very simple Hasidim preferred Reb Yekhiel Meirl. The average ones clung to Reb Mordkhe Yosef, and the most intensely devoted hung by the door of the Rebbe's private room, waiting for Reb Itshe Meirl to convince the Rebbe to begin seeing them again.

A Fire Burns in Kotsk

And once when Reb Itshe Meirl came into the study house, he saw the leading Hasidim rush toward him, and on all their faces a single question could be read: "What's it going to be? When will he start acting like a rebbe?"

But Reb Itshe Meirl brushed them off, and his eyes sought out Reb Mordkhe Yosef. And since he didn't spot him right away, he asked, "Is Mordkhe Yosef here?"

"Yes, he's with us. He hasn't been allowed to leave yet, either."

At that, Reb Itshe Meirl saw Reb Mordkhe Yosef sitting in a corner with a few Hasidim. He sensed that he was about to begin a real war against Reb Mordkhe Yosef, that it wouldn't be easy to keep Reb Mordkhe Yosef in the Kotsk study house until the Rebbe opened his doors.

But the first thing Reb Itshe Meirl wanted to do was go into the Rebbe's private room and see what was happening there.

When Reb Itshe Meirl strode through the long study house to get to the door that led into the secretary's room, Reb Mordkhe Yosef shouted after him, loud enough for all of the Hasidim to hear: "They brought him down again. He thinks this is some difficult passage in Maimonides that he can figure out with his brilliant mind. We're talking about reality now, about the actual truth of the world. And none of his clever dialectics are going to help now!"

Reb Itshe Meirl found Reb Hersh Tomashover sitting in the secretary's room like a mourner. He wanted to put his hand on the knob of the Rebbe's door. But Reb Hersh Tomashover indicated that he shouldn't do it. He stood up, approached Reb Itshe Meirl, greeted him sorrowfully, and said: "He ordered me not to let anyone in."

Reb Itshe Meirl hesitated a while, then returned to the study house and said, "Well, we'll get in tomorrow."

When Reb Itshe Meirl returned to the study house he saw Reb Mordkhe Yosef surrounded by a group of the leading, most passionate young Hasidim. Reb Mordkhe Yosef was saying to them: "At the beginning, every approach is new, so of course it's true. There's no force of habit. Whatever is done is done from the heart, with one's own will. But it must be done in public, not in solitude. We're going to do it together, and let it be done in solitude over there," he concluded, pointing toward the locked door.

Reb Itshe Meirl approached the circle of Hasidim and spoke up: "But first you have to be a Tomashover Rebbe.[73] Otherwise you can break your neck. It's no small matter to initiate a new approach!"

"If you create new things, you grow higher and stronger," answered Reb Mordkhe Yosef. "But everything has to be done openly in front of the entire world. But here we are waiting to see what will come from 'over there,' to see if 'he' will share with us a word that will make the world easier to bear. We don't want to live on what's already prepared. We don't want to live on leftovers, waiting for someone to throw us bits of already-baked Torah. Together we'll sharpen our sayings, together we'll create the light . . ."

Reb Itshe Meirl did not reply further. He sighed deeply and said more to himself than to Reb Mordkhe Yosef: "It's hard to be the leader of a generation. You have to arm yourself well. You need a lot of strength."

Meanwhile the Hasidim slipped off to the side. They made way for Reb Itshe Meirl, and soon the two men were standing in the middle of a circle of Hasidim.

Reb Mordkhe Yosef kept the dialogue going. It was clear that he wanted to share with Reb Itshe Meirl the thoughts that had been preoccupying him for these last weeks, so that everyone in the court of Kotsk would know.

And he answered Reb Itshe Meirl's last statement: "If you have something new to say, then you find you have supernatural power!"

"But we are after all flesh and blood. Sometimes we think we're saying something and it turns out to be nothing, just hot air—and then the abyss of Sheol threatens."

"No one's talking about falsehood here," answered Reb Mordkhe Yosef. "But if you're afraid, God forbid, then nothing gets done. A person has to be able to rely on himself."

"A person can go astray even unintentionally," answered Reb Itshe Meirl. "That's why one must not rely on himself but listen to what the Rebbe says."

"By all means, it's good to listen to what the Rebbe says," retorted Reb Mordkhe Yosef. "But what are we hearing here? For weeks on end

---

73. A reference to R. Menachem Mendel, the Kotsker—who was of course first Rebbe in Tomashov.

the Rebbe's been secluded. We don't see him and we don't hear a single word of Torah. If you put your ear against the door of his room, you hear sorrowful muttering that makes your heart tremble. If you ask Reb Hersh Tomashover, he doesn't answer. So, tell me what we should do. You have entrée to him, and a favored place at his table . . ."

"I myself haven't been inside there. But I think we have to wait. We have to ask him about everything first. When the prophet Samuel heard the voice of the Holy One, he too first went to his rebbe, to Eli the Priest, to ask what to do. Satan has many ways to deceive."

"Every day new worlds are created," answered Reb Mordkhe Yosef, and he sensed that the Hasidim were gradually leaning toward his side. "Every day hew concepts come into being. What was considered yesterday the highest truth has ceased being true today . . . That's the power that created the way of Pshiskhe. If it weren't for that, we'd all still be stuck in the way of Lublin, and we'd still be getting fat on miracles and prophecies."

"Do you really mean to compare this crowd to the Pshiskhe Hasidim?" answered Reb Itshe Meirl, raising his voice.

"Every generation is worthy of a new approach, if only their leader is worthy and truly leads the generation, without thinking only of himself," answered Reb Mordkhe Yosef.

"Sometimes you run into a difficult passage in Maimonides," continued Reb Itshe Meirl, "so you work on it, you look for solutions, until you figure it out. You always have to struggle to find the right interpretation."

"Interpretations you have to struggle for aren't worth anything," Reb Mordkhe Yosef interrupted. "All your limbs have to grasp the truth. All your limbs have to dance joyfully toward the truth. If you feel any doubt, you have to keep looking, not try to come up with excuses. You have to keep looking until you see that light has been revealed."

"Do you really think that illumination is found on every street corner? You have to work for it! You have to prepare yourself!" shouted Reb Itshe Meirl in exasperation.

"We'll work! We'll search! We can't be scared off. When we left Pshiskhe, we set off on even bolder paths in Tomashov," Reb Mordkhe Yosef replied even louder.

Reb Itshe Meirl walked away in anger. Reb Mordkhe Yosef himself seemed to sense that he should not have conducted his dialogue in public, before the entire crowd, and he ended by saying to the Hasidim who surrounded him: "He wants to patch everything over. His intentions are pure as well. But an entire community of Hasidim can't be left without a shepherd. We can't stay shut out like this forever. Meanwhile we'll wait to see what he'll bring us from 'there.' They'll let Reb Itshe Meirl in. Let's wait until tomorrow."

The Hasidim together with Reb Mordkhe Yosef gradually went away to their inns, and Reb Itshe Meirl remained in the study house with a few simple Jews, who recited Psalms in a sobbing voice.

28

The Kotsker Rebbe in His Private Room

When Reb Itshe Meirl later went into the secretary's room, he approached Reb Hersh Tomashover, who sat in a corner sadly smoking a pipe.

"Can I go in?" asked Reb Itshe Meirl.

"What do I know," answered Reb Hersh Tomashover in a resigned voice. "If you want, try—I won't stop you anymore."

Reb Itshe Meirl pulled his belt tighter, smoothed out his earlocks, ran his fingers through his beard, and, with his heart pounding, opened the door to the Rebbe's room.

The Rebbe's room was filled with smoke. A large candle was burning on the table, throwing shadows on the walls.

The Kotsker Rebbe stood in a large skullcap and a cotton shirt at the edge of the table, bent over a religious text.

And although Reb Itshe Meirl opened the door as quietly as he could, the Kotsker Rebbe nevertheless heard that someone had come in. Lately his ears had become so sensitive that he noticed every rustle.

The Rebbe rose from the table and muttered angrily, "What more do they want of me?"

But when he saw Reb Itshe Meirl standing in the doorway in terror, his voice immediately changed and he said in a quiet, cheerful tone: "Itshe Meirl, it's you? It's good that you came."

The Kotsker Rebbe greeted him formally and led him to the table.

Various books covered the table, half-opened and full of creases. Near them lay several sheets of paper scattered about and a number of goose quill pens.

At first Reb Itshe Meirl didn't recognize the Kotsker Rebbe. The light in his eyes was overcast by a sad fire; his sidelocks were wildly disheveled, and the right half of his greying beard was bent to the side, since he'd been resting his right hand on his chin for so long. His high forehead was full of creases and his voice had a certain alien quality, as if it were coming from far away.

Reb Itshe Meirl thought that after the first friendly words the Kotsker Rebbe had said to him, the conversation would continue, so he stood waiting for the Rebbe to ask him something. He was afraid to venture anything himself, because anything he said might cause pain. But the Kotsker Rebbe didn't say anything else to Reb Itshe Meirl. He quickly became totally absorbed in his thinking and utterly forgot that Reb Itshe Meirl was there. He began walking quickly around the room, saying incomprehensible things to himself: "So where do we stand? Go further, or start again?"

From these few words it could be deduced that they came after a long chain of thoughts that the Kotsker Rebbe had been mulling over in his mind for quite some time.

The Kotsker Rebbe continued pacing the room. Suddenly he began shouting in a strange voice: "Well, where's the way out? We always come back to the same thing! Will we always be stuck in the void, in 'He creates worlds and destroys them'? Will we really never reach a genuine order?"

Reb Itshe Meirl was terrified listening to these words. Only now did he understand why the Rebbe didn't want to see anyone, only now did he understand where the Rebbe's thinking lay. Reb Itshe Meirl slipped over to the side, behind a chair, and in awe and fear he waited for the Rebbe to notice him again.

But suddenly the Kotsker Rebbe stopped next to him, stared at him hard and said: "Who are you? Who dares to enter my room? What do strangers want from me? Tell me, who are you?"

Reb Itshe Meirl's fright only increased. Huge drops of sweat broke out on his brow, and in a trembling voice he answered: "How do I know who I am?"

At this the Kotsker Rebbe caught himself, and as if he'd just tumbled down from a high mountain he began suddenly speaking in a broken voice: "I am embittered, dear Itshe Meirl, very embittered."

And in his great weakness he fell onto the chair.

Reb Itshe Meirl gave him a bit of water. The Rebbe barely wet his lips, wiped the sweat from his face with a large flowered kerchief. His intense concentration had so exhausted him that he looked like he had just completed a long and difficult prayer service.

When the Kotsker Rebbe had calmed down a bit, he began speaking to Reb Itshe Meirl as though he wanted to bare his heart in confession.

"We can't find a way out," the Kotsker Rebbe began in a broken voice. "We're both reaching for the same point, I and Mendl Lubavitsher.[74] The difference is that we started with the heart and he started with the brain. Pshiskhe started with the innermost center of the heart, and Chabad started with the very source of the brain. And while we were reaching up toward the brain, they were lowering themselves down toward the heart. Now we've met. Each of us stuck to his own path until we encountered each other. We approached from opposite sides, and now we've met in the middle, and now neither of us knows where to go next."

Then the Kotsker Rebbe thought deeply again. Reb Itshe Meirl was reminded of the saying of an old Pshiskhe Hasid who had seen the Lubavitsher Rebbe: "Mendel and Mendel can be compared—both want the same thing, but they have different approaches."

The Kotsker Rebbe glanced at Reb Itshe Meirl as if at a stranger again, but he soon recognized his friend and continued his discourse: "But he, Reb Mendele Lubavitsher, is in a better situation. He's approaching the heart, and the heart has no end. But what can we accomplish with our poor intellect?"

Reb Itshe Meirl stood with a bowed head without answering, as if he had lost the power of speech. "And while I've been struggling for weeks to find the way out, they've been distracting me with their petitions for advice," the Kotsker Rebbe repeated.

"And is that why the Rebbe is in seclusion?" Reb Itshe Meirl asked tentatively.

"Who told you that I'm in seclusion?" shouted the Kotsker Rebbe. "I want to come to them with something new to say."

"Wasn't the path until now a good one?" asked Reb Itshe Meirl again, when he saw that the Rebbe was willing to converse.

"It's good, but it leads nowhere. I do know that when I do find the new insight, they won't want to listen to me. Now you want me to go

---

74. R. Menachem Mendel Schneersohn of Lubavitch (1789–1866), known as the "Tsemah Tzedek."

out to them, and when I'm ready to go out, you won't let me! Even you yourself, Reb Itshe Meirl, won't allow me.

"We have to start again. Only now do I see things I couldn't see before. We have to see the 'internal light,' but until now we've wasted so much time around the 'internal light' that its light doesn't shine out at all. Do you see the heap of books lying on the table? All of them only conceal the light, rather than peeling away the shells covering it. Someone needs to write a commentary to reveal the light. A single folio will be enough."

Throughout this discourse the Kotsker Rebbe's voice changed continuously, and suddenly he rushed to the table and angrily swept away all the books lying there. He grabbed a piece of parchment and began writing, "This is the new commentary, called 'These are the Generations of Man.' The entire Torah can be contained on one sheet," he shouted in a wild voice, "and they keep stuffing us with their stories about how our teacher Moses ordered us to count Gentile women, stories about the daughters of Zelaphehad!"

Reb Itshe Meirl clapped his hands over his ears listening to the Kotsker Rebbe's last words. He leaned down and quickly picked up all the books lying on the ground.

Meanwhile the Kotsker Rebbe collected himself and helped pick up the books, kissing each one and asking in amazement, "Who threw them down?"

But since Reb Itshe Meirl didn't answer at all, the Kotsker Rebbe evidently understood what had happened, and he began once again unburdening his broken heart.

"Dear Itshe Meirl! My body is being consumed by fire; my heart is bursting into pieces from all these doubts; they dig into my soul like a worm and won't let me rest."

"But the Rebbe never meant to bring the masses along. His way was always meant for individuals."

"Certainly, that's what I always wanted," answered the Kotsker Rebbe, "but what can I do when they collect around me like fleas? The more you send them away, the more they come back. So I'm going to go to them with something new to say, and anyone who doesn't want to come along with me will run away behind the Mountains of Darkness to avoid seeing me again."

A Fire Burns in Kotsk

"And was that the way of the holy Baal Shem Tov?"

"Certainly that was his way. First of all he got rid of the waste and prepared the way for his disciples. But the purification process was continuous."

But in the middle of the conversation the Kotsker Rebbe extended his hand to Reb Itshe Meirl and said, "Well, we've talked enough, one mustn't tell everything. It's necessary to think everything through on one's own and fully resolve the matter. Meanwhile go in health and peace. One must work through one's doubts on his own."

And Reb Itshe Meirl left the Rebbe's room.

Hundreds of Hasidim stood on the other side of the door waiting to hear what Reb Itshe Meirl would have to say. But Reb Itshe Meirl passed through the big crowd in silence, and returned to his inn to consider what to do.

He still heard Reb Mordkhe Yosef shouting at him: "Well, why won't he tell? He kept on yelling that we have to ask the Rebbe. And now he's coming from there, so why won't he tell us what he heard?"

And when Reb Itshe Meirl was ready to leave the study house he was stopped by a group of Hasidim who pulled at his sleeve and pleaded: "Tell us, Itshe Meir, what did you say to each other? We want to know where we are in the world. When will the Rebbe start saying goodbye again? We want to know when we can see him!" came the questions from all sides.

"Not now, tomorrow I'll speak to you and tell you. I'm tired now, let me go. Everything tomorrow!" Reb Itshe Meir begged them, and he left the study house bowed down with care. Reb Itshe Meirl strode into a big puddle that surrounded the courtyard of Kotsk, and thought about what to do:

"We can't leave the whole assembly without leadership," he thought. "Reb Mordkhe Yosef Izhbitser is ready to attract everyone to himself, if the Rebbe won't come out to see them. And can we let him talk to them and say such things? It will rock the world. And everybody's looking at me, waiting for me to tell them what's going on 'there.' But what can I tell them?"

With these heavy thoughts Reb Itshe Meirl reached his inn, thinking that the next day he would speak to Reb Hersh Tomashover and consider together what to do.

29

The Society of "Watchers" at the Court of Kotsk

The next day Reb Itshe Meirl didn't appear in the study house as he had promised his Hasidim. He sent for Reb Hersh Tomashover, the Kotsker's loyal assistant.

Reb Hersh Tomashover came to Reb Itshe Meirl's inn, locked himself and Reb Itshe Meirl into a small room, and strictly ordered the Hasidim not to dare come in or eavesdrop.

When Reb Itshe Meirl had sealed the door, he began explaining in a sad voice: "Hersh, I was there yesterday, and I was frightened by his new approach."

"What did you see there?" asked Reb Hersh.

"I can't repeat what I saw and heard, but I'm afraid that no good will come of it," answered Reb Itshe Meir with a sigh.

"But what did you see there?" asked Reb Hersh.

"He threw all the books down from the table," Reb Itshe Meirl whispered.

"Is that all you saw?" asked Reb Hersh with a teasing smile.

"He also said things that an ordinary person mustn't hear," whispered Reb Itshe Meirl in a frightened tone.

"Is that all you saw and heard?" asked Reb Hersh again. "And that's what you're afraid of? And what can I say, since I go into his room twice a day to bring him food and he says such things to me that you could tear your clothes in mourning, if you didn't try to reinterpret them. Just yesterday when I went in with a plate of porridge, he said to me: 'Hersh, do you really think that the Baal Shem Tov's new approach was to continue worrying endless about the "ox that gored?"' (Exodus 21:28–32, 35–36). I didn't respond at all, and just stood there trembling. He looked at me and said, 'Well, Hersh, you don't have an answer, so I'll tell you. The Baal Shem Tov certainly didn't have that in mind. He wanted to rearrange everything, to change the work of creation, but he was afraid the other side might be too strong, so he left it to his disciples. Many who came after him have tried to complete the work, but they brought their ideas to the public too soon. Don't think that I've secluded myself because I don't want to be among the Hasidim. No, first of all I want to polish every word I plan to say so that it will be pure when I come to them. Let my words be so sharp and glowing that all of the simpletons will burn themselves and run away. The only ones who should stay are the individuals who are worthy of hearing the new Torah.' And he concluded: 'Every Jew can reach the level of our teacher Moses, who received the Torah from God.' Well, what can I tell you?" Reb Hersh Tomashover finished with a sigh.

"It's a bitter situation, and we need to figure something out," replied Reb Itshe Meirl.

"But I'm not afraid," Reb Hersh said as if to give himself strength. "You have to encourage yourself, once you've harnessed yourself to the wagon. You have to be able to pull it all the way and not get stuck in the middle."

"But we could be misled," said Reb Itshe Meirl. "More than once the leader has thought that he knew everything. The disciples followed blindly, and that leader and his disciples sank into such a deep puddle that no one could drag them out of it."

"Don't provide an opening to Satan!" angrily shot back Reb Hersh. "Anyone who doesn't trust our leader should get away. But I'm holding on to his belt, and whatever happens to him will happen to all of us."

"Certainly I have faith," Reb Itshe Meirl said to himself. "Reb Mordkhe Yosef's doubts are alien to me, but the difference between me and you is that you are always in the Kotsker court and you don't know what they say in the background. But I'm in Warsaw and I meet other Hasidim. Don't think they don't know what's going on here. The walls have ears, and in other rebbes' courts they tell bizarre stories about him. Many rebbes from Galicia, those who once wanted to excommunicate the Rebbe Reb Bunem, are rubbing their bellies with delight. They don't hesitate to point out that they were right. They even want to call a conference and sentence all of us to such a severe punishment that a Jew is forbidden to say it. And here comes Mordkhe Yosef adding fuel to the fire, trying to get 'him' to come out as soon as possible to say goodbye to the Hasidim and say in public what he's thinking in private. So how can we let him out?"

"We have to do whatever he wants. We dare not oppose him, but as long as we can prevent it, we'll prevent it."

"But what should we do meanwhile? They're waiting for an answer in the study house. I promised them that I'd tell them what he said tomorrow."

"We need to stall for as long as we can. It won't take long. Probably he told you, too, that he would soon be opening his door."

"If so," Reb Itshe Meirl concluded, "we can return to the study house."

It was late at night. At the Kotsk study house they weren't so particular about saying their prayers with a minyan or saying them on time, so little groups of Hasidim were standing scattered about the study house discussing Hasidism. At the lectern stood Reb Mordkhe Yosef surrounded by a group of Hasidim. He was conducting a Hasidic discourse around the theme of the leader's obligation not to separate from the community but to do everything together with them.

When Reb Itshe Meirl came into the study house, he approached the group of Hasidim surrounding Reb Mordkhe Yosef without being detected, and he heard Reb Mordkhe Yosef telling a story: "I'll tell you a story in order to reinforce what I said earlier. It happened to the Rebbe Reb Elimelekh of Lizhensk. Once upon a time someone came and told the Rebbe Reb Elimelekh that a Jew had appeared in the synagogue dressed in a sack, thin from fasting for years and sitting locked up in a cave, away from the world.

"'I don't want to see him,' shouted the Rebbe Reb Elimelekh. 'It is written: "If a man hides in secret places will I not see him?" (Jeremiah 23:24). This means: if a person hides in a cave and avoids everyone, then God says, "I don't want to see him."'

"And the Rebbe Reb Elimelekh concluded by explaining that the discipline of solitude doesn't mean removing oneself from the entire world and having nothing to do with anyone else. True solitude is when a person finds himself in a room with a thousand others and yet feels as though he's entirely alone—that is the highest level of solitude."

Reb Itshe Meirl well understood the moral of Reb Mordkhe Yosef's story. He wanted to reply but suddenly he heard a dreadful wailing coming from the vestibule. Reb Itshe Meirl quickly went into the vestibule to see what had happened there. He saw Reb Velvele the Judge standing surrounded by a group of Hasidim. They kept shouting and banging their hearts as if they were praying on Rosh Hashanah.

This was the new society of "watchers" assembled by Reb Velvele since the Rebbe had locked himself in his room and ceased to conduct himself in public.

The watchers kept fasts, imposed all sorts of strictures on themselves, observed celibacy, didn't go home to sleep at night but stayed awake in the study house. In the middle of the night they put on sackcloth, sprinkled ashes on their heads, and recited the special Kabbalistic midnight prayer service. They stayed by the Rebbe's house guarding the door. Reb Velvele the Judge, a Jew thin as a willow branch, with a lemon yellow face and an amber beard, had found a passage in the Zohar that clearly hinted a new light would be revealed this very year.

"You see, when the Rebbe opens the door," Reb Velvele said in a voice choked with weeping, "and reveals the new light to us, we won't be worthy of that light. The Rebbe secluded himself from the entire world because the new light will be revealed through him. We also need to be ready to receive it. We need to purify ourselves, repent, so that we'll be fit to perceive the light. This year, 5600, is a propitious year for the beginnings of redemption, as the holy Zohar hints in its commentary on the Torah portion Vayera (117): 'In the six hundredth year of the sixth millennium the gates of wisdom will be opened.' Reb Shimon bar Yochai, the author of the Zohar, meant this year, and only through 'him,'" he said, indicating the door of the Kotsker Rebbe's private room, "will the sources of wisdom be opened, and only through 'him' will the new light be revealed. And therefore," he concluded mournfully, "we must prepare ourselves with fasts, purify ourselves and repent."

Reb Itshe Meirl propelled himself toward Reb Velvele the Judge and began shouting: "Who has to fast? The Hasidic approach is against that. The Baal Shem Tov abolished fasting. Pshiskhe didn't believe in it. Sure, you've got to keep your head away from the vain things of this world—but fasting? God forbid!"

"But you can accomplish a lot by fasting," spoke up a young Hasid.

"If you fast," answered Reb Itshe Meirl, "then you're thinking about your body. You want to torment it, humiliate it, but it's still important to you. It has substance, but really you shouldn't be thinking about your body at all; it shouldn't take up any space . . . it has to be ignored completely."

And Reb Itshe Meirl concluded: "Fasts are good for pious people, but we say—pious is crooked! And we have a rule that a diligent person has no time to study, and a pious person doesn't have God in mind because he's always full of doubts. Perhaps he didn't pronounce a word properly, perhaps he didn't wash his hands, his skullcap isn't back far enough on his head . . . Meanwhile, he forgets the larger truth; he forgets about the final redemption."

"Absolutely, we want to prepare ourselves for the final redemption," shouted Reb Velvele in a throaty voice. "We know that when he opens the door, the new light will appear and we won't be able to perceive it, so we have to prepare for it. Friends, it's almost time for the midnight ceremony.[75] Let's go to the mikvah to prepare ourselves!"

And the watchers, a few dozen youngsters and a few older Jews, left the vestibule to go to the mikvah.

Reb Itshe Meirl stood by a bookcase with a heavy heart. He sensed that everything was falling apart at once. "In the Rebbe's private room," he thought to himself, "sits the 'Column of Fire' spitting sparks which could, God forbid, consume any lesser mind and send it down to the abyss. Here Reb Mordkhe Yosef is teaching that it's time to close the school and start over. Yekhiel Meir of Gostinin has turned into an old woman, saying Psalms with village Jews, and Velvele the Judge is disciplining himself with these mystical intentions and practices that could lead him far astray . . . And all around them there's a crowd of Hasidim who don't know what to do. They've abandoned their homes. They're waiting for the door to open so they can take their leave. And in there he's sitting, preparing a new Torah that could burn up the world. Everybody's sitting waiting for me to tell them what he said to me."

In his anguish and exhaustion Reb Itshe Meirl dozed off next to the bookcase, leaning his head on a book, until the Watchers returned from the mikvah and began the midnight ceremony.

---

75. Midnight devotions (*tikkun hatzot*) originated in the 16th century kabbalistic school of Safed, consisting of the recitation of psalms, confessional prayer, affirmations of faith, and dirges. The Safed kabbalists held that the forces of evil were most powerful at midnight, and thus needed to be neutralized in this manner.

30

The Watchers Are Driven Out

When the Watchers came back in from the mikvah they gathered in the women's section, so that the other Hasidim wouldn't harass them.

It was deathy quiet in the women's section. Every few minutes another Watcher would come in with sackcloth over his shoulders and a candle in his hands, and sit down on the ground sighing.

They sat down in a circle. In the middle sat Reb Velvele the Judge. They all looked as though they had just been exiled from Jerusalem.

And Reb Velvele began to speak: "Before we observe the midnight ceremony, I want to announce to you that our redemption is very near, that very soon the door to the Rebbe's room is going to open, and the Light will certainly be revealed. We can already hear the footsteps of Messiah, but we aren't at all ready for his coming. Before the Torah was given there were three days of separation. Now we have to be even more pure than back then because now the true redemption is coming. So we have to be altogether separate until the Light is revealed. Once upon a time 'he,' too, secluded himself completely. We have to do the same thing. The more we separate ourselves, the more we punish our bodies, the quicker will be the footsteps of the true redeemer!"

And suddenly the women's section in Kotsk was filled with weeping as if it were time for Kol Nidrei on Yom Kippur.

Each of the Watchers found his own way to torment himself. One of them sat on sharp rocks, another put dry chickpeas into his boots, and a third put a rough sack onto his naked body and over that his shirt, so none of the Hasidim would know about it. One of the watchers vowed not to speak a word to anyone but only to answer if someone spoke first. One of them vowed to stand up whenever he was awake and to sleep in a sitting position.

Everyone wanted to best his neighbor. They found new ways to torment themselves, and they were all certain that it would help them hasten the redemption.

Immediately after the midnight ceremony the Watchers began to recite Psalms. Reb Velvele the Judge stood in the middle screaming each verse separately, with contorted facial expressions. It was enough to rip your heart in pieces. Tears the size of beans poured down their faces as the women's section resounded with wailing.

Reb Itshe Meirl, who had stood in the vestibule for a long time absorbed in a book, heard the wailing coming from the women's section and sensed that if the Watchers were left on their own, nothing good would come of it. He went into the study house and assembled a couple of dozen young men. Together they went to the women's section.

"Madmen," shouted Reb Itshe Meirl, "what are you howling for? Do you want to turn the Kotsk study house into a women's synagogue? Are you going to stop crying? I promise you that soon the Rebbe will once again meet with his Hasidim and say goodbye to them! It's true, we need to be ready, but not this way. We shouldn't have the hearts of women. Our hearts have to be hard as a stone, to be able to bear everything, but what you're doing will lead you astray and who knows whether you'll be able to make your way back if you don't realize in time how lost you are."

And the Hasidim who had rushed to the women's section began driving out the pious fasters with their belts and kerchiefs.

The watchers ran away on all sides, and they were driven out from every corner: "Get out of the Kotsk study house! There's nothing for you here. Kotsk isn't the place for you." And a few young men grabbed Reb Velvele and carried out his sentence then and there:

His arms and legs were tied with belts, and he was beaten with wet kerchiefs. Then they opened his mouth, poured a glass of pure eau de vie into his mouth and pushed some food in.

"But he didn't pray today!" shouted some Hasidim.

"That's even better," shot back others, "let him know what his sin was and why he needs to repent."

But Reb Velvele the Judge accepted his punishment willingly, and while the Hasidim were beating him, he kept pounding his heart, murmuring through pale lips, "I have sinned, I have rebelled, let it be recompense for my sins, and may by soul be purified, so that I may better perceive the Rebbe's new direction."

A Fire Burns in Kotsk

▲▼▲▼▲▼

After the Hasidim had carried out their sentence against the society of Watchers, Reb Velvele the Judge dissolved the society, and everyone began fasting on his own. Reb Velvele became more discrete and only rarely appeared in the synagogue. Hasidim said that he was secretly gathering select individuals, going to the forest with them and there continuing his practices, preparing them to meet with their souls purified the new light which they expected to shine from the Rebbe's private room.

But most of the former Watchers and fasters hung around the big study house suffering from hunger. Fewer and fewer village Jews came to the court of Kotsk, and very rarely did someone provide money for drinks. If a village Jew did happen to come to Kotsk, the regulars attacked him like flies. They did everything they could think of to get a few coins out of him for drinks.

The specialist in this matter was Reb Leybush Sokhatshever, a young man who had a rich father-in-law who still supported him. He had discovered various ways to obtain poultry and make a little meal.

One time he disguised himself as a rebbe and told a village Jew who had come to the court of Kotsk to give the Rebbe a note, that "since the Rebbe isn't seeing anyone, I'm serving as his substitute. And I'll take the note." The village Jew believed everything Leybush Sokhatshever said to him, especially when he saw that a number of Jews were pushing toward Leybush and pressing notes into his hands. Seeing that, the village Jew likewise gave Leybush a note with a significant contribution, began complaining and weeping that his cows had stopped giving milk and he would be ruined if the cows didn't start giving as much milk as they used to.

"The nerve of those cows of yours!" said Leybush just like he was a rebbe. "What do you mean, they don't want to give any milk? And why were they giving it until now? If they were dumb cattle until now, then I decree that they shall remain dumb cattle."

But in order to make sure that his blessing would come to fruition, he asked the village Jew straightaway to bring a gift of a few chickens for the Hasidim; if not, the blessing would have no effect.

The village Jew, who thought the young man was a rebbe, believed everything and immediately brought several hens for the Hasidim.

One time he hit upon the idea of tricking the Hasidim themselves: He disguised himself as a rebbe, and when a rural leaseholder came to Kotsk, he told the man that he could clearly see that the leaseholder would only be helped if he invited a couple of dozen Hasidim to his home in the country and made a dairy feast for them. The leaseholder did exactly as the "rebbe" had asked, and soon all the Hasidim found out that Leybush Sokhatshever had organized a big feast for them at the home of a broker in a nearby village.

But Leybush was more interested in tricking the Hasidim than in the feast itself. He spent his last few pennies at the butcher shop, buying a liver that he broiled in the oven. When the Hasidim got into the wagons to ride to the nearest inn, Leybush, acting like a rebbe, handed out liquor and bits of broiled liver to the Hasidim. And a half hour later, when the Hasidim arrived at the inn ready to rush at the food, they were bitterly disappointed. All the tables in the inn were covered with delicious treats fit for a king—but it was all dairy food, and those who had tasted the liver sat downcast, unable to taste a thing until they had waited for six hours . . .

Eventually even Leybush got tired of begging the village Jews for a meal, and he too hung around downcast, until one day Reb Itshe Meirl came to him in the study house and said, "Leybush, you look like you're lost in a shapeless world."

"I can't sit still anywhere."

"What happened?"

"I'm barely human," Leybush boldly answered.

"Don't be ashamed. Tell me," Reb Itshe Meirl drew him out.

"I'm thinking about home," Leybush admitted, avoiding Reb Itshe Meirl's gaze.

"Why all of a sudden?"

"I don't know myself," Leybush unburdened himself. "When I came to Kotsk, at first the whole world seemed like an obsolete text to me. I never thought about home, and I never worried. But lately I just can't sit still."

Reb Itshe Meirl was profoundly moved by Leybush's simple and honest words. He felt even more strongly how black the clouds were over Kotsk, and he began speaking intimately: "You think you're the only one?"

"I know, the Rebbe says that if you really want something, if you have true will, you can overcome all distractions. But I'm such a cripple, that I can't even want it anymore..."

"Everybody stumbles," Reb Itshe Meirl set out to comfort him. His words sounded as though he were trying to comfort himself. "But you have to help yourself. You're not alone here. We'll have to find a solution to the troubles we share."

"But lately my heart is so torn with doubts. Mordkhe Yosef teaches us a new doctrine and says, 'The Rebbe thinks that every Jew perceives the vanity of the world like he does. He thinks that the fire of redemption burns as brightly in everyone's heart as it does in his... But the beginners need beginner's teachers, and also—what about home, the family; what are we supposed to do about them?'"

Suddenly the door of the study house opened, and the head of a prematurely aged woman could be seen, wrapped in a scarf. It was Leybush's wife. She stood bent over at the door, trembling all over. Then she began calling in a weak voice: "Leybush, Leybush!"

Leybush ran to the door. He saw his wife and fearfully asked her: "When did you come?"

"Just now."

"Why all of a sudden?" he asked.

"A disaster" was all she answered, for she was choked by tears.

"My father," she began telling him as she wept, "my father, may he be a good intercessor for us..."

But she couldn't say anything more, and the tears poured down from her eyes.

"Blessed is the true Judge," murmured Leybush, and his wife Dvoyrele told him, "He was sick for several weeks. His sickness cost us his entire fortune. I avoided disturbing you for as long as I could. Probably you know better than I do. But now I have no choice."

"What should I do? How can I help?" Leybush pleaded with his wife.

"You'll come home and look for a way to earn some money to support us."

"Go home? And that will be my end? To be buried alive in the mud?"

"You have to! There's no other choice. I can't do anything more. My father's illness, may he rest in Paradise, ruined me, and I spend all day begging with Shloymele."

Leybush recalled that she was talking about his own son, and he asked in embarrassment, "Tell me, how is Shloymele? Grown up into a wild kid?"

"A dear child," his wife reported with maternal warmth. "All day long he keeps shouting, 'Daddy! Daddy!'"

"Oh, how I'd like to see him!" Leybush exclaimed. "But how can I go home? How can I spend a single hour in that darkness?"

"Well, are you ready to let us starve from hunger, me and your only child?"

Leybush's wife burst into tears, and she ran out of the study house in shame.

31

The Kotsker Rebbe Agrees to Open the Door

All the Hasidim who were still in Kotsk gathered at the study house. A rumor had quickly spread through the town that something was going to happen. At first people thought the Rebbe had decided to open his door, but later they found out unofficially that the Rebbe had asked for Reb Itshe Meir to be sent to him.

The Hasidim gathered in the study house saw Reb Itshe Meirl enter the secretary's room in agitation together with a stranger, and holding a secret meeting with Reb Hersh Tomashover. The Hasidim looked at the messenger curiously. They knew that he was a Kotsker Hasid, but his dress and appearance struck them as bizarre.

They could tell the messenger wasn't Polish, but rather a Hungarian from the long mohair overcoat with large, crooked pockets in back that he wore, and by the long curly sidelocks that hung down from his large satin hat, blending with his long beard. He looked more like a Polish rabbi than a simple Cracow lumber merchant. And he spoke with a curious, soft "l" sound, and instead of pronouncing the Yiddish word for "I" as *yakh,* he said *yekh.* "*Yekh hob nisht ken tsaat,*" I don't have any time, he replied to someone who offered him a greeting.

And the curiosity of the Hasidim was not for nothing. The messenger from Cracow came with sad news. It was news he didn't want to tell anyone except Reb Itshe Meirl and Reb Hersh Tomashover. Reb Hersh Tomashover quickly chased all the Hasidim out of the secretary's room. Those who were reluctant to go weren't given a choice. The caps or tall fur hats they wore on their heads were thrown out of the secretary's room, and the Hasidim themselves went after them.

And when the secretary's room had been cleared, the Hasid from Cracow explained that he had been sent by the Kotsk Hasidim from Cracow to announce that the Galician rebbes intended to call a conference to discuss the Rebbe's conduct.

Word had spread through the various courts of Galicia that the Kotsker had secluded himself and wouldn't see anyone, that he was preparing to teach a new way that doesn't follow the Torah. "And for that," the messenger concluded, "they want, God forbid . . ." At that he stopped and couldn't say anything further.

"I understand," said Reb Itshe Meirl. "They want to do the same thing they tried to do in the days of the old Apter Rabbi of blessed memory—they want to excommunicate us. Well, Hersh, what do you say about it?"

"Not only that," the messenger from Cracow spoke up again, "not only excommunication, but they want to ban him from the Jewish people altogether."

"God preserve us!" they all spit out at once.

And the messenger from Cracow further reported how the rebbes in Galicia planned to influence the Kotsker Rebbe to speak openly, so that the whole world would know what he had in mind. "And then they'll go to war against us, if we don't turn away from him."

"Hersh!" spoke Reb Itshe Meirl in agitation. "Do you know what it sounds like? Like ap . . ."

Reb Itshe Meirl didn't want to say the word "apostasy," but he was fuming. They wouldn't succeed, he would go to 'him' today and convince him to begin conducting himself like a rebbe again, so that the entire world would see what his statements were, what his new path really meant. "Hersh! Let's go talk to him."

"I don't know if we'll be able to," sadly answered Reb Hersh Tomashover. "First, you need to go back into the study house, and I'll try to go into his room. If it's possible I'll summon you."

"But I don't want to meet Reb Mordkhe Yosef now. He'll start asking questions. Well, it can't be helped," Reb Itshe Meirl waved his hand. "You've got to be strong!" He turned to the messenger from Cracow: "Don't say anything! Not a word to anyone! Go out this way to your room," Reb Itshe Meirl pointed to the back door leading to the synagogue lane.

Reb Itshe Meirl went into the study house to wait until Reb Hersh Tomashover called him.

In the study house, which was packed full of Hasidim, Reb Itshe Meirl encountered Reb Mordkhe Yosef standing at a table insisting:

"We can't be patient any longer. We need an answer. Is the door going to open or not?"

"Whoever comes to Kotsk and wants to follow the way of Kotsk," said Reb Itshe Meirl from the other side of the table, "has to be able to withstand anything. We don't play in Kotsk!"

"But if the whole congregation is hanging around without even understanding what they're told, don't you call that playing?"

"Mordkhe Yosef," said Reb Itshe Meirl in a firm, loud voice, "you are a rebel against the Rebbe."

"Whatever I am, I am, but I'll never be afraid to pronounce the truth before the whole world. I won't hide in a back room! And I won't abandon the congregation."

"Since when are you afraid of the mixed multitude, and when did you become their spokesman? Who prevents them from understanding the Rebbe's way, and who's keeping them here? If they can't stand it, let them go home."

"Who's afraid?" Reb Mordkhe retorted angrily. "As long as the passion and enthusiasm were there, it was possible to overcome every stumbling block. But now, when we see the fire slowly going out, what are we supposed to do? Are we supposed to sit still and watch everything fall apart? Just look at the young men," he stretched out his hand around the room. "Is this Kotsk? It's turned into a city of refuge for those who have nothing better to do. They hang around looking for a way to keep body and soul together. Velvele the Judge teaches the society of Watchers that they have to torment themselves even more in order to be worthy of understanding the Rebbe's teaching. And do we have a Rebbe now? We have a seraph who isn't ready to descend from the heights for a second, and there's nobody here to begin teaching them the alphabet. They torment themselves, they stay away from their wives, they want to imitate him. I say that it will lead . . ."

"Mordkhe Yosef, calm down," Reb Itshe Meirl heatedly interrupted. "Consider what you're saying."

"A fire is burning in my soul. It isn't interested in calming down," answered Reb Mordkhe Yosef, his face covered with sweat. "If you want to accomplish something, you need the fire burning in your soul. That's the column of fire that can illuminate the world. But the Hasidim need a leader who can heal their lost souls, be good to them, be a father to them, encourage them, and help them bear the burden of livelihood and the burden of exile."

Reb Itshe Meirl wanted to reply further, but suddenly the door of the secretary's room opened up and Reb Hersh Tomashover called: "Itshe Meir! Where's Itshe Meirl? The Rebbe is calling him!"

Reb Itshe Meirl immediately set off toward the door of the Rebbe's private room, calling back to Reb Mordkhe Yosef as he did so: "Mordkhe Yosef, retract! Think about what you want to do! You're playing with fire. You're a rebel."

▲▽▲▽▲

The Kotsker Rebbe sat in his private room, engrossed in his own thoughts. He could no longer even comprehend ordinary human worries.

"Itshe Meirl, what do they want from me?" asked the Kotsker Rebbe.

Reb Itshe Meirl, who had come into the room walking slowly and full of awe and fear, looked sideways.

"Itshe Meir, why are they harassing me?" the Kotsker Rebbe asked once again.

"The Hasidim want to go home. They want to take their leave of you. They want blessings from the Rebbe. There was terrible inflation this year and food is very scarce."

"Why is food so expensive?" the Kotsker Rebbe asked, and answered his own question in humorous fashion. "Because everybody wants to eat. Let everybody decide they want to study instead. Then study will be expensive and food will be cheap."

But suddenly his face changed. He forgot what Reb Itshe Meirl had said to him earlier, and he began speaking in a strange voice. "Itshe Meir, who can assure me that I will at least have Gehennom? In order to grasp that, one must have great faith!"

The Kotsker Rebbe was silent for a moment, and then he said: "But do you know what I'm going to do when I'm led into Gehennom? I'm going to climb onto the roof of Gehennom and start discoursing on Torah. The tzaddikim in Paradise will hear it, they'll come down to where I am, and it will turn into Paradise. I'm not afraid of Gehennom."

A Fire Burns in Kotsk

Reb Itshe Meirl, who had come in intending to ask the Kotsker Rebbe to resume holding court and taking leave of his Hasidim, regretted the whole idea as he listened to these words. He was afraid lest the Hasidim hear such radical words, and especially of the rumor reaching the Hasidic courts in Galicia. So he kept silent the whole time, waiting for the Kotsker Rebbe to tell him why he had been summoned.

The Kotsker Rebbe continued to sit lost in thought. He took his goose quill pen in his hand, wrote a letter on a piece of parchment that lay open before him, and his face was full of pain. Then he suddenly threw away the quill and turned to Reb Itshe Meirl:

"Itshe Meir! Do you think I don't know that things aren't all right in the study house, that Mordkhe Yosef is dissatisfied? But what do I want from the Hasidim? I want three things from them: not to look outside of themselves, not to look into anyone else, and not to have themselves in mind.

"And if they can't reach that level," the Kotsker Rebbe continued, "then you don't have to be a Hasid. Do you know the meaning of the Talmudic saying, 'The needs of your people are many and their intellect is lacking' (Berachot 29b)? Because their intellect is lacking, that's why their needs are many. Believe me, Itshe Meir, this wasn't what I had in mind when I left Pshiskhe. I thought," here he stood up and seized the laces of his cotton jacket, "that I would have a minyan of Hasidim who would wear shirts made of chains and they would be able to look straight into Heaven, without a veil . . . But I didn't get them. I know that the world will despise me when people find out that I don't agree with the current approach. The world is accustomed to disguising the truth, and whoever wants to uncover it they hate. But I'm not afraid of anything. Here," he pointed to a piece of parchment, "the whole Torah will stand written! Nevertheless I will try one more time. This Friday night I'll come to the table. We'll see whether there is even a minyan of Jews who agree with my approach."

When Reb Itshe Meirl heard why the Rebbe wanted to see his Hasidim, he spoke up anxiously: "But the Hasidim aren't at all prepared for this. They won't understand the Rebbe's ways."

"That's exactly my claim!" shouted the Kotsker Rebbe. "But once and for all the wager has to be made. If they don't understand, what do I need them for? And you, on the other hand, this is already the second time you've come in to ask me to open the door. I just told you that I'm not ready to do that, and now, when I'm agreeing, you yell back at me that the Hasidim aren't ready. But I can't wait any longer. Tell them that this Friday night we will gather at the table."

With that, the Kotsker Rebbe said goodbye to Reb Itshe Meir and locked himself back into his room.

The Hasidim who were waiting for Reb Itshe Meirl in the study house surrounded him as soon as he left the Rebbe's room. All of the Hasidim posed the same question: "Well? When is the Rebbe going to open the door?"

"He'll open, he'll open! Mordkhe Yosef got his way, but I just hope he won't regret it."

When the Hasidim heard that the Kotsker Rebbe would gather his Hasidim around him at the Sabbath table, they immediately set out for all the inns to share the good news.

Soon Hasidim began gathering in the study house. The young men drank a bit of liquor to express their joy. Reb Velvele the Judge sat on a stone in front of the study house dressed in sacking, calling on the Hasidim to repent.

"Jews!" he shouted. "Our Rebbe has agreed to open the door. The ways of the Rebbe will be a burning coal. Soon a new light will be revealed. We have to prepare for it, so that we will understand every word. Woe to anyone who doesn't grasp the Rebbe's discourses properly."

And Reb Mordkhe Yosef stood with a group of Hasidim and said, "Now, when he comes out, we'll hear what he has to say to us. And if his discourse surpasses our comprehension, we'll say that we're not angels, we're only human, and we won't let Itshe Meir lead us around."

32

The Terrible Friday Night

The news that on the coming Friday night the Kotsker Rebbe would conduct a ceremonial Sabbath table spread quickly through the entire region. From all the nearby cities and towns people traveled to spend the Sabbath in Kotsk.

Leading Hasidim such as Reb Henekh (later to become the Aleksander Rebbe), Reb Volf Strikover, and other future rebbes came as well.

▲▼▲▼▲▼

Immediately after the prayers ushering in the Sabbath the Hasidim filled the whole study house, waiting for the Rebbe to enter from his private room. Reb Velvele and his society of Watchers slipped under the table so that they would be able to hear better every word of the Rebbe. Hundreds of Hasidim tied their belts to the iron hooks that protruded from the walls, and they hung that way until the Rebbe came in. Crowds of young men who wanted to be as close to the Rebbe as possible pushed toward the head of the table. A number of elderly Hasidim fainted even before the Rebbe opened the door, and suddenly Reb Hersh Tomashover shouted: "Quiet! The Rebbe is coming!" And suddenly it became so quiet that you could have heard a fly buzzing.

The Kotsker Rebbe quickly opened the door to his room and moved directly toward the table.

Anyone who had known the Rebbe before could see that he had changed entirely. His beard was gray, his eyes were sunken and burned with a dark fire. His face was sorrowful and pale. He looked at everyone as though they were strangers, and it seemed as though he was looking for at least one familiar face among the thousands of Hasidim.

His brother-in-law Reb Itshe Meirl stood by him the whole time and didn't take his eyes off the Rebbe for a second but carefully noted every motion. On the other side stood Reb Hersh Tomashover.

And Reb Mordkhe Yosef Izhbitser stood with his followers far away from the Rebbe clear on the other side of the room, looking like he was preparing for a great battle.

The Hasidim pressed in from all sides. Everyone wanted to see the holy face of the Rebbe. As soon as Reb Hersh Tomashover poured the goblet of wine so that the Kotsker Rebbe could make a blessing over it, the Rebbe concentrated his thoughts and began his discourse.

At that the huge crowd of Hasidim in and around the building pressed even closer to the table. They hung in the air, they stood on each other's heads. Reb Velvele crawled from under the table with his society of Watchers making weird gestures, as though they were getting ready to receive a new Torah. The Rebbe's strong voice could be heard: "'And Jacob sent messengers to Esau his brother.' How long will they keep telling us stories about Jacob sending messengers to Esau?" The Rebbe's voice suddenly changed, and his face lit up like a lick of fire. He began saying things that none of the Hasidim could understand. He began a complex discussion of the meanings of "worship out of fear" and "worship out of love," and he shouted: "Certainly I'm right—worship out of love is the main thing; could it really be that the important thing is to be afraid? Pfooey! I'm not afraid of anything." With that he blew so hard that the candles nearly went out, and he continued in the same passionate tone.

"I have a new way to fulfill the entire Torah, and it won't require telling any stories about Jacob sending messengers to his brother Esau..."

But suddenly a shout like a thunderclap could be heard from the other side of the building: "Jews, don't listen to him! Jews, let's save ourselves!"

It was Mordkhe Yosef, who stood with his followers on the other side of the room. A deadly silence filled the room, until Reb Mordkhe Yosef's voice rang out once again: "Woe to the ears that hear such as this! Jews, let's save ourselves."

"Respect!" rang out another voice from near the second table.

"Wherever the Divine Name is being desecrated one need not honor the master," Reb Mordkhe Yosef quoted the Talmud (Berachot 19b).

Chaos broke out. People started pressing toward Reb Mordkhe Yosef.

A Fire Burns in Kotsk

Reb Mordkhe Yosef left through a window, and hundreds of Hasidim began leaving through all the doors and windows. They grabbed onto each other's belts, jumped over chairs and tables in their rush to get outside. And in a few minutes the big room was almost entirely empty. Fur hats, caps, and belts lay scattered on the tables. Only a few Hasidim remained inside, including Reb Velvele and his Watchers, who shouted: "Let the Rebbe finish teaching! Let's hear the new approach, let's see the new light!"

But the Kotsker Rebbe remained quiet for a few minutes. Suddenly he felt very weak. He leaned his head to one side, as if he had suddenly fallen into a deep sleep. Murmured words could be heard: "There is no Law and there is no Judge." But the Kotsker Rebbe quickly came to and shouted: "What are you all running away for?" He wanted to continue his discourse, but Reb Itshe Meirl and Reb Hersh Tomashover took his arms and practically carried him back into his private room.

Reb Velvele and his society, along with the few loyal Hasidim, stood in astonishment. They could still hear the Kotsker Rebbe shouting to Reb Itshe Meirl: "Well, didn't I tell you they wouldn't understand me? And even you, who kept asking me to appear in public, even you want to tear me away from them? Did they understand a single word I said?"

Right away Reb Mordkhe Yosef set off for his inn. But he didn't want to hold court in Kotsk, and he only waited for the Sabbath to end so that he could get away.

The news quickly spread through the court of Kotsk that the Rebbe had gone back into seclusion and wouldn't see anyone.

And as soon as three stars appeared in the sky on Saturday evening, Reb Mordkhe Yosef called for the horses to be harnassed, and sped away from Kotsk. Reb Itshe Meirl only managed to get him to promise not to say anything about what had happened the previous evening.

Either the Kotsker Rebbe went back into seclusion or perhaps he was locked away. And that's how he remained for some twenty-three years.

At first the Kotsker Rebbe wouldn't let anyone in to see him, but in later years he would open the door from time to time, speak angrily to the Hasidim and then close the door again.

Almost everyone, including the leading Hasidim, departed with Reb Mordkhe Yosef. Only a few remained loyal to Kotsk, including the

Aleksander Rebbe and other leading lights. The leader for all practical purposes was Reb Itshe Meirl.

Immediately after the Sabbath the Kotsker Rebbe burned his manuscript, the piece of parchment with the title: "These are the Generations of Man." Afterward the Kotsker Rebbe kept writing down his new insights, but every Eve of Passover he would burn his manuscripts together with the last bits of leavening, and after Passover he would begin writing again.

Reb Mordkhe Yosef became Rebbe in Izhbitse, and the divide between Izhbitse and Kotsk was complete.

33

The Rebbe of Gostinin Doesn't Know to Whom to Go

The Kotsker Rebbe had shut himself back up in his private room. His disciple Reb Mordkhe Yosef had begun his reign in Izhbitse, and Reb Yekhiel Meir, the future Gostininer Rebbe, absolutely could not decide which one to choose and to travel to see. Whenever he had doubts or troubles he had one solution for them: reciting Psalms. "A Psalm can break through every wall, can open up all the Heavens," he used to say. And this time too, Hasidim relate, he relied on his tried-and-true method and said Psalms. He hired a coach and set off to "go to the Rebbe," although he still didn't know which one. But he believed with perfect faith that as he traveled it would be revealed to him.

Reb Yekhiel Meir kept traveling until he reached a crossroads: one way led to Kotsk and the other to Izhbitse. Heaven had still not revealed to him which way to go. In his anguish he sat at the crossroads for three days and three nights. He sent the coach back home empty. Reb Yekhiel Meir sat on a rock with his pack on his back, with his volume of Psalms in his hand, and didn't want to move.

Wagonloads of Hasidim drove by Reb Yekhiel Meir's spot in a hurry, in joyful song. The Hasidim saw someone sitting on a rock. They got down from their coaches and recognized Reb Yekhiel Meir, and asked him to ride with them. But Reb Yekhiel Meir didn't budge. "I don't know where my Rebbe lives yet," he answered.

The Hasidim, who were well acquainted with him from Kotsk, shouted: "What do you mean, Reb Yekhiel Meir? You've been going to Kotsk for years, and suddenly you don't know where your Rebbe lives?"

But Reb Yekhiel Meir had just one answer: "I've lost the way to the Rebbe," and tears poured from his eyes.

The wagonloads of Hasidim galloped further down the road that leads to Kotsk, and Reb Yekhiel Meir resumed reciting Psalms in a weeping voice. More wagonloads of Hasidim appeared. They saw a

Jew standing on a stone. They got down and asked the same question: "Why are you sitting here by yourself, Reb Yekhiel Meir?"

"I've lost the way to the Rebbe," he wept in response.

"Come with us, we'll show you the way," the Hasidim tried to convince him. "We're going for the first time, too. Right here we turn right, and the road leads straight to Izhbitse!" they pointed.

"I have to wait until someone else shows me the way," Reb Yekhiel Meir answered sadly.

The Hasidim drove off singing down the road that leads to Izhbitse. And Reb Yekhiel Meir sat on his stone as before, reciting Psalms.

And so it went for three days. Day and night Reb Yekhiel Meir sat in the same spot waiting for someone to show him the way. Finally one evening when he was in the middle of saying Psalms, a fiery column appeared before his eyes, shining up to the sky. He was very eager to see where the column was. He got up from the rock and walked toward the place it seemed to come from. At first it seemed very close, but the closer he came to the column of fire, the further it moved away from him. He walked and walked, through untrod byways, through fields and forests. The fiery column kept ahead of him and he followed it, until he suddenly saw that he was in the marketplace of Kotsk, and that the fiery column arose from the room where the Kotsker Rebbe was secluded.

And Reb Yekhiel Meir went into the synagogue of Kotsk. He heard Hasidim relating that they had met Reb Yekhiel Meir of Gostinin sitting on a rock, and he didn't want to accompany them to Kotsk because "he didn't know which road led to his Rebbe."

Kotsker regulars were ready to take a coach and ride back there. They were afraid that Izhbitser Hasidim would convince him to go to Izhbitse instead. But suddenly they heard a voice: "You don't have to go back there! I found the way."

The Hasidim looked around, and at first they didn't recognize Reb Yekhiel Meir, so wasted was he from fasting and weeping. But soon they realized it was indeed Reb Yekhiel Meir himself. There was great joy in the Kotsker synagogue, and from that point on Reb Yekhiel Meir remained a Kotsker Hasid.

But not all the Hasidim received the same "revelation" from Heaven. Many of them set off for Izhbitse.

And to tell the truth, the Izhbitser Rebbe also continued the way of Kotsk but with less fire. The Izhbitser himself was more approachable than the Kotsker. He didn't shout at people but instead made light of their petty passions with a witty saying.

Yet the Izhbitser Hasidim didn't understand what had led to this. They didn't know why the Rebbe Reb Mordkhe Yosef, the greatest Hasid of the Kotsker, had broken with the Rebbe, and the younger Hasidim who had never seen the Kotsker allowed themselves to speak mockingly of him.

A major dispute broke out between Izhibitse and Kotsk. The new Izhbitse Hasidim told incredible stories about the Kotsker Rebbe and about Kotsker Hasidim. They said that in Kotsk, no one prayed anymore and that they had stopped observing Judaism there.

On the other hand, the Hasidim who kept going to Kotsk didn't keep silent either. They didn't spare the Izhbitser Rebbe's reputation, and it is said that on practically every holiday Hasidim would get up on the lectern of the Kotsk study house and publicly mock the Izhbitser Rebbe.

The Kotsker Hasidim related that the Izhbitser Rebbe said things just to get others angry. They claimed that he explicitly said in his discourses that Korah was justified in his rebellion against our teacher Moses; that Zimri was correct, not Phineas; and that King Menashe of Israel, whom the Talmud reports as having set up an idol in the Holy of Holies, meant well.

It reached a point where the Izhbiter Rebbe's book *Mei Hashiloach* (so named because the Rebbe Reb Bunem had said of Reb Mordkhe Yosef that he was like the waters of the Shiloah spring, which flow slowly and dig deep) was referred to by the Kotsker Hasidim with the derogatory name *Mei Raglayim* (urine).

The enmity between Izhbitse and Kotsk led to Izhbitse Hasidim standing on the roads leading to Kotsk, tugging at the sleeves of Hasidim and blocking them from going to Kotsk. Later, according to some, they claimed that if the Kotsker Hasidim who kept going to Kotsk were rewarded in the World to Come, it would only be because they went halfway to Izhbitse.

At first the big study house in Kotsk was almost empty. Once when Reb Hersh Tomashover was checking to see whether there was a minyan for the Sabbath, he said: "Well, and if we've still got a minyan, then we've got nothing to be afraid of."

But Reb Itshe Meirl didn't want to content himself with a mere minyan. He was obsessed with finding ways to draw people back to Kotsk. Especially since among the current minyan there were some that didn't belong at Kotsk at all.

Reb Yekhiel Meir of Gostinin himself, even though he had looked for a sign from Heaven to tell him which way to travel, had perhaps been looking more for the Kotsk study house than for the Kotsker Rebbe. He had always considered himself a simple Psalm Jew, and he didn't need the Kotsker Rebbe and his incisive aphorisms. For him it was enough that he found himself in the vicinity of the Kotsker and could go on saying Psalms as he used to.

Another of the ten Jews was Reb Velvele the Judge, who looked hardly human due to his constant fast and self-torments. He contended that the guilty ones were the Hasidim themselves because they hadn't sufficiently purified themselves to be ready to understand the Rebbe's exalted ways.

And when Izhbitser Hasidim kept coming to Kotsk seeking to entice away the remaining Kotsker Hasidim, the Izhibitser Hasidim discretely asked Reb Velvele the Judge how he could still be loyal to someone who had said such things. Reb Velvele the Judge answered that it's not always the case that the Rebbe has to elevate his Hasidim. Sometimes it's the opposite: the Hasidim have to elevate the Rebbe ... Relative to the Hasidim, the Rebbe is a superman, and therefore his agonies and his doubts are greater than those of ordinary flesh and blood. If you leave the Rebbe all by himself, he may fall into Sheol below, God forbid. So the only solution, concluded Reb Velvele, is to repent even more in order to elevate him, so that he can regain his elevated level, while we Hasidim will better understand what the Rebbe means.

But the kind of ideas that Reb Yekhiel Meir held on one side and Reb Velvele the Judge held on the other side couldn't attract Hasidim back to Kotsk, and if Kotsk gradually regained its luster, that was only thanks to Reb Itshe Meirl.

Reb Itshe Meirl began once again to recruit young men to Kotsk.

"What's the point of going to the Rebbe," the young men asked, "if you don't get to see the Rebbe himself, and if he does sometimes open the door, all he says is something short and angry enough to make you wish he hadn't opened the door?"

It was very hard for Reb Itshe Meirl to bring any new Hasidim to Kotsk. It was only due to his spiritual strengths and his readiness for self-sacrifice that after a few years Kotsk was once again what it had been: The study house of Polish Hasidim, which drew thousands of Hasidim from every corner of the land.

The notion arose that sometimes the tzaddik himself is so great that he cannot connect with his Hasidim. The Kotsker Hasidim came to believe that their Rebbe was so great that just touching the handle of the door to his private room was enough for someone to be helped.

Reb Itshe Meirl would take the notes the Hasidim wrote and bring them to the Rebbe, and everyone believed that they had been answered.

34

The Kotsker Rebbe Escapes from His Private Room

The Kotsker Rebbe sat in his room like an angry lion locked in a cage, despairing of the entire world. From time to time he would be overcome by the sense that his own courtiers were against him. He wanted to go out and see the Hasidim, tell them what he thought of them and of those close to him, but guards always stood in front of his door, preventing him from going out. Even his loyal secretary, Reb Hersh Tomashover, blocked his way more than once.

Those in the inner circle told the simple Hasidim that the Rebbe had secluded himself out of good motives and didn't want to see the world, but they knew that the Kotsker Rebbe had been locked in.

More than once the Kotsker Rebbe would hear a Hasidic song reaching his ears from the study house. He would move toward the door, but he found it locked. Then he would howl so terribly that the walls trembled. The Hasidim would run to hide on all sides.

Those closest to the Kotsker Rebbe worked extra hard to make the court of Kotsk appear like a normal Hasidic court.

They kept raising money from the Hasidim and constructing building after building. The wealthy Hasidim who had once felt like stepchildren in Kotsk became the big shots. Whoever provided the most wine for the celebratory meals led by Reb Itshe Meirl; whoever donated more money to the secretaries; whoever made the largest contributions and wrote the largest pledges—was the most important person, and was drawn closer to the inner circle.

They also began building a house for the Kotsker Rebbe's children. The house was built right in front of the windows of the Rebbe's private room.

Some days the Kotsker Rebbe would spend hours standing at his window looking out at the fields, which spread all the way to the river. The last few years he hadn't gone up to the window, but sometimes he would look out through a chink, lost in thought as he watched a white cloud hovering in the pure sky. And once the Kotsker Rebbe suddenly saw bricks and mortar spread out in front of his window. Gentiles were coming with axes and shovels. The Kotsker Rebbe asked Reb Hersh Tomashover what was going on. But Reb Hersh Tomashover didn't give him a clear answer. Since the Kotsker Rebbe was in any case preoccupied with other thoughts, he himself quickly forgot about the matter.

Most hours of the day the Kotsker Rebbe sat on his chair lost in thought or dozing off. He smoked his long tobacco pipe and the whole room was filled with smoke. He could spend entire days like that without saying a word, until Reb Hersh Tomashover would come in and tell him to get out of his chair.

And often the Kotsker Rebbe would get an idea in his head, hold onto the idea for a few days, play with it and caress it as one caresses a small child. Then he would draw and quarter the idea, smash it into a thousand pieces, throw away the junk and just keep the core, and once again polish and break it, until he could tell that it would lead him nowhere, that somewhere the insight had been interrupted and he couldn't draw it out any longer. Then he would grow angry at himself, trying to tear out the nerves from his head, in his anger to drive the insight away altogether like one tries to get rid of an annoying fly. But the insight didn't want to leave him; it tormented and persecuted him. Then the Kotsker Rebbe would run back and forth across his room, agitated and exhausted.

One Saturday night, after he'd been sitting in his chair lost in thought for a few days, the Kotsker Rebbe angrily ran to the window. And there he suddenly saw a wall before his window. The brick wall had arisen over the previous few days. It blocked his few of the wide open fields which used to calm his mood. "Now I won't even be able to see the sky," he thought to himself.

The Kotsker Rebbe tried once again to ask his secretary, Reb Hersh Tomashover, what building was going up, and failing once again to get a clear answer, he decided that he would have to go see himself what was going on outside.

That same Saturday night, when the Kotsker study house was full of Jews as usual, and they were drinking and making little post-Sabbath feasts, the Kotsker Rebbe put on his cotton jacket, pulled his lambskin cap down over his ears, and set out to see the world! His secretary, who used to sleep near his room watching to see that no harm came to him and to make sure that the Kotsker Rebbe could never escape from his locked room and "ruin everything," was fast asleep. He knew that the Rebbe had long since despaired of seeing the world, and he had let his guard down.

Therefore the Kotsker Rebbe freely made his way out of his private room, and this is what he saw: Before his fallen-down wooden house stood building upon building. All of the open area where he had once strolled with his Hasidim, teaching them secrets of the Torah, had been developed. The fine brick houses that had been constructed here looked like the court of a Polish nobleman, and everywhere laugher and cheerful voices could be heard. There was dancing, singing, and general partying. He kept walking until he met a half-drunk young man, a Kotsker Hasid who had never seen the Kotsker Rebbe. The Kotsker Rebbe asked the Hasid to tell him whose houses these were, and why everybody was singing so loudly. The Hasid answered: "What do you mean? Don't you know that the Kotsker Rebbe lives here, and that his Hasidim are having a good time?" The Kotsker Rebbe answered that he had heard nothing about it.

The young man became angry and said, "If you don't know that the Kotsker Rebbe lives here, then you deserve to be thoroughly beaten!" He concluded, "And I don't want to talk to you anymore," and went away.

The Kotsker Rebbe kept walking until he came to the newly built study house. He entered and saw hundreds of Hasidim at tables laden with good food. They were eating fish and meat, and wine flowed from bottles. Dozens of young men were rushing around handing out large portions of meat, and the room was filled with shouts like a tavern full of drunks. From time to time the study house would grow quiet and a certain Hasid whom the Kotsker Rebbe didn't even know would toast the crowd "Lechaim!" and shout, "Serve the Lord joyfully! Our Rebbe, may he live, told us to be joyful! He himself is in seclusion and torments himself and doesn't want to see the light of day, in order to redeem us Jews from sin, in order to take away our heavy yoke. So we have to be even more joyful, and wish the Rebbe long years! So, lechaim for our Rebbe!"

A Fire Burns in Kotsk

"Lechaim for our Rebbe!" voices could be heard in response. And the wine flowed once again.

The Kotsker Rebbe stood at the door, shot through with anger. Every limb was trembling. People pushed him from all sides, and no one recognized him.

"Aha, aha," he said to himself. "They've created a new idol for themselves and locked it away. They've turned me into an object of worship, and they serve me by eating chicken thighs and drinking buckets of wine... That's what I accomplished in my life, which I'm now spending locked away, and that's why they didn't want to let me out. The good-for-nothings have multiplied. They've built palaces and do whatever they feel like, and they hope that I'll atone for everything... That's the approach they're being taught now."

And suddenly a huge cry could be heard in the study hall: "Vermin, debauchers, get out of here! Who told you, you muddy worms, to twist my word and desecrate my way?"

Panic spread through the half-drunken crowd. Reb Hersh Tomashoever and a few of the old men, who immediately recognized the Rebbe's voice, headed for the door. The young men who didn't recognize the Kotsker Rebbe thought that a madman had entered the study hall. They moved toward the door, ready to give him what for. But when Reb Hersh Tomashover and the veterans blocked their way and reached the door of the study house first, they found the Kotsker Rebbe lying in the doorway in a faint. They didn't understand how the Rebbe had gotten out of his room.

Chaos broke out among the crowd. The drunken Hasidim who wanted to beat the Rebbe dispersed in terror. The Rebbe was brought into the study house. Throughout Kotsk the word spread: "The Rebbe fainted!"

All the Hasidim hurred to the spot where the Rebbe lay just so they could see him because by now there were thousands of Hasidim who had been going "to the Rebbe" for years and had never seen him in person. Healers also approached the Rebbe and began to revive him.

After some time the Rebbe opened his eyes. He looked around at everyone as though he'd never seen them before. His shriveled body trembled with cold. He twisted his head to all sides as if looking for just one friendly face among the huge crowd. Next to him stood Reb

Hersh Tomashover and a few elderly Hasidim. The Rebbe raised his head again, once again cast an alien, angry look at everyone in the large study house, and shouted "the world stinks!"

The Hasidim immediately took the Rebbe into his private room and sent for the gentile doctor. After intense efforts, the Rebbe was revived before daybreak. Before he left, the doctor said to the Hasidim, "Your Rabbi is dangerously ill. Pray to your God, and perhaps you will save his life."

The half-drunken Hasidim quickly sobered up. They made their way quickly into the study house. And among the empty bottles of wine, among the platters of meat and other dishes that lay on the table, they began reciting Psalms.

Every few minutes a Jewish woman from town would come in with a group of ladies to grab hold of the curtain over the Holy Ark, and their desperate pleas were loud enough to deafen everyone in the room. Another group of women left the study house for the cemetery to supplicate the dead there. And there was a great tumult throughout the town. As soon as day broke, messengers set off toward various towns and cities to announce the sad news that the Kotsker Rebbe was dangerously ill. A special messenger went to Warsaw with a letter for Reb Itshe Meirl, who happened to be away from Kotsk just then, telling him that for God's sake he had to come to Kotsk.

35

The Passing of the Kotsker Rebbe

On Sunday morning, as Reb Itshe Meirl returned from the synagogue, he encountered the messenger. Seeing someone from Kotsk in Warsaw so early, he immediately understood that it was a serious matter, and he asked the messenger in an anxious voice: "What happened?"

But the messenger didn't say anything. He took out of his pocket the letter that Reb Hersh Tomashover and Reb Dovidl, the Kotsker's son, had sent.

And Reb Itshe Meirl read:

With Divine assistance, Saturday night, the week of the Torah portion of Mishpatim, at Kotsk.

For a few weeks my father has been suffering from his illnesses, and since last Sabbath eve he has been very ill. May God send him healing. It would be helpful if you could come.

Your faithful friend, Dovid son of the Holy Rabbi may he live Morgenstern.

The Rebbe's wife and Reb Hersh Tomashover added:

The Rebbe's wife and I urgently beg you to come immediately.

Reb Itshe Meirl understood that although the letter stated explicitly that the Rebbe had been sick for several weeks "from his illnesses," something new had happened. Only a few weeks earlier he had been in Kotsk, and just a couple of days earlier he had seen a Hasid who had been in Kotsk. The Rabbi's wife had sent him regards, and the message that "The illnesses that her husband, the Kotsker Rebbe, suffers from chronically are as usual, and he continues the same." And now, all of a sudden—a letter like this!

Reb Itshe Meirl went to a quiet place with the messenger and began asking him about what had happened. But the messenger didn't want to provide any details. He only let Reb Itshe Meirl know that the previous night, while the Hasidim were celebrating the departure of the Sabbath, the Rebbe had suddenly appeared at the threshold of the study house, shouted angrily at the crowd, and when they hurried toward the door, they found him lying in the doorway in a faint.

Reb Itshe Meirl began talking to himself in great agitation: "Who let him out? Why didn't Hersh Tomashover guard him? I knew it would happen, that he wouldn't stand it when he found out what was going on outside." And in a broken tone he continued, still to himself: "Who bears more guilt than I do? It was my actions that led to this. Yet," he tried to comfort himself, "what else could I have done? What other choice did I have, when I wanted to keep the Hasidim in Kotsk and not have them scatter to other courts?"

And Reb Itshe Meirl turned to the messenger: "Perhaps you can tell me what the Rebbe said?"

"I don't know," said the messenger. "I didn't hear it clearly."

"But perhaps you can repeat at least a few words that you did hear?"

The messenger confided, as if betraying a secret, "The Rebbe shouted something like 'vermin, worms, out! You are desecrating the way!'"

"Really? What happened next?"

"Then they revived the Rebbe a bit, he raised his head and suddenly shouted: 'The world stinks,' and fainted away again. Next they took the Rebbe back into his private room. The town doctor was immediately brought in, and the Rebbe was revived early in the morning. I was told to travel straight to Warsaw to see you and to deliver this letter."

Reb Itshe Meirl didn't even go home. He rushed back into the Kotsker prayer room to tell the Hasidim the sad news.

At the prayer room they immediately lit candles and began reciting Psalms.

The sexton of the Kotsker prayer room went to all of the Hasidic synagogues in Warsaw, and told them about the disaster. The town sexton went from house to house in the Jewish neighborhood, knocking three times on every door with a wooden hammer, ordering everyone to go to the synagogue.

Jews abandoned their houses and stores, and asked the sexton what the bad news was, what was the evil decree, and the sexton answered in a sorrowful tone: "Jews, Jews, God's anger has been poured out upon us. The Kotsker Rebbe is deathly ill. Go to the synagogue and plead with Heaven!"

His weeping voice echoed through all the lanes in the Grzybow neighborhood. The Jewish artisans closed their workshops and went to their various little synagogues, and their workers and apprentices quietly enjoyed the unexpected free time.

The women left their baskets of eggs and fruit on the sidewalk and got themselves ready to set off en masse for the cemetery.

The teachers gathered their pupils and took them to the study houses. All of the synagogues, study houses, and prayer rooms were full of Jews. Thousands of candles burned, and it looked like the evening of Yom Kippur. Jews wept like small children and their wailing reached up to the heart of Heaven.

Meanwhile the Kotsker Hasidim, including Reb Itshe Meirl, immediately hired coaches and set off for Kotsk.

The closer they came to Kotsk, the more wagonloads of Hasidim they met, and when they were about to enter the town itself, the roads were jammed as though it was a market day. All of the streets and open areas were occupied by wagons and coaches. Hasidim came from all the distant cities and towns in Poland, in order to see the Rebbe's face one more time.

And when Reb Itshe Meirl came into the courtyard of Kotsk, he saw that the door leading to the Rebbe's private room was propped open and all the Hasidim were pushing in to see the Rebbe one last time. They walked straight in without even asking the secretaries.

Reb Itshe Meirl pushed in along with the rest of the crowd. No one paid any attention to him. When he entered the Rebbe's room he saw the Rebbe lying on his bed in a large skullcap. The right side of his beard was compressed from his lying facing the wall. His eyes were glazed, and his breathing came hard. From time to time he would open his eyes, sigh deeply and say a few incomprehensible words.

Reb Itshe Meirl stood to the side, unable to move, seeing what had become of the Kotsker Rebbe. For years he had been secluded from the world. He had dedicated his whole life to spiritual wholeness, sent the masses away, seeking only select individuals, and now everything was upside down. Jews went in and out without seeking permission. The Rebbe suddenly raised his head and in a weak voice asked Reb Hersh Tomashover, who didn't leave his besides the whole time: "Is he still not here?"

Reb Hersh answered, "He came! He came!"

"Where is he?"

"Here he comes," Reb Hersh Tomashover nodded to Reb Itshe Meirl and told him to approach.

Reb Itshe Meirl came up to the bed. The Kotsker Rebbe tried his hardest to sit up, and finally Reb Hersh Tomashover had to help him. He supported himself on the pillows at the head of his bed and said, "We were waiting for you, Itshe Meirl!"

The Kotsker Rebbe felt a bit better and asked for some black coffee. He swallowed a few spoonfuls and had them put the dish away. But Hasidim quickly hurried in, grabbed the dish, and began handing out tastes from it as the Rebbe's leftovers. In his anger the Rebbe closed his eyes again. But everyone could see that he had no more strength to speak. Village Jews stood with bottles in their hands, asking for a few drops of the coffee to heal their sick wives and children.

Next to the bed stood an old Hasid. The Kotsker Rebbe touched his belt, and saw the belt immediately shred into bits. Everyone wanted a piece of the belt the Rebbe had touched. The Kotsker Rebbe turned to Reb Itshe Meirl and said to him, "Don't you see what they turned me into, Itshe Meirl? Don't you see how my way is being ground into the earth?"

And suddenly the Kotsker Rebbe shouted, as if in someone else's borrowed voice: "My Rebbe, the Holy Jew, said, 'the meaning of the verse "dwell in the land and enjoy safe pasture" (Psalm 37:3) is, "lie in the ground and graze on faith."'"

The Hasidim thought that the Rebbe was going to teach them Torah, and they began pressing closer, but when the Kotsker Rebbe saw this, he shouted: "What are you all rushing for? What do you want to see? A Tatar, a magician? Hair will grow here," he pointed to the palm of his hand, "before a fool reaches the World to Come. Get out of my room, and don't let me see you anymore." With that, the Kotsker Rebbe fell back into a state of near unconsciousness.

Reb Itshe Meirl and the Rebbe's children, who were standing around the bed, immediately ordered everyone to leave the Rebbe's room, and added that no one except particular individuals were to be allowed in.

The Kotsker Rebbe lay in his sickbed until Thursday morning. He kept talking to himself, remembering the names of his former Hasidim, the first young men from Pshiskhe, and he repeated the same words a few times: "The Rebbe [meaning the Holy Jew] himself is guilty . . . He shouldn't have stopped in the middle. He started a war, and he should have conducted it until the end, instead of stopping. All or nothing! Compromises are not possible."

Reb Itshe Meirl, who had been up all night with the Rebbe's sons and grandchildren and with a minyan of the old Kotsk and Pshiskhe Hasidim, saw that the time was approaching. He couldn't understand how the Rebbe held fast to his approach, though he was so terribly weak and must realize that he hadn't won. The Kotsker Rebbe looked at Reb Itshe Meirl and asked: "Itshe Meir, why are you looking at me like that?"

"I want to know what the Rebbe is working on now."

"I can't tell you," the Kotsker Rebbe answered. "I'm looking through the generations from Moses on, to see who could have accomplished it and why they were all unsuccessful. I've just been conversing with . . ."

And here, old Kotsk Hasidim relate, the Kotsker Rebbe began saying things that cannot be repeated. Then he turned to Reb Itshe Meirl and asked him to take a certain manuscript from his drawer.

Reb Itshe Meirl brought a piece of parchment covered with tiny writing.

The Kotsker Rebbe ordered a candle to be brought. He got them to put his eyeglasses on and began reading the manuscript. Then he said to Reb Itshe Meirl: "You see, Itshe Meirl, for twenty years I've been struggling with this manuscript. Every year I've burned it before Passover, and started writing again. I wanted to write the entire Torah of the Generations of Man in one folio, but I wasn't successful." And the Kotsker Rebbe burned the bit of parchment with the candle. "May this Torah be burned together with me!" the Rebbe cried, and then fell back exhausted.

Reb Itshe Meirl wanted to give the Rebbe some medicine that the doctor had prescribed, but the Kotsker rejected it with his hand. Reb

Itshe Meirl and the Rebbe's children began begging the Kotsker to take at least a spoonful to calm his heart, but the Kotsker Rebbe clamped his teeth shut and shook his head "No."

At that Reb Itshe Meirl declared, "When it comes to life and death, it is permitted to force open the mouth and pour in the medicine."

And when the Kotsker heard this, he lifted himself up and said in a voice that could barely be heard: "Has it come to this? I have no say any more? 'There is no authority in the day of death . . .'"

And he turned his face toward the wall and said to his Hasidim, "I can begin saying . . ." and with that his death throes began.

Wailing filled the entire court. All the doors leading to the Rebbe's room were opened. The Kotsker Rebbe's last words were heard: "I am connected to the Hidden Light . . . to the Infinite."

And a half hour later the Kotsker Rebbe passed away.

It was Thursday, the Torah portion of Mishpatim, the 22nd of the Hebrew month of Shevat, in the year 5619—January 27, 1859.

www.ingramcontent.com/pod-product-compliance
Lightning Source LLC
Chambersburg PA
CBHW071816230426
43670CB00013B/2470